Giuseppe Rossi and Paola Carbone
The Law and Comedy

Law & Literature

Edited by
Daniela Carpi and Klaus Stierstorfer

Volume 24

Giuseppe Rossi
and Paola Carbone

The Law and Comedy

—

DE GRUYTER

ISBN 978-3-11-128539-9
e-ISBN (PDF) 978-3-11-128677-8
e-ISBN (EPUB) 978-3-11-128776-8
ISSN 2191-8457

Library of Congress Control Number: 2023939391

Bibliographic information published by the Deutsche Nationalbibliothek
The Deutsche Nationalbibliothek lists this publication in the Deutsche Nationalbibliografie; detailed bibliographic data are available on the internet at http://dnb.dnb.de.

First published in Italian under the title *Diritto e comicità* by Giappichelli © 2021 Paola Carbone and Giuseppe Rossi. English translation by the authors.

Printing and binding: CPI books GmbH, Leck

www.degruyter.com

In memoria di Paolo Villaggio
Che la terra le *sii* lieve, Maestro

Foreword to the English edition

This is the English edition of our study *Diritto e comicità*, first published in 2021 by Giappichelli, Turin, in the series *Studi e ricerche*, edited by the Centro di Ricerca per l'Estetica del Diritto (Research Centre for Aesthetics of Law) – CRED of the Università Mediterranea di Reggio Calabria, under the direction of Daniele Cananzi and Ettore Rocca.

The text is unchanged, with the sole exception of some minor adaptations in order to make some examples related to Italian literary and film works more understandable for English-speaking readers.

Two appendixes by Giuseppe Rossi were added, thanks to suggestions by Vincenzo Zeno-Zencovich and Paolo Heritier.

We would like to thank the directors of the *Law and Literature* series, Daniela Carpi and Klaus Stierstorfer, for hosting our volume, the Director of the Department of Humanities, Giovanna Rocca, and the Director of the Department of Business, Luca Pellegrini, of IULM University for funding our research, Myrto Aspioti, Stella Diedrich, and everybody at De Gruyter for their valuable help, and, of course, our readers, for their time, attention, and, hopefully, critical remarks. This is but a first step in the largely uncharted territory of law and comedy.

The essay is dedicated to the memory of Paolo Villaggio (Genoa, 1932 – Rome, 2017). Villaggio was an Italian writer and comedian, whose work, besides casting an invaluable light on the Italian society of the 1970s–1990s, is an original reflection on the condition of humans who must cope with the hostile determinism of existence, without losing their capacity to imagine that some change may be about to come. In a sense, Villaggio's work is a perfect synthesis of the law and comedy relationship.

Milan, March 18, 2023

Giuseppe Rossi and Paola Carbone

https://doi.org/10.1515/9783111286778-001

Preface

This book has taken its cue from some impromptu conversations: law, despite its innate seriousness, and the instinctive association with justice that it arouses, constitutes one of the areas most frequented by comedy, in all its forms. Not only farces, but more or less elegant comedies, satire, jokes, cartoons, humorous comics often feature politicians, judges, lawyers, policemen, bureaucrats and other characters from the world of law. Sometimes it is the rule of law itself or the legal way of thinking (not to say the legal worldview) that provides the subject matter, or the pretext, that comedy uses to provoke laughter.

Joseph Heller's oft-cited anti-militarist satirical novel *Catch 22* is an example:

> There was only one catch and that was Catch-22, which specified that a concern for one's safety in the face of dangers that were real and immediate was the process of a rational mind. Orr was crazy and could be grounded. All he had to do was ask; and as soon as he did, he would no longer be crazy and would have to fly more missions. Orr would be crazy to fly more missions and sane if he didn't, but if he was sane he had to fly them. If he flew them he was crazy and didn't have to; but if he didn't want to he was sane and had to. Yossarian was moved very deeply by the absolute simplicity of this clause of Catch-22 and let out a respectful whistle
> 'That's some catch, that Catch-22,' he observed.
> 'It's the best there is,' Doc Daneeka agreed.[1]

The ridiculousness of the rule that triggers the short circuit of the "catch 22" lies not only in its bureaucratism, or in its circular structure, but in highlighting, finally, the absurdity of the idea of normativity as the expression of a power: the rule decides that aviators cannot avoid flying missions, even though these are foolish, and therefore sane individuals are naturally inclined to avoid them. So, the rule tells us that taking part in flying missions, risking one's life to kill other human beings, is madness that must be committed because someone, who has the legal power to do so, has decided it. That power finds its foundation in a certain worldview, which that law makes its own, and which it makes binding on those subject to it. War is a legitimate part of such worldview.

The rule of law not only obliges one to set aside all ethical perplexity, but also supersedes the very rule of rationality and self-preservation, which dictates that one must avoid madness. All this, besides being disturbing, is actually a little ridiculous.

To oppose it, by the way, would be childish. It is no surprise, however, that the gaze of childhood, with its mixture of astonishment and judgment (in the sense, of

1 Joseph Heller, *Catch 22: A Novel* (1961) (New York: Simon & Schuster, 2011), 52.

https://doi.org/10.1515/9783111286778-002

course, not of experience, nor of technique, but of some innate and intransigent capacity for evaluation), is among those congenial to the comedian. To adults alone, children's speech often appears unintentionally comic. In reality, the child cannot but be a child, and in the same way, a comedian cannot but be comic. As Paolo Villaggio recalled when he was awarded the Golden Lion for Lifetime Achievement by the Venice Film Festival in 1992: comic talent is

> a genetic quality, impossible to invent. But the comedian never becomes an adult, he always remains a child, he never loses his childish behavior: like Laurel and Hardy, like the Marx Brothers. A comedian never kisses his partner: if he falls in love, he is not successful.[2]

A character like Pierre Bezuchov comes to mind, not without some grotesque traits. When he appears at Anna Pavlovna Schérer's *soirée*, he is "a stout, heavily built young man, with close-cropped hair, spectacles, the light-coloured breeches fashionable at that time, a very high ruffle and a brown dress coat," who arouses in the hostess "a look of anxiety and fear, as at the sight of something too large and unsuited to the place." However, "her anxiety could only have reference to the clever though shy, but observant and natural, expression which distinguished him from everyone else in that drawing room."[3]

The childishness (very affluent and somewhat profligate), and the sharp as well as arbitrary judgements that characterise Pierre at the beginning of the novel (from which he will develop some wisdom, through experience) shine through in his dialogue about the war with Prince Andrew, who is about to leave to join his unit:

> '[...] this is what I have been thinking and wanted to tell you. There is a war now against Napoleon. If it were a war for freedom I could understand it and should be the first to enter the army; but to help England and Austria against the greatest man in the world is not right.'
>
> Prince Andrew only shrugged his shoulders at Pierre's childish words. He put on the air of one who finds it, impossible to reply to such nonsense, but it would in fact have been difficult to give any other answer than the one that Prince Andrew gave to this naïve question.
>
> 'If no one fought except on his own conviction, there would be no wars,' he said.
>
> 'And that would be splendid,' said Pierre.
>
> Prince Andrew smiled ironically.
> 'Very likely it would be splendid, but it will never come about ...'
> 'Well, why are you going to the war?' asked Pierre.

2 Quoted by Natalia Aspesi, "Villaggio in cerca d'amore," *La Repubblica*, September 8, 1992.
3 Leo Tolstoy, *War and Peace* (1865–1869) (London: Penguin, 1997), 9.

> 'What for? I don't know. I must. Besides that I am going ...' He paused. 'I am going because the life I am leading here does not suit me!'[4]

Prince Andrew invokes the juridical dutifulness of war ("What for? I don't know. I must"), but from Pierre's "childish" interlocution (depicted in an ironic, not overtly comic manner) humanity emerges in the form of the young man's dissatisfaction and desire for action and fulfilment ("I am going because the life I am leading here does not suit me!"). Thus, the non-juridical, but comical (childish) view of the dutifulness of war leads one to wonder whether law, by its normativity, imposes war as something irrational, unwanted, and ultimately inhuman, or whether it merely embraces the innate irrationality of the human, giving it a semblance of rationality, and with it a basis of dutifulness.

Of course, not all rules of law compel one to do something as ethically questionable as war. Rules of law, in general, aim to prevent injustice, which is a very worthy thing to do. So, at least in terms of intentions, they belong to the realm of the good. Yet, strangely enough, the comedian does not laugh at injustice (at evil), but at law (at the remedy), and at those who attempt to administer it, such as legislators, judges, lawyers, policemen. From this standpoint, law and medicine share the same fate. Since antiquity and the *commedia dell'arte*, it is not the disease that is mocked, but the physician who attempts to cure it, perhaps by flaunting a science he does not possess, or which he overestimates.

The first attempts to investigate the relationship between law and comedy have revealed another significant aspect. Laughter, and the comedy that arouses it, are extremely complex phenomena, which have always engaged many areas of thought, starting with philosophy. It may well be said, from this point of view, that laughter and comedy are very serious things. Thus, a singular and unexpected inversion takes place: the serious law turns out to be an easy object of comedy, while laughter and comedy display an almost unfathomable complexity and variety.

The book attempts to explore the many facets of this inversion, through legal reflection and the analysis of various literary and cinematic examples from different periods and cultures. The approach followed is not entirely linear. This does not suit law, which loves logicality (at least to distinguish itself from arbitrariness), but it does suit, and indeed is perhaps inevitable, a subject such as comedy, characterized, as it will be seen, by a close link with errancy.

Comedy thwarts the law's aspiration to expel errancy and irrationality, which are essential and ineradicable aspects of the human. Comedy brings

4 Leo Tolstoy, *War and Peace*, 25.

law back to the dimension of the human, denounces and depotentiates the threats that are implicit in the coercive capacity (though not necessarily in the nature) of law itself, even if aimed at the noblest aspirations. Finally, comedy makes us realise that it is precisely the inability of the law to avoid errancy that not only makes the law itself tolerable, but ultimately ensures its function, preventing it from getting lost in an unlikely and useless fixity.

The considerations set forth in this book, therefore, are errant, and certainly largely erroneous. We submit them, however, for the attention of our readers, counting not on their benevolence, but on their criticism, which will provide us with inspiration for new and perhaps different analyses.

The various chapters have acquired, almost spontaneously, a dialogical structure, in which literary analysis responds, sometimes dialectically or problematically, to legal reflection. The conception and layout of the book are the result (and this is not a note of style) of joint reflection between the authors. The odd-numbered chapters were written by Giuseppe Rossi, the even-numbered ones by Paola Carbone.

In the course of writing the book, we presented some elements of our analysis, here carried out in a broader form, at the sixteenth edition of the Giornate Tridentine di Retorica (Tridentine Days of Rhetoric), in 2016, at the University of Trento, and at the 2017 Annual Conference of the Italian Association of Law and Literature – AIDEL, at the University of Verona. The essay presented at the Verona Conference is published in the volume *Monsters and Monstrosity: From the Canon to the Anti-Canon: Literary and Juridical Subversions*, edited by Daniela Carpi, with the title "Who is the Monster? Laughing at Friends and Foes."[5]

We thank the colleagues who, on those occasions, paid attention to our work, and the editor of the cited volume, who hosted our essay. We thank Daniele Cananzi, Ettore Rocca, and the Research Centre for the Aesthetics of Law of the Mediterranean University of Reggio Calabria for hosting our volume in their series.

We would like to thank the Director of the Department of Humanities, Giovanna Rocca, and the Director of the Department of Business, Luca Barbarito, of IULM University, for funding our research.

Finally, we would like to thank the friends and colleagues who provided comments and suggestions, including by reading partial and provisional drafts of the work: Carla Barbati, Daniela Carpi, Valentina Garavaglia, Davide Grill, Paolo Her-

5 Paola Carbone and Giuseppe Rossi, "Who is the Monster? Laughing at Friends and Foes," in *Monsters and Monstrosity. From the Canon to the Anti-Canon: Literary and Juridical Subversions*, ed. Daniela Carpi (Berlin/Boston: De Gruyter, 2019), 157–179.

itier, Mara Logaldo, Maria Migliazza, Federico Regaldo, Paolo Revigliono, Laura Salmon, Luca Salvadori, Martina Treu.

Milan, March 18, 2021

Giuseppe Rossi and Paola Carbone

Contents

Chapter 1
Law, comedy, justice

Law and comedy: an unnatural combination or an unavoidable pair?

Laws, judgments, wills, contracts, damages, the legitimate use of state force against those who do not respect its rules, fines, prison, or even capital punishment: none of this is funny. By definition, law belongs to the domain of seriousness. The language of law is refined, specialized, and technical to the point of sometimes being incomprehensible to those who have not studied it, and it can even arouse a sense of mystery and distance that is typical of initiatory knowledge. The subjects who shape or enforce the law are cloaked in solemnity, bear titles, wear uniforms, carry badges and inspire the respect and fear that is due to those who have the power to define what is good, and to impose that observance on the unruly and sluggard. Nothing is less ridiculous than constitutions, parliaments, and supreme courts. No one is amused on the stairs and in the hallways of a courthouse, as they go to meet their judge.

Law and comedy represent an unnatural, illogical juxtaposition, and their terms are not related at all. Law is never nonsense; if it were, it would cease to be law. Law and silly, predictable jokes about lawyers have nothing to do with each other; rather, it is a combination born of chance, or at most, childishness. Law is serious, whereas jokes are a diversion: amusing, perhaps, but harmless and above all brief. One laughs about law the same way children laugh at their teacher's tics during the school break, or perhaps as mice plan to tie a bell around a cat's neck. Laughing at law is a carnival. In a 1981 essay on the relationship between comedy and rules, Umberto Eco[6] writes that "the comic seems to belong to the people, liberating, subversive, because it gives license to violate the rule. But it gives such license precisely to those who have so absorbed the rule that they also presume it is inviolable." Moreover, "the comedian doesn't have to reiterate the rule because he is sure it is known, accepted without discussion, and it will remain all the more so after the comic license has allowed, within a given space and through an intermediary mask, violating it in jest."[7] If this were the case, the

6 Umberto Eco, "The Comic and the Rule" [1981], trans. William Weaver, in Umberto Eco, *Travels in Hyperreality. Essays* (San Diego: Harcourt Brace Jovanovich, 1986), 269–278, 275.

7 Eco's argument seems to refer to characteristics of comic acts from the medieval period. "The medieval man laughs a double, contradictory laughter: the festive, collective laughter, that shows

https://doi.org/10.1515/9783111286778-003

feigned violation achieved with laughter would be entirely negligible and unworthy of attention. This essay could end here.

One may encounter the law during one's lifetime, but then, as with medicine, one must rely on the knowledge of an expert. The jurist, lawyer, and judge, above all, are among the most authoritative figures. They are necessary, like a physician. Laughing is useless. They are necessary like Doctor Balanzone in the *commedia dell'arte*, a jurist, lawyer and, if necessary, a physician, or vice versa.

In truth, the axiom that "law is serious" may be misleading; the laughter that law and its actors – legislators, judges, lawyers, notaries, policemen – have been arousing in large numbers for a very long time may not just be a harmless carnival. Law, like medicine, needs seriousness in order to be believed and respected. This does not mean that it is always serious, just as it is not always good. Just to give an example, the racial laws were certainly legal but it is equally certain they were not good.

This essay intends to reflect on the relationship between the claim/need for seriousness, typical of law, and the capacity for laughter, typical of humans, which comedy stimulates. As a starting point, we have assumed one extreme of the range between these two elements: the assertion that law is always serious. At the other extreme is the opposite assertion: law is always ridiculous. In this case, law and comedy would not, as noted at the outset, give rise to an unnatural juxtaposition but, on the contrary, to an inevitable combination. Laughter would be the direct and ineliminable consequence of the comic nature of law. The congenital nonsense of law could find its natural foundation in its human nature, which would make it the inevitable recipient of the laughter of Democritus, in the apocryphal narration traditionally attributed to Hippocrates. Democritus laughs at a single object, the human being who is full of nonsense, empty of righteous works, puerile in all his projects, who endures endless trials without benefit. Democritus mocks what should be apparently more serious, respected and feared; this includes, along with suffering and death, even honors and magistratures.[8]

From this standpoint, the only remaining hope of seriousness for law would be its total, or at least partial, detachment from the human dimension, in order

---

trust in his cultural environment through parody; the individual, personal laughter, that shows the pleasure of breaking individually what is respected when in the community": Georges Minois, *Histoire du rire et de la dérision* (Fayard: Paris, 2000) [my translation]. Eco himself, however, in his 1980 novel *The Name of the Rose*, which is set in the Middle Ages, implied a far less innocuous reconstruction of laughter.

8 Hippocrates, "The Democritus Letters," in *Pseudepigraphic Writings: Letters-Embassy-Speech from the Altar-Decree. Studies in Ancient Medicine*, trans. and ed. Wesley D. Smith (Leiden/New York: Brill, 1990), 47–125.

to transfer it to the divine one. Legal experience has never shied away from this hypothesis, which it sometimes still follows, entailing the subordination of law to faith, and the vanishing of the former as the latter fades. Laughter, in this extreme logic, is subversive and blasphemous; it deserves the condemnation inflicted on it by Christianity's interpretation that was widespread during the Middle Ages: by emphasizing the misery of the human condition, it removes any hope of redemption through faith (and of justice through law, which is grounded in it).[9]

Laughing at law is evil. Baudelaire writes that "human laughter is intimately linked with the accident of an ancient Fall, of a debasement both physical and moral," and again that "there is then, according to the Sage, a certain secret contradiction between his special nature as Sage and the primordial nature of laughter," to the point that "the Sage par excellence, the Word Incarnate, never laughed. In the eyes of the One who has all knowledge and all power, the comic does not exist. And yet the Word Incarnate knew anger; He even knew tears."[10]

If law is an instrument that enables man to counter evil, and is, therefore, both a result and a means of a civilization's progress, to laugh at it is not only a blatant act of pride (Baudelaire adopts the idea of laughter as a manifestation of superiority, which will be discussed later). Rather, it weakens humanity, it moves humans further and further away from the earthly paradise (where "it seemed to man that all created things were good," and "joy did not find its dwelling in laughter"), it reduces their confidence in their ability to break free from a primitive state, of which laughter is a characteristic expression. Fortunately, according to the poet of *spleen*, "as humanity uplifts itself, it wins for evil, and for the understanding of evil, a power that is proportionate to that which it has won for good," and "the comic changes its nature too": therefore "the angelic and the diabolic elements function at the same time." After all, it is with laughter – although satanic – that humans "sometimes soothe and charm their hearts," while "it is with tears that humans wash the afflictions of humans": thus, "the phenomena engendered by the Fall will become the means of redemption."[11]

It follows, then, that even law, as an expression of the aspiration for goodness (if not properly angelic) has some hope of surviving the comedy. This cannot deprive humans of the intelligence of goodness, and in return it will "sweeten" their hearts, and "soothe" them, making them less intransigent towards their own weaknesses, including the fallacies of law. On the other hand, to assume

---

9 Jacques Le Goff, "Rire au Moyen Âge," *Cahiers du Centre de Recherches Historiques* 3 (1989): 1–14; Letizia Ercoli, *Filosofia dell'umorismo* (Rome: Inschibolleth, 2013), 31.

10 Charles Baudelaire, "On the Essence of Laughter" [1885], trans. and ed. Jonathan Mayne, in *The Mirror of Art. Critical Studies by Charles Baudelaire* (New York: Doubleday, 1956), 131–155, 134–135.

11 Baudelaire, "On the Essence of Laughter," 97.

that law is always serious would be to deny its human nature, or to absurdly elevate the human condition to that of a god, thus setting humanity free from error.

This way, the legal rules that humanity sets and enforces, by coercing people to follow them and suffer the consequences of their infringements, would become infallible. Of course, this is unrealistic. One can take it as an axiom that error is inevitable, in law as in any other human activity. If error were a negative element by its very nature (but this cannot be taken for granted) law would contain an unavoidable and unpredictable number of dramatic errors, and thus would not only always be serious but, indeed, tragic.

Thus, if the relationship between law and comedy were limited to the two extremes of the interval described above, the only choice that would remain would be between the laughter of Democritus and the wailing of Heraclitus, the "philosopher of weeping," in which the human condition brings about the opposite of hilarity, i. e., constant pain. One might, then, conclude with Seneca: *"Adice quod de humano quoque genere melius meretur qui ridet illud quam qui luget: ille et spei bonae aliquid relinquit, hic autem stulte deflet quae corrigi posse desperate."*[12] Human law is ridiculous, but humankind could still improve…

Or, with Diderot, one might prefer "le rôle compatissant d'Heraclite, qui pleurait sur la folie de ses frères" to the "rôle cruel de Démocrite, qui se rit des malheureux humains."[13] The tragedy of the errors of law would at least generate solidarity among human beings. Humans are "the only creatures that laugh," writes Aristotle.[14] Giambattista Vico, in his *Vici vindiciae* ("Vindication of Vico"), takes Aristotle's cue to further conclusions. While thanks to "acute remarks," which reveal non-ob-

---

12 Seneca, "Of Peace of Mind," trans. Aubrey Stewart, *Minor Dialogues together with the Dialogue on Clemency* (London: Bell & Sons, 1889), 250–287, 282: "Add to this that he who laughs at the human race deserves better of it than he who mourns for it, for the former leaves it some good hopes of improvement, while the latter stupidly weeps over what he has given up all hopes of mending."

13 Denis Diderot, *Essai sur les règnes de Claude et de Néron, et sur la vie et les écrits de Sénéque, pour servir d'introduction à la lecture de ce philosophe* (1782), available online: https://obvil.sorbonne-universite.fr/corpus/critique/diderot_claude-neron/#body-2 (last access January 2023), 286. On the dualism between the Democritean and Heraclitean approaches, Letizia Ercoli, *Filosofia dell'umorismo*, 19; Massimo Donà, *Filosofia dell'errore. Le forme dell'inciampo* (Milan: Bompiani, 2012), 181.

14 Aristotle, *Parts of Animals*, trans. A.L. Peck (Cambridge, MA: Harvard Univ. Press, 1961), 52–436, 281. The Stagirite identifies the emergence of humanity in the first laughter of infants. Contemporary zoology has long been aware that laughter is actually an attitude shared by humans and other primates. The same goes for the 'spontaneous smile' of infants, during sleep, which is the antecedent of conscious smiling and laughter. This phenomenon is also observed in newborns of chimpanzees and some species of macaques. See Fumito Kawakami, Masaki Tomonaga, and Juri Suzuki, "The First Smile: Spontaneous Smiles in Newborn Japanese Macaques (Macaca fuscata)," *Primates* 58 (2017): 93–101.

vious connections, "our mind, which by its very nature hungers for truth, learns many things in the brief span of a moment,"

> argute remarks are the product of a feeble and narrow imagination that either compares mere names of things, regarding only their external appearances (and not all of them), or presents some of them absurdly or unsuitably to an unthinking mind that, while expecting appropriate and suitable ones, is deluded and frustrated in its expectation.[15]

Animals, according to Vico, do not know how to laugh

> because they have one sense only, which enables them to pay attention to but one object at a time. Hence, any one object is continuously expelled and deleted by the subsequent one. It is thus perfectly obvious that since animals have been denied by nature the ability to laugh, they are also deprived of all reason.

The *risores* ("cacklers": those who "laugh immoderately and without reason") are therefore characterized by a kind of attenuated rationality, which places them between humans and beasts. If laughter shows the embryo of the capacity to grasp the connections between types of knowledge, without isolating each of them from the others as it happens with animals, humans reach the truth only when they go beyond the superficiality and false appearances that arouse laughter. This "comes from our feeble human nature, which 'deceives us by the semblance of right.'" Because laughter is affected by this same "instability of mind" that is "the principal cause of foolishness,"[16] "philosophy dedicates itself to overcoming this instability above all else and principally aims at reinforcing the wise." The minds of the wise man, indeed, "tend always toward the uniform, suitable, and appropriate."[17]

15 "... Therefore, when the brain fibers, focused on an appropriate and suitable object, are disturbed by an unexpected one, they become disordered. Being agitated, they transmit their restless motion to all branches of the nervous system. This shakes the whole body and removes man from his normal state" (Giambattista Vico, "Vindication of Vico," in *Keys to the "New Science": Translations, Commentaries, and Essays*, eds. Thora Ilin Bayer and Donald Phillip Verene (Ithaca/New York: Cornell Univ. Press, 2008), 107–135, 118).

16 *Risus abundat in ore stultorum.* A locution that Vico traces back to 'Divine Wisdom'. The only formula 'in ore stultorum' actually appears in the *Vulgate.* See also Renzo Tosi, "Sulla genesi di alcuni proverbi," in *Καλὸς καὶ ἀγαθὸς ἀνήρ· διδασκάλου παράδειγμα – Homenaje al Profesor Juan Antonio López Férez*, eds. Luis Miguel Pino Campos and Germán Santana Henriquez (Madrid: Ediciones Clásicas, 2013), 813–819.

17 "[...] this delight is in intensity the same as that which pervades the spectator at a game, as for example, when he sees the trajectory of a ball finish exactly where the player had directed it and to where the ball should go" (Giambattista Vico, "Vindication of Vico," 121). The delight in the game of the ball, at least in today's version of football, seems to lie, instead, above all in the possibility of

These and similar reflections are the starting point for philosophy's suspicion of laughter, which prevailed until Friedrich Nietzsche's great rehabilitation of laughter, as well as for the dualism between comedy and humor (moderate laughter, a possible precursor to knowledge, and thoughtless laughter, coarse and an end in itself), which is characteristic of many famous theories about comedy, including that of Luigi Pirandello. Baudelaire's thoughts are along the same lines, according to which "[...] since laughter is essentially human, it is, in fact, essentially contradictory; that is to say that it is at once a token of an infinite grandeur and an infinite misery – the latter in relation to the absolute Being of whom man has an inkling, the former in relation to the beasts."[18]

If laughing is foolish, then laughing at the law is supremely foolish, not only because law is serious, but also because law, at least according to the Western conception, represents first and foremost a logical order. This should be ensured by the coherence of concepts and rules aimed at guaranteeing social order, whether it is understood as a reflection of the worldly and otherworldly order of creation, or not. While laughter is by essence contradictory, law should be by essence coherent, exalting the value of certainty and the logical link that binds its concepts and rules. Laughing at law would therefore mean denying the very uniformity and congruence that philosophy and the sage's mind should aim for, or exalting incoherence as an essential human trait, with repudiation of the value of *firmitas* as an attribute that is typical of humans as subjects of law. The mockery of law would thus have a strong potential for social disintegration. It would undermine institutions, which would find themselves deprived not only of consensus, but also of logical sense. We may admit, in light of the successive evolutions of philosophical and legal thought, that coherence and logical order are neither the sole nor the highest objective of both philosophy and law. Anyway, the fact remains that laughing at law implies, if not the denial of the possibility for order, the at least temporary dominance of the disorder in regard to order, which is still one of the qualifying aspects of legal systems. Both the theme of the relationship between the seriousness and the ridiculousness of law, and that between the order of the law and the disorder of the comedy lead intuitively to a problem of measure, or balance. According to the Stagirite, excessive laughter is reprehensible and typical of "vulgar buffoons" who "strive for humor at all costs, [...] aiming rather at raising a laugh, than at say-

the unexpected, if not the impossible or the magical, which it shares with the fairy tale (cf. Paola Carbone and Giuseppe Rossi, "Ethics and Law at Play on the Football Pitch," in *Fables of the Law. Fairy Tales in a Legal Context*, eds. Daniela Carpi and Marett Leiboff (Berlin/Boston: De Gruyter, 2016), 209–243.

18 Baudelaire, "On the Essence of Laughter," 140.

ing what is becoming and at avoiding pain to the object of their fun."[19] On the contrary, *eutrapelìa* is typical of the sage, who has the ability to joke in an appropriate way at the right time, without exceeding or offending the recipient of the joke.[20] Does eutrapelia exist between the extremes of the relationship between law and comedy? Where does it lie? It is essential, therefore, to explore the full extent of the interval. First of all, however, there is another problem. If eutrapelia is the ability to joke, and therefore to laugh and make others laugh at the right time, in an appropriate way, and with respect for the sensibilities of others, it is a matter of rules to establish when a moment is right for a joke, when the manner and style of the comic act are appropriate and what the boundaries beyond which laughter becomes intolerable are. Since law is nothing more than a set of rules, when we laugh at law, eutrapelia is the result of rules that tell us when we can laugh at other rules. Thus, the relationship between law and comedy apparently shows the characteristics of a comparison between sets of rules; these same rules indicate when laughing at law does not automatically lead to a spiral into chaos.

The third element: the phantom of justice

If eutrapelia is the outcome of rules that establish when one can laugh at law, it is evident that the source of these rules cannot be law itself. Otherwise, the answer would most likely be that laughter at the law, and especially at the expense of the law, is never socially or legally permitted. The same Aristotelian text points to ethics as the source of rules of behavior that sanction the actions of the virtuous person, including the limits of their laughing and joking. As a consequence, the relationship between law and comedy conceals a third element, which concerns the definition of ethical rules of conduct. However, the fact that one of the terms of the relationship is precisely law leads to broadening the reference to ethics, understood as the source of rules of conduct in the context of social relations (including those regulated by law, as well as the activities of forming and enforcing legal rules), to something broader and decidedly more elusive, which one instinctively associates with law. I am referring, of course, to justice.

In this work it is not necessary to delve into the complex issue of a theoretical definition of justice, or even just a reconstruction of the theories of justice. We

19 Aristotle, *The Nicomachean Ethics*, trans. David Ross (Oxford: Oxford Univ. Press, 1998), 103.
20 But Rabelais, as an epigraph to his masterpiece, writes that "Mieulx est de risque de larmes escripre | Pour ce que rire est le propre de l'homme."

need only observe how any individual, or community, believes that they can affirm (not necessarily on the basis of legal rules) what is just or unjust – perhaps without being able to formulate even the vaguest and most uncertain definition of what is meant by 'justice.' Both the comedians and their audience possess a knowledge (or more precisely a feeling) of justice, which may converge or diverge. This knowledge-feeling of justice appears to be highly variable in time and space. Historically, individuals and social groups have manifested the most varied attitudes to the justice of even extreme choices, such as capital punishment or massacres, and continue to do so today.

While reassuring, it would be misleading to conceal the profound variability of human feelings as to what is just or unjust in our relationship with the world and with our fellow human beings, behind the veneer of unanimity in international organizations, or behind the proclamations of human rights charters. To give just one example, think of how complex and uncertain the answer is to the question of whether there is a 'just war', and what its reasons and characteristics should be. The achievements of civilization, of each culture, although they may seem universally agreed upon, are transitory and circumscribed.

The law, in all its manifestations, can never escape comparison with this individual and social knowledge of justice, and the continuous judgment that ensues, which is less technical than social, moral, ethical, and even aesthetic (think of the humor of the circumvoluted language of legislation, court decisions, and legal doctrine, or of the ornaments and trappings of jurists). The law formulates judgments based on rules, which are in turn constantly judged on the basis of other rules. These latter rules often constitute objects of uncertain, if not impossible, enunciation, but of certain perception on the part of those individuals or social bodies, who apply them. The relationship between law and comedy is thus configured as a relationship between sets of rules, and between claims of judgment that, on closer inspection, can sometimes be conflicting. While the legal rule and its instruments of application are, at least for the most part,[21] formed by explicit statements and by formal and tangible apparatuses (institutions), on the contrary the rules of judgment to which the individual and the community submit the law and its results are often unspoken, difficult to enunciate, and perceived as an ectoplasmic but constant presence.[22]

21 The reference to cryptotypes, investigated by Rodolfo Sacco, cannot be ignored. See in particular Rodolfo Sacco, *Introduzione al diritto comparato*, 4th ed. (Turin: Giappichelli, 1990), 155 who defines "cryptotypes" as "implicit models," characterized by not taking verbal form.

22 The comic laughter of the legal often implies the question that opens an essay by the magistrate and writer Salvatore Mannuzzu, published in 1998 (in the aftermath of the series of trials for bribery against outstanding politicians and managers called "Tangentopoli" (Briberyland) and at the

The law, its symbolism and its serious representations (when they are not denunciatory...) tend to constantly recall the idea of justice, to the point of suggesting the equivalence of the two terms. This equivalence is often found in both institutional language (the Ministry of Justice) and in everyday language, where the word "justice" is often used as a metaphor for "jurisdiction." On the contrary, comic representations of legal themes often portray the law and its actors as symbols of incapacity, vacuous formalism, dishonesty, uselessness, arbitrariness, denouncing the betrayal of justice. Perhaps the most obvious example is offered by the comic comparison between jurisdiction, as practiced in each context, and the aspiration that the trial should be an instrument of justice. An oft-repeated sketch from theater comedy and comic cinema shows a criminal trial of a poor man accused of minor offenses assisted by a court-appointed lawyer who reads a newspaper during the hearing. The defendant proclaims his innocence, but when the judge invites the lawyer to make his plea, the lawyer, after stating that "the defendant pleads guilty," "appeals to the clemency of the court" to the obvious dismay of the defendant (who utters, perhaps in some vernacular, a resigned comment such as "oh, what a lawyer ..."). The final judgment, in this way, is known in advance and is no longer perceived by the spectator as the result of the juridical, of which the trial in the adversarial process of the parties is at the same time expression and condition,[23] but of mere clemency, that is to say of a sense of justice. The judge may possess and want to use such a sense, or may not possess it or may not want to use it depending on the good fortune of the accused. The state of law in each legal system and in a given historical moment is not a fact of nature, but the result of a balance of forces between sets of rules and demands for judgment.

---

beginning of the 'second Republic' in Italy: "do Justice and justice have something in common? Meaning by the former not the heavenly one which, as we know, is not of this earth, but the justice possible according to the historical aspirations of men, written or not in laws; and meaning by the latter, the product of institutional operations that adapt concrete cases to the models of the given orders, perhaps ne cives ad arma veniant: a public service rendered also so that citizens do not fight each other too much": Salvatore Mannuzzu, *Il fantasma della giustizia* (Bologna: Il Mulino, 1998), 7 [my translation]. The image of the phantom of justice is taken from *The History of the Human Race*, in which Leopardi narrates how Jupiter "gave laws, injunctions, and legal status to the new peoples; and finally, wishing to bestow an incomparable gift upon them, he sent among them certain phantoms of the most excellent and superhuman appearance, ceding to these a very great of the government and administration of these peoples: and they were called Justice, Virtue, Renown, Patriotism, and names of that sort" (Giacomo Leopardi, *The Moral Essays (Operette morali)* [1827], trans. Patrick Creagh (New York: Columbia Univ. Press, 1983), 38).

23 It is the "dialogical method that requires seeking the truth through confrontation between the parties (and not through a 'tyrannical' injunction)": Maurizio Manzin, "Del contraddittorio come *principio* e come *metodo*," in *Audiatur et altera pars. Il contraddittorio tra principio e regola*, eds. Maurizio Manzin and Federico Puppo (Milan: Giuffrè, 2008), 5.

Eutrapelia, which is laughter "at the right time and in the right way" in the face of the law and its actors, is one of the possible revenges that the phantom of justice can inspire or impose on humans in the face of unjust law, and it is not necessarily harmless.

Protest aimed at changing the law is another possible form of revenge inspired, or demanded, by the phantom of justice. Rebellion is the most extreme one of all. Just as the phantom of justice is constantly changing shape and form in time and space, when it comes to laughing at law, eutrapelia manifests itself differently depending on place and context. The fact that a comic act can be very funny to an audience of a certain nationality, and boring – if not pathetic – to spectators from another country,[24] is the result of the ethical tension, of approval or blame, that laughter implies. This tension becomes more intense when the object of the comic act is the law (or religion, morality, death, suffering or other aspects that are intuitively associated with the domain of the serious or tragic), and so the phantom of justice begins to hover.

The upside-down world: laughter as a sanction of the injustice of law

According to Bergson,[25] laughter is a social phenomenon that has a sanctioning value: by expressing society's disapproval, it punishes behavior that deviates from what is socially expected in certain situations. The idea of laughter as a stigma, whether individual or social, goes back to Thomas Hobbes who, in the part of *Elements of Law, Natural and Politic* concerned with *Human Nature*, establishes the well-known theory of laughter as a manifestation of superiority:

> Men laugh often (especially such as are greedy of applause from every thing they do well) at their own actions performed never so little beyond their own expectation; as also at their own jests: and in this case it is manifest, that the passion of laughter proceedeth from a sudden conception of some ability in himself that laughet. Also men laugh at the infirmities of others, by comparison of which their own abilities are set off and illustrated … I may therefore conclude, that the passion of laughter is nothing else but a sudden glory arising from

24 On which Umberto Eco, "The Comic and the Rule," dwells, contrasting the geographical and cultural relativity of the comic with the universality of the tragic. Even the latter, however, may not be taken for granted.

25 Henri Bergson, *Laughter. An Essay on the Meaning of the Comic* [1900], trans. Cloudesley Brereton and Fred Rothwell (London: McMillan, 1911), 19–20. For a critical reconstruction of the so-called 'superiority theory' see John Morreal, *Comic Relief. A Comprehensive Philosophy of Humor* (New York: Wiley Blackwell, 2009), 4ff.

> sudden conception of some eminency in ourselves, by comparison with the infirmities of others, or with our own formerly ... It is no wonder therefore that men take it heinously to be laughed at or derided, that is, triumphed over.[26]

In the sixth chapter of the first part of *Leviathan*, the theme is taken up again with some important clarifications:

> Sudden glory, is the passion which maketh those grimaces called laughter; and is caused either by some sudden act of their own, that pleaseth them; or by the apprehension of some deformed thing in another, by comparison whereof they suddenly applaud themselves. And it is incident most to them, that are conscious of the fewest abilities in themselves; who are forced to keep themselves in their own favor, by observing the imperfections of other men. And therefore much laughter at the defects of others, is a sign of pusillanimity. For of great minds, one of the proper works is, to help and free others from scorn; and compare themselves only with the most able.[27]

Baudelaire shares the idea that laughter arises from the feeling of someone's superiority over somebody else, or people over nature (in the case of the grotesque, which he calls "absolute comic"). In the latter case, the joy of superiority expressed by laughter would arise from the recognition of people's ability to perform acts of creation: "faboulous creations, beings whose authority and raison d'être cannot be drawn from the code of common sense, often provoke in us an insane and excessive mirth, which expresses itself in insane paroxysms and swoons."[28]

Bergsonian theory seems to explain the mockery of the juridical in a particularly felicitous way: in the case of comedy about law and its protagonists, the laughing spectators disapprove of the legal rule and/or its application, noting its distance from their expectations in that particular situation. It goes without saying that their expectations are inspired by the phantom of justice, so eager for revenge. While Bergson observes that the transgressions of social mores that are sanctioned by laughter are of such a minor nature that they do not affect the rules of law, the comedian who laughs at law judges and condemns law itself and its enforcement mechanisms, in the name of a higher order. The laughter stems from the fact that the comedian and audience share this order, at least at the level of intuition or in-

---

26 Thomas Hobbes, *Elements of Law, Natural and Politic* (1650), ed. Ferdinand Tönnies, 2nd ed. (London: Frank Cass & Co., 1969), 41 – 42. For a reconstruction of Hobbes' thought and the subsequent debate that developed in English philosophy between the seventeenth and eighteenth centuries see Andrea Gatti, "Egoismi e incongruenze. Estetiche del riso in età moderna," in *Animal Ridens, I castelli di Yale online* 5.2 (2017), 289–303.

27 Thomas Hobbes, *Leviathan, or The Matter, Forme and Power of a Common Wealth Ecclesiastical and Civil* (1651), ed. J.C.A. Gaskin (Oxford: Oxford Univ. Press, 1996), 38.

28 Baudelaire, "On the Essence of Laughter," 104.

spiration (they are under the influence of the phantom of justice), and they grasp the distance between it and the reality of law. If this were not the case, comedy about law would not be funny. Think, for example, of the Collodian judge-gorilla who tries and condemns Pinocchio in the land of Acchiappacitrulli (Trap for Blockheads):[29] "The judge was a big ape of the gorilla tribe – an old ape respected for his age, his white beard, but especially for his gold spectacles without glasses that he was always obliged to wear on account of an inflammation of the eyes that had tormented him for many years."

The judge who imprisons a victim by diverting the law and the trial at court from their function (it is no coincidence that he has been suffering from "inflammation of the eyes" for many years) commits a blatant injustice: he therefore deserves to be laughed at and depicted as a clumsy animal, even though he is ironically described as "respectable." At the same time, however, Collodi intends to teach a lesson that goes beyond warning against the danger of judicial arbitrariness: he wants to make the reader aware that the law does not protect (or did not protect at the time) against excesses of gullibleness.

The comedian invites the audience to reflect on the goodness of those rules that they have, perhaps, "incorporated," by posing the question, for example with Dworkin, whether a good, law-abiding citizen has any duty to obey an unjust rule. Laughing at the juridical means laughing at the pretended good rules and the pretended justice achieved by those who apply these rules in reality, and not only in comic fiction. From this perspective, the comedy is a revenge inspired by the phantom of justice against the unjust legal system.

This approach can explain, at least in part, the fact that satire often makes use of the grotesque as a means of expression. Behind the appearance of justice and order, the absurd is thus disclosed and the truly unjust or chaotic revealed. In the case of satire, the tension between the legal need for seriousness and the comedian's subversive derision reaches its apex, and the conflict between sets of rules (of law and eutrapelia) and claims for judgment becomes particularly manifest, to the point of setting law against comedy. A later chapter of this essay will be devoted to this issue. However, this theoretical approach is not exhaustive: it does not explain the entire phenomenon of comedy and laughter, nor, as far as we are interested here, the entire phenomenon of law and comedy.

A parallel can perhaps be established between the superiority-sanction theory of comedy, according to which laughter is the result of a judgment and a punishment (the act of laughing itself) expressed by the one who laughs, and the typical way law is enforced. This leads to a kind of legalization/juridification of laughter,

29 Carlo Collodi, *Pinocchio* [1881] (London: Bloomsbury Books, 1994), 67–68.

which goes hand in hand with its politicization. These are elements, at least sometimes, of satire rather than comedy. Moreover, the same Hobbesian passage in *Leviathan* makes it clear that the superiority of those who laugh is only illusory, it is a superiority attributed to "them, that are conscious of the fewest abilities in themselves; who are forced to keep themselves in their own favor, by observing the imperfections of other men. And therefore, much laughter at the defects of others, is a sign of pusillanimity." Assigning the laughing person the function of avenger of justice, *per se*, means assuming that the phantom of justice can only be a Shakespearean specter, which demands revenge and places the human being in constant dilemmas and tragic choices between right and wrong, and that laughter is the deadly weapon through which revenge is consumed.

Even simply describing a person who laughs as a "maieuta of a new order," as Eco proposes with reference to Franti in *Cuore* ("Heart"),[30] can lead to attributing greater merits to laughter than it actually possesses. In the novel, Franti laughs at everything and everyone, even at the king's funeral, and is therefore detested by the diarist Bottini.[31] However, his laugh is not maieutic, but foolish and unrealistic. Once expelled from school, he disappears from the book, which foreshadows for him a destiny of definitive marginalization and probable life imprisonment. The most significant aspect, from a legal point of view, of Franti's expulsion from school is the teacher's final despair: "the master bore him thus, heavy as he was, to the principal, and then came back alone and seated himself at his little table, with his head clutched in his hands, out of breath, and with a look of such weariness and trouble that it was painful to see him. 'After teaching school for thirty years!,' he exclaimed sadly, shaking his head."

The teacher's discouragement provides a significant representation of the failure of the rule (and of the institution), which is unable to be embraced and, even more importantly, to establish communication with the addressee. Franti laughs not because he criticizes or sanctions the rules, but simply because he is indiffer-

---

30 Umberto Eco, "Elogio di Franti," in Umberto Eco, *Diario minimo* (Milan: Bompiani, 1963), 153. In the same essay, Eco compares Franti to Gaetano Bresci; later, in *Il costume di casa. Evidenze e misteri dell'ideologia italiana negli anni sessanta* (Milan: Bompiani, 1973, reprint 2012), 90, he compares Franti to the boys of the Barbiana school, to the author of the 1968 manifesto "Contro l'Università" (Against University) Guido Viale, to the anarchist activist Pietro Valpreda.

31 "Only one boy was capable of laughing while Derossi was declaiming the funeral oration of the King. It was Franti. I detest that fellow. He is wicked. When a father comes to school to reprove his son, he enjoys it; when anyone cries, he laughs. He cowers before Garrone, and he strikes the little mason, because he is small. He torments Crossi because he has an helpless arm. He ridicules Precossi, whom everyone respects. He even jeers at Robetti, that boy in the second grade who walks on crutches, through having saved a child" (Edmondo De Amicis, *Heart. A School-Boy's Journal* [1886], trans. Isabel F. Hapgood (New York: Crowell & Co., 1901), 102, 104).

ent to them and their inherent punishments,[32] up to the outcome: his expulsion from school (from the legal order), which enshrines the latter's definitive failure. De Amici's words, inevitably dated, are influenced by Cesare Lombroso's positivist theories on the genetic predisposition to delinquency of certain individuals, who are therefore irredeemable. The master's despair, however, partly reverses this perspective. The sanction/expulsion from the legal order is not the natural fulfillment of the law (even the substance, according to positivist thought of law as the legitimate use of force), but the symptom of his failure.

On the other hand, there is also no necessary correlation between the idea of laughter as a manifestation of superiority and the idea of laughter as a punishment. Although the person that laughs deems himself superior to the one who laughs at, this does not necessarily imply that the latter deserves to be punished, or that, by laughing, one aims at punishing others, rather that amusing himself. Therefore, when the object of laughter is law, the one who laughs does not necessarily aim at punishing the law because of some implicit or explicit grievance of injustice of the law itself. As we will see below, the law may just look (involuntarily) funny, though not unjust.

Referring to the absolute comic, Baudelaire identifies in it an art[33] capable of arousing joy associated with the perception of man's creative/transformative capacity, and thus man's superiority over nature, from whose conditioning he is capable of freeing himself. Laughing at law, including laughter provoked by satire's grotesque deformations, could also be a manifestation of joy at the effectiveness of the real law (and not the deformed one mocked by the comedian) to contribute to the progress of mankind, manifesting man's superiority over nature, which would relegate him to the feral state. Laughter, therefore, not as a denunciation of law's injustice, but as an exaltation of the capacity of law to produce what is just, to ensure an order that contributes to the progress of civilization. Laughter, in itself, has no positive or negative value: the reasons that induce it can be commendable or futile, even stupid, or cruel. The mockery of the juridical, like any mockery, can be empty and foolish, the result of ignorance, cynicism, barbarism.

The person who laughs can announce the advent of a new order, preceded by the de-legitimization of the previous one, or be pleased with the "superiority of humanity over nature." But those who laugh can also commit a mere brutality, being deaf to fundamental moral or ethical impulses. Think, for example, of the

32 "The master sometimes pretends not to see his rascalities, and he behaves all the worse. The master tried to get a hold on him by kind treatment, and the boy ridiculed him for for it. The master said terrible things to him, and the boy covered his face with his hands, as though he was crying; but he was laughing" (De Amicis, *Heart*, 103).

33 Baudelaire, "On the Essence of Laughter," 103–104.

mocking laughter and jokes that the House of Lords set forth in the peroration by the grotesquely disfigured protagonist of the *Homme qui rit,* who complained of serious injustices and announced forthcoming rebellions:

> How could they stand such nonsense? The laughter burst out afresh; and now it was overwhelming. Of all the lava which that crater, the human mouth, ejects, the most corrosive is joy. To inflict evil gaily is a contagion which no crowd can resist. All executions do not take place in the scaffold; and men, from the moment they are in a body, whether in mobs or in senates, have always a ready executioner among them, called sarcasm.[34]

Foolish and brutal laughter, anyway, is not the prerogative of crowds, assemblies, or people who are detached from reality, like Franti. Somebody may continue, foolishly, to laugh alone, because his hilarity, as Vico taught, arises from the misunderstanding of order, or because his phantom of justice is a personal specter which no one else sees or even senses.[35] Not only that: in addition to having a subversive charge, laughter also has an opposite, conservative one of sublimation of clash and victory. Starting from Hobbes' reflections, Elias Canetti wrote, in *Crowds and Power*, that

> Originally laughter contained a feeling of pleasure in prey or food which seemed certain. A human being who falls down reminds us of an animal we might have hunted and brought down ourselves. Every sudden fall which arouses laughter does so because it suggests helplessness and reminds us that the fallen can, if we want, be treated as prey. If we went further and actually ate it, we would not laugh. We laugh instead of eating it. Laughter is our physical reaction to the escape of potential food. As Hobbes said, laughter expresses a sudden feeling of superiority, but he did not add that it only occurs when the normal consequences of this superiority do not ensue. His conception contains only half the truth [...].[36]

It must be added that Canetti assigned a very different symbolic value to laughter in his only fictional work, the 1935 novel *Auto da fé*, which we will deal with in a following chapter.

Baudelaire himself noted that: "the Being who sought to multiply his own image has in no wise put the teeth of the lion into the mouth of man – yet man

---

34 Victor Hugo, *The Man Who Laughs* [1869] (New York: Sears & Co.), 449–450.

35 Think of the protagonist of the Italian songwriter Francesco Guccini's song, *Il matto* (The Madman), included in the 1996 album *D'amore, morte e altre sciocchezze* (EMI): "They said I was mad / because I took life / as a jester, as a madman / with infinite gaiety. / Actually, it is much better, / within this tragedy, / to laugh on oneself, not to cry, / and to turn it into comedy... but it does not seem normal to me / to always laugh alone."

36 Elias Canetti, *Crowds and Power* [1960], trans. Carol Stewart (New York: Seabury Press, 1978), 223. See Marco Bertozzi, "Hobbes e Canetti. Il riso come maschera dell'arcaico," *Animal Ridens – I castelli di Yale online* 5.2 (2017): 279–287.

rends with his laughter; nor all the seductive cunning of the serpent into his eyes – yet he beguiles with his tears."[37]

Laughter still represents a symbolic, sublimated bite, which leaves unharmed the physical body of the victim as well as the metaphorical bodies of the institutions and the just or unjust rules that the latter apply. Laughter is never the revolution. At the most, it can bring about the revolution (Canetti's "overthrowing crowd"), and therefore the transformation of law par excellence. But laughter can also avert the revolution by acting as a substitute, as Eco reminded writing about carnival or medieval festival laughter. In any case, even the assumption that there is a necessary link between laughter and context, and between a comic act and something outside it, could be an incorrect starting point. The laughing face, as in the works of the famous Chinese artist Yue Minjun,[38] can be a logo or a mask – a sign that is indifferent to the context, which can be affixed to anything, always remaining the same, without judging anything. A laughing face can simply be produced, bought, and sold, like any commodity. In the case of comedy dealing with law, perhaps this happens more rarely because of the value content that the juridical naturally carries with it, and because of the inherent capacity of comedy that laughs at law – even the most banal or trivial – to somehow awaken the phantom of justice.

Incongruity: who is "good"?

Schopenhauer maintains that

> In every case, laughter results from nothing but the suddenly perceived incongruity between a concept and the real objects that had been thought through it in some relation; and laughter itself is just the expression of this incongruity. If often occurs through two or more real objects being thought through one concept, and the identity of the concept being transferred to the objects. But then a complete difference of the objects in other respects makes it strikingly clear that the concept fitted them only from a one-sided point of view. It occurs just as often,

---

37 Baudelaire, "On the Essence of Laughter," 135.

38 Ben Davis, "Guy Smiling," review of the exhibition *Yue Minjun and the Symbolic Smile*, Oct. 14, 2007–Jan. 6, 2008, at Queens Museum of Art, in http://www.artnet.com/magazineus/reviews/davis/davis11-12-07.asp (last access February 2021): "Yue's style is thus fused to ideas about cartoons, mascots, logos and the like. It is a brand identity, and a successful one [...] the truth of Yue's art is in the whole and not in any of the individual works, in the way that, as he says, his grinning self-portraits 'propagate their own image everywhere.' Yue Minjun's artistic project is less a painterly one than it is a conceptual one about the market, image and self-marketing –– something his successful mass self-fabrication as a sculpture already suggests. The content of his art cannot be separated from its inherent marketability. He is laughing all the way to the bank."

> however, that the incongruity between a single real object and the concept under which, on the one hand, it has been rightly subsumed, is suddenly felt ... All laughter, therefore is occasioned by a paradoxical, and hence unexpected, subsumption, it matters not whether this is expressed in words or in deeds.[39]

The essence of comedy, then, is incongruity. In rebuttal to Hobbes, in 1725 the Scottish philosopher Francis Hutcheson formalized his incongruity theory, emphasizing the moral/ethical incongruity from which laughter arises. The latter is said to originate from the contradictory assimilation of images that suggest opposite judgments within a single main idea

> [...] generally the cause of laughter is the bringing together of images which have contrary additional ideas, as well as some resemblance in the principal idea: this contrast between ideas of grandeur, dignity, sanctity, perfection, and ideas of meanness, baseness, profanity, seems to be the very spirit of the burlesque; and the greatest part of our raillery and jest is founded upon it.[40]

Incongruity, therefore, can take on a dual significance: it can be either logical or ethical, or even show both aspects. A key element in Schopenhauer's thought is the dualism between reason and intuition, based on the observation of the inevitable fallacy of all conceptualization.[41] As a matter of fact, laughter is the consequence of the sudden perception[42] of this fallacy, which arises from the dystonia between the fact and the concept within which it can be subsumed. This happens

---

39 Arthur Schopenhauer, *The World as Will and Representation* [1818], trans. E.F.J. Payne (New York: Dover Inc., 1969), I, 59; Arthur Schopenhauer, *Supplements to "The World as Will and Representation"* [1844], trans. E.F.J. Payne (New York: Dover Inc., 1969), II, 91. See once again John Morreal, *Comic Relief*, 30 ff.; John Morreal, *Taking Laughter Seriously* (Albany: State Univ. of New York Press, 1983), chap. 3; Luca Mori, "Il 'ridere' come rottura nelle cornici di senso: esplorazione filosofica a partire da un chiasma platonico," *Itinera* 6 (2013), 156–174.

40 Francis Hutcheson, *Reflections Upon Laughter and Remarks Upon the Fable of the Bees* [1725] (Glasgow: D. Baxter, 1750), 19. These are the three essays on laughter published in *The Dublin Journal* in 1725. Schopenhauer, *Supplements to 'The World,'* 93 identifies Hutcheson's *Introduction into Moral Philosophy* as the earliest known attempt at a psychological explanation of laughter. For comments see Gatti, "Egoismi e incongruenze"; Elizabeth Telfer, "Hutcheson's Reflections upon Laughter," *The Journal of Aesthetics and Art Criticism* 53.4 (1995): 359–369.

41 As observed by Giovanni Piana, *Interpretazione del 'Mondo come volontà e rappresentazione' di Schopenhauer* (London: Lulu, 2013), 80: "if there were no concepts, there would be no laughter"; from this perspective, the Aristotelian-Scholastic observation that laughter is proper to man becomes even more significant, since laughter is associated with man's ability to conceptualise, through reason, and at the same time to perceive the limits of his own conceptualizations, through intuition."[my translation]

42 Hobbes too emphasizes the sudden nature of what causes laughter.

in the type of comedy that Schopenhauer calls "wit" (*Witz*). A similar fallacy may arise also from the dystonia between the concept and the vastness and variety of facts that it aspires to subsume, which make the concept itself inevitably inadequate, as is the case with "buffoonery" (*Narrheit*).

Law considers reason and logic as its instruments par excellence, among its cornerstones. This can be understood as the product of history, in an idealistic or factual-social key. But it can hardly be considered the result of intuition. Indeed, aspiring to conform reality to abstract models if not to actual concepts, law often appears counter-intuitive. In law, actually, conceptualization is not merely interpretative or descriptive, but it aspires to be transformative and even conformative: the rule of law (not always, but often) is a command, which, through the obedience of the addressees, aims to transform reality in accordance with a model.

The subsumption of facts within the abstract scheme (*Tatbestand*) drafted by the legal norm, using syllogisms (the means employed by legal systems based on general and abstract provisos: *Tatbeständen*) is the logical instrument of such conformative function.[43] The witticism that strikes the juridical emphasizes precisely the limits of the mechanism of subsumption, to the point that it acquires the connotations of paradox,[44] and thus it highlights the structural inability of the law to achieve its objectives (i. e., to make the world comply with the logical schemes underpinning the legal system). This is not necessarily an exhortation to revolution, or even just to change the rule of law, nor is it political criticism in comic form, but it is simply an acknowledgment of the coexistence (not necessarily the coincidence) between the juridical and the just.

Although without explicitly linking the two themes of law and comedy, it is Schopenhauer himself who points to the trial as an example of the possible arbitrary reduction of facts to concepts unsuitable for subsumption, and thus a source of comedy:

> before a tribunal the dispute is one between authorities alone, – such authoritative statements, I mean, as are laid down by legal experts; and here the exercise of judgment consists in discovering what law or authority applies to the case in question. There is, however, plenty

43 The situation is partly different when legal rules are stated by judicial precedents, as it happens in the common law systems. Enforcement of legal rules stated in judicial precedents requires comparison between different facts as a necessary logical operation. The identification of similarities and differences between the facts of the precedent case and the facts of the new case is necessary in order to assess whether the rule stated in the precedent is applicable to the new case. It is the *distinguishing* technique. See Ugo Mattei, "Common law. Il diritto anglo-americano," in *Trattato di diritto comparato*, ed. Rodolfo Sacco (Turin: Utet, 1992), 229 ff.

44 See once again Giovanni Piana, *Interpretazione*, 80.

> of room for Dialectic; for should the case in question and the law not really fit each other, they can, if necessary, be twisted until they appear to do so, or vice versa.[45]

For some reason, the authority of the law, compared to other intellectual activities, appears to Schopenhauer to be able to create concepts that are more explanatory of what is real. Schopenhauer's emphasis on the concept of authority implies that the characteristic of legal command lies in the force of the state. However, the author suggests that this is only apparent strength, as it is fragile in the face of the wiles of dialectics, and thus, in essence, inconsistent, and therefore comical. Indeed, the legal rule is, by its very nature, no more able of subsuming, and *a fortiori* of transforming-conforming the real, than other conceptualizations. This, however, is not necessarily a bad thing, nor an indication of the inherent evil of humanity and the futility of any dialectical contradiction on the rule and its application. Consider one of the examples proposed by Schopenhauer, namely the paradox generated by a particularly dull preacher: "Bav is the true shepherd of whom the Bible spake: if his flock be asleep, he alone remains awake." This epigram "subsumes under the concept of a shepherd watching over his sleeping flock, the tedious preacher who has sent his whole congregation to sleep, and then goes on bellowing without being heard."[46] The paradox arises not only from the metaphor of the shepherd of souls or of a flock, but from the inability of the term of judgment – established by the set of rules that define being a good shepherd – to subsume the concrete case of the soporific preacher. Let us therefore ask ourselves whether Azzeccagarbugli (Dr. Quibbler) in Alessandro Manzoni's *The Bethroted* is a good lawyer, starting with Agnese's exhortation:

> 'Listen, children, and take my advice,' said Agnese a few moments later. 'I've been in this world longer than you, and I know something about it. We mustn't lose our heads – thing

45 Arthur Schopenhauer, "The Art of Controversy" [1831], trans. T. Bailey Saunders, in Arthur Schopenhauer, *The Art of Controversy and Other Posthumous Papers* (London: Swan Sonneschein, 1896), 1–48, 40. The observation should be read in the context of the philosopher's highly critical stance towards dialectics, which he considers mere eristic, intellectual fencing indifferent to truth: "Dialectic, then, need have nothing to do with truth, as little as the fencing master considers who is in the right when a dispute leads to a duel. Thrust and parry is the whole business" (Schopenhauer, "The Art," 11). For this reason, the philosopher considers dialectics unworthy of study, and arguing "with people like almost everyone is" (dishonest), something to be avoided. Arthur Schopenhauer, *Essays from the Parerga and Paralipomena* [1851], trans. T. Bailey Saunders (London: Allen & Unwin, 1951), 54: "in making his way through life, a man will find it useful to be ready and able to do two things: to look ahead and to overlook: the one will protect him from loss and injury, the other from disputes and squabbles."

46 Schopenhauer, *Supplements to "The World,"* 93.

> aren't always as bad as they seem. Poor folk like us see troubles as more tangled that they really are, because we haven't got the key to them; but then sometimes the advice of a man who knows his books, just a couple of words from him … I know what I'm talking about.'[47]

Agnese, who claims for herself the knowledge that stems from experience, and thus at least an embryo of the capacity to conceptualize, trusts in the skills of those who have honed this capacity through study, that is to say, in Schopenhauer's terms, in the (illusory) superiority of the intellect and, legally, in the conformative capacity of law. Azzeccagarbugli, after having meticulously relied on the *gride*, namely the rules of formal law (the law in the books), regarding the punishment that is due to a person who has threatened a curate by preventing him from doing his duty, completely overturns Agnese's perspective: "It's your job to tell us the plain facts; it's our job to confuse the issue." Contrary to Agnese's wishes, according to Azzeccagarbugli the practitioner's task is not to unravel the skein, in order to bring disordered facts back to the juridical order (of reason). Contradicting his own nickname, which, not surprisingly, he does not like at all, Azzeccagarbugli believes that his real job is to entangle what was originally clear by exploiting the weaknesses of juridical norms and their instruments of enforcement. Azzeccagarbugli may be a good lawyer from his client's point of view (or of the "persons of consideration" whose interests he serves), but from the point of view of objective law he is certainly a bad lawyer, one who repeatedly practices and recommends illegality. However, the comic incongruity in Azzeccarbugli's speech reaches its climax (just before the unraveling of the misunderstanding and Renzo's expulsion), with a famous phrase: "if you really know your way around the proclamations (*gride*), d'you follow me, there's no such thing as guilty, and no such thing as innocence." The rule of law is by its nature limited, first of all from a structural point of view, since it makes use of concepts and words, which are only partly capable of describing reality. Yet even more, the limitation of the rule of law is evident considering that it is never self-sufficient. In fact, it requires enforcement instruments that cannot just be mere concepts and rational operations, rather they must inevitably trespass on reality in order to attempt to transform it. The less the rule of law is agreed upon by citizens (or among those citizens who can most influence the law's application apparatus), the weaker its ethical basis, and the more intense the transformative effort becomes, the greater the risk of failure. Azzeccarbugli is well aware of all of this. Does this awareness make him a bad lawyer? So, is it necessary for a good lawyer to do without it? Given that experience can only lead the lawyer to an awareness of the limits of the law (the only difference may lie in the

47 Alessandro Manzoni, *The Bethroted* [1825], trans. B. Penman (London: Penguin, 1972), 61.

time required), it will follow that, just as with eutrapelia, the lawyer's goodness is not a mere consequence of the rule of law, but it will arise from an intersection of rules: the rules of law, and the ethical (deontological) and moral (personal) rules that will enable him to identify a limit beyond which using the weakness of the law for the benefit of his client represents a 'bad' choice.

Back to Agnese and her expectations:

> 'Good – well, he's a wonderful man! I've known several people who were caught by the feet like a wasp in honey, and didn't know which wall to bang their heads against next – well, after an hour alone with old Quibbler (mind you don't call him that!) I've actually seen them laughing about the very same thing."[48]

"Laughing about the very same thing": Azzeccagarbugli – Quibbler is the medium that makes one perceive the risk of comic incongruity that arises whenever one attempts to subsume reality into the abstract schemes of the law and, through them, to transform it.

Another incongruity: the "just" law in the books and the "unjust" law in action

About the kind of comedy called *Narrheit*, Schopenhauer writes:

> Or, conversely, the concept first of all exists in knowledge, and from it we pass to reality and to operation on reality, to action. Objects in other respects fundamentally different, but all thought in that concept, are now regarded and treated the same way, until, to the astonishment of the person acting, their great difference in other respects stands out; this species of the ludicrous is called folly [49]

An example of *Narrheit* ("folly") proposed by the Danzig philosopher is the tale of laughter in which the renowned tragic actor David Garrick bursts out,

> because a butcher, standing in front of the pit, had put his wig for a while on his large dog, so as to wipe the sweat from his own head. The dog was supported by his fore-feet on the pit railings, and was looking towards the stage. This laughter was occasioned by the fact that Garrick started from the concept of a spectator, which was added in his own mind.

---

48 Manzoni, *The Bethroted*, 61–62.

49 Schopenhauer, *The World*, 59–60. The following quotation in the text is from Schopenhauer, *Supplements to The World*, 97.

No matter how broad his concept of the audience was, the actor could never have imagined that the audience could also include a periwigged dog. The incongruity that 'naturally' can generate *Narrheit*, when it comes to law, is one between its formal expressions (the law in the books) contained in norms or judicial decisions and its applied results (the law in action). As already mentioned, it is not by chance that the trial is one of the favorite targets of comedy: it is perhaps the most regulated legal activity of all, and at the same time the one in which the clash between abstract formulas and concrete reality becomes more acute, opening up spaces for (easy) comedy.

Substantive law, however, is also often condemned to be ineffective and possibly the object of comic derision, or of biting and somewhat cynical irony, arising from the comparison between what ought to be, as the rules impose (at times even pompously), and the unchanged, and perhaps sometimes unchanging, reality. In such cases, comedy is generated by the sudden discovery of incongruity. Once again Manzoni offers a significant example in the first chapter of *The Betrothed* dedicated to the *gride* (proclamations) against the *bravi* (bravoes).

> As early as 8 April 1583, the most illustrious and excellent Lord don Carlos of Aragon, Prince of Castelvetrano, Duke of Terranuova, Marquis of Avola, Count of Burgeto, Grand Admiral and Grand Constable of Sicily, Governor of Milan and Captain General of His Most Catholic Majesty in Italy, 'being fully informed of the intolerable affliction in which this City of Milan has lived and still lives on the account of bravoes and vagabonds', published an edict against them. 'We decree and pronounce – he went on – 'all men to be affected by this edict, and to be rightly esteemed as bravoes and vagabonds ... who, whether they be foreigners of local residents, have no lawful occupation, or if they have such, are not employed therein ... but devote themselves, either with or without payment, to the service of some noble or gentleman, or officer or merchant ... to give him support and help, or rather, it may be supposed, to lay snares for other men' ... The edict formally instructs all such persons to quit the country within six days, prescribes the galleys to those who fail to comply, and gives all officers of justice the most strangely arbitrary and loosely defined powers to enforce these orders. But on 12 April the following year, the same noble Lord remarked that 'the city is still full of the aforesaid bravoes, who have returned to their former way of life, without changing their habits or decreasing in number'. So he put out another edict, of a still more forceful and memorable kind [...].[50]

It is questionable whether, once the six days of the first ultimatum had expired, some bravo had changed his life, except to "return to his former way of life" sometime before 12 April of the following year. Manzoni, in any case, makes explicit the comic (ironic) incongruity between the solemn "this must be" (command) of the law and the occurrence of norms without any concrete effectiveness. Anyway, in-

50 Manzoni, *The Betrothed*, 28–29.

effective norms do not cease to be legal norms, just as the audience of a theater that includes a dog with a wig on his head does not cease to be 'an audience'.

> Such words, coming from so great a lord, so bold and confident in their tone and accompanied by such specific orders, can only inspire us with the wish to believe that their very utterance in those resounding terms may have been enough to make the bravoes vanish for ever.

It goes without saying that "a wish to believe" is not synonymous with "a rational conviction": the attempt to trace the theme under analysis back to the Schopenhauerian scheme seems a little far-fetched. One must, however, take into account the phantom of justice, which does not belong to the world of the senses, but nevertheless is much closer to intuition than to reason. The aspiration for justice is as essential as it is indefinite. It infers, it cannot be seen or touched, but nevertheless it engenders a perception just like the ghost of the metaphor. Individuals and social bodies know what is just, but they are often unable to think about it rationally or express it in words (or even in coherent and logical concepts). Yet, one senses the justice of a rule of formal law, and at the same time the injustice – or inanity[51] – of its application. However, we laugh (or rather, more often we smile bitterly) at how the law, just like the audience in Schopenhauer's theater, includes, in an irrational albeit ineradicable way, the just and the unjust, the useful and the useless, the effective and the vain, men and canids with or without wigs.

Luckily, we are readers of *The Betrothed*, and not Don Abbondio, who, when he: "[...] came round the bend, and looked straight ahead towards the shrine, as was his custom ... saw something he did not expect or want to see at all"[52], namely the bravoes lurking at the crossroads. No victim of injustice or inanity of laws can laugh, just as the man who, by tumbling and perhaps injuring himself, arouses the laughter of others, does not laugh.

Baudelaire writes:

> To take one of the most commonplace examples in life, what is there so delightful in the sight of a man falling on the ice or in the street, or stumbling at the end of the pavement, that the

51 Vittorio Italia, "Alessandro Manzoni, le 'grida' contro i 'bravi' e le 'linee guida' sugli appalti pubblici," *Società e diritti – rivista elettronica* 2.3 (2017): 23–24, maintains that the proclamations, though effective against some crimes, were actually powerless against bravoes, who relied on the protection by their lords to escape any punishment. A real fight against bravoes required an overall change of the social structure, via a radical constitutional reform. Indeed, one has to wonder whether a constitutional reform is sufficient to "change the existing social order," or whether the opposite is not rather true, i. e., that a constitutional reform, to be effective, must be preceded by a change in the social order.

52 Manzoni, *The Bethroted*, 28.

> countenance of his brother in Christ should contract in such an intemperate manner, and the muscles of his face should suddenly leap into life like a timepiece at midday or a clockwork toy? The poor old devil has disfigured himself, at the very least; he may even have broken an essential member. Nevertheless the laugh has gone forth, sudden and irrepressible.[53]

According to the French poet:

> It is certain that if you care to explore this situation, you will find a certain pride at the core of the laughter's thought. That is the point of departure. 'Look at me! I am not falling!,' he seems to say. 'Look at me! I am walking upright. I would never be so silly as to fail to see a gap in the pavement or a cobblestone blocking the way.'

In fact, one laughs at the fall, not at the injury: as an example, it is no coincidence that slapstick cinema never shows injuries, and indeed the laughing spectators are aware (or hopeful) that no one has ever really been hurt.[54] Similarly, comic incongruity is provoked by the impotence of law, not by the injustice that is its effect. This, on the contrary, never makes one laugh, but arouses pain and sympathy. If laughter presupposes a judgment (and this is a stretch and an undue generalization, as noted above), this is not directed at the victim, but at what makes, or contributes to making the victim a victim. More often, it is more likely that there is no judgment behind the laughter, but the intuitive observation of the limits of the human, from which no one is immune, including the one who laughs, whether he is walking on a sidewalk or attempting to conform the reality of humans and things to a model, as is the case with law.

Another incongruity: the ridiculousness of serious law

Schopenhauer observes that while wit is always voluntary, *Narrheit* is the result of unconscious ridicule. In witticism, laughter is the result of an act performed in order to make people laugh; conversely, in the case of "buffoonery," laughter is involuntarily provoked by someone who wishes to be taken seriously. Also Baudelaire maintains that

53 Baudelaire, "The Essence of Laughter," 138.

54 Actually, acting in slapstick cinema required a certain degree of acrobatic skills, and the scenes were often really dangerous. Buster Keaton recalls in his autobiography: "We seldom rehearsed bone-breaking scenes ...It was too easy for someone on the scene to be hurt or badly injured. Even if not put out of action the bruised man might dog his work the second time. For the same reason we tried to avoid retakes" (Buster Keaton and Charles Samuels, *My Wonderful World of Slapstick* (New York: Doubleday & Co., 1960) 150).

> The comic and the capacity for laughter are situated in the laugher and by no means in the object of his laughter. The man who trips would be the last to laugh on his own fall, unless he happens to be a philosopher, one who has acquired by habit a power of self-division and thus of assisting as a disinterested spectator at the phenomena of his own ego. But such cases are rare. The most comic animals are the most serious – monkeys, for example, and parrots.[55]

In the famous anecdote reported in the *Theaetetus*, Plato recounts that one day Thales raised the laughter of a "Thracian serving-girl with a nice sense of humor" as he "was looking upwards in the course of his astronomical investigations, and fell into a pothole" because he was "concerned with knowing about what was up in the sky and not noticing what was right in front of him at his feet."[56] The anecdote does not specify whether Thales laughed in turn with the girl, as Baudelaire seems to suppose, nor, moreover, do we know whether monkeys and parrots are really the most serious animals. Certainly, according to Plato, the scholar who, like Thales in the anecdote, ignores his surroundings,

> when he is compelled, in a law court or anywhere else, to speak about things that are right in front of his feet or in his direct line of vision, he becomes a source of amusement, not just to Thracian girls, but to the general public. His impracticality pitches him into potholes and a whole pack of problems and he is terribly gauche, which earns him the reputation of stupidity.[57]

I wonder whether law, in pursuing the ambition to know and regulate (at least human) existence, can run into the same accident as Thales, falling into the pothole and making a fool of itself. Since we are talking about, hereto, *Narrheit*, the ridiculousness should derive not from the witticism that some beautiful spirit indulges in the law, but from the legal rule, or rather from its application, both considered *in* and *per se.* The seriousness of law originates from the authoritativeness which arises from the ethical foundation of a rule that is shared or capable of obtaining shared understanding.

Weak law, which lacks this capacity, sometimes tends to resort to authoritarianism through the pomposity and muscular display of some mighty sanction or exemplary punishment, as in the case of the *gride* against the bravoes. Actually, economic analysis of law shows that the deterrence of a sanction is not in *re ipsa,* but depends on the profit that the offender can derive from the violation, and on the

55 Baudelaire, "The Essence of Laughter," 140.

56 Plato, *Theaetetus*, trans. Robin A.H. Waterfield (London: Penguin, 1987), 70. About the anecdote, its dissemination and interpretations Hans Blumenberg, *The Laughter of the Thracian Woman. A Protohistory of Theory* [1987], trans. Spencer Hawkins (London: Bloomsbury, 2015).

57 Plato, *Theaetetus*, 70.

likelihood of the discovery of the offence and the actual infliction of the sanction itself.[58] Once again, the *gride* against the bravoes are a good example.

Another tool that the weak law, being unable to gain consensus, uses to satisfy its need for seriousness is technical language. The function of the latter exhausts itself in the need for accuracy. When there is no real need for accuracy, or when the limits of this need are trespassed, technical language degrades to institutional-bureaucratic raving. It becomes a gimmick which hides the weakness of the legal rule, and/or of its drafters or enforcers, behind the initiatory veil of unintelligibility.

In the second chapter of *The Betrothed*, Renzo asks Don Abbondio to explain his refusal to officiate at the wedding:

> 'But tell me what this other formality is, that you say we've got to attend to, and we'll do it at once'
> 'Do you know what the effective impediments are?'
> 'What would I know about impediments?'
> '*Error, conditio, votum, cognatio, crimen,*
> *Cultus disparitas, vis, ordo, ligamen, honestas,*
> *Si sis affinis, ...*"
> began Don Abbondio, counting the points on his fingers.
> 'Are you making fun of me, your Reverence?,' interrupted the young man. 'What good do you think your Latin is going to do me?'
> 'Well, if you don't understand these things, you must be patient, and leave it to those that do'[59]

The *latinorum* (an expression used in the Italian original, meaning macaronic Latin) together with Don Abbondio's counting the points on his fingers, gives the dramatic scene an obvious comic effect. The priest's recourse to an incomprehensible language is a clear means of dissimulating the weakness of both the pretext put forward by Don Abbondio and the curate himself.

Don Abbondio's knowledge is illusory, as is made clear by his need to count the *impedimenta* on his fingertips in order to remember them. In the final sentence ("be patient, and leave it to those who know") such an illusory knowledge is used as a weapon (an ineffective one, as will be seen shortly thereafter) against an unskilled victim, like Renzo. According to Don Abbondio, the technicality of the law should deceive Renzo, but this does not happen because the betrothed, who is ignorant of any legal technicalities but inspired by the phantom of justice,

---

58 Gary S. Becker, "Crime and Punishment: An Economic Approach," *Journal of Political Economy* 76 (1968): 169–217.
59 Manzoni, *The Betrothed*, 48.

perceives precisely the injustice, and leaves the parsonage all but convinced. The stratagem did not reinforce the rule of law, which, moreover, was invoked out of hand. On the contrary, it made it ridiculous, at least in the eyes of the reader if not of Renzo, due to the same mechanism of incongruity discussed above, regarding the *gride* (proclamations) against the bravoes and the bravoes lurking at the crossroads.

Even outside of self-interested exploitation of the law's weaknesses, the law itself is still generous with unintentional comic effects, whenever the pursuit of seriousness degenerates into squareness and thus into ridiculousness. To mention just one Italian example, a fair amount of irony has been made about Article 66 paragraph 4 of the Highway Code (legislative decree 285/1992), which claims to define nothing less than the shape of the wheel: "the rolling surface of the wheel must be cylindrical without edges, protrusions or discontinuities."[60] In fact, the rule is part of a broader provision devoted to animal-drawn vehicles and in particular to metal rims, with which their wheels may be fitted. In essence, this is a technical rule, which differentiates this type of vehicle from others, such as agricultural machinery (Art. 57) or operating machinery (Art. 58), which can be fitted with tracks. The fact remains that, even if art. 66 para. 4 did not exist, we would hardly see crawler tracked *botticelle* (typical Roman carriages) around Rome.

The comical incongruities of law are shown when the rule pretends, more or less consciously, that a fact of reality (the fact that the metal rims of carts are smooth and without discontinuity) is the result of a norm. In other words, the law can disguise its futility behind an apparent effectiveness, as if, for example, a legal rule required a text written in Italian to be read from left to right. The same often happens with norms stating definitions, with which EU legislation and national rules implementing them abound, as well as for certain interpretative rules. Not even the study of the history and theory of statutory interpretation[61] can restrain a smile when reading Art. 8 of the English Interpretation Act, 1978 (still in force): "In the measurement of any distance for the purposes of an Act, that distance shall, unless the contrary intention appears, be measured in a straight line on a horizontal plane."

---

60 In the pamphlet by Gian Antonio Stella, *Bolli, sempre bolli, fortissimamente bolli. La guerra infinita alla burocrazia* (Milan: Feltrinelli, 2014), 1.

61 See, e.g., Willian Twining and David Myers, *How to Do Things with Rules. A Primer of Interpretation* (Cambridge: Cambridge Univ. Press, 1976) and the classical work by Frank B. Cross, *The Theory and Practice of Statutory Interpretation* (Stanford, CA: Stanford Univ. Press, 2009).

Another incongruity. The ridiculousness of law without communication. Rabelais

In the tenth chapter of *Pantagruel*, the eponymous giant "equitably decided a cause which was wonderfully intricate and obscure," "whereby he was reputed to have a most admirable judgment."[62] When this happened, Pantagruel had already put his knowledge to the test, since:

> in all the carrefours (cross-ways) streets and corners of the city he set up conclusions to the number of nine thousand seven hundred sixty and four, in all manner of learning, touching in them the hardest doubts that are in any science [...] he held dispute against all the regents, professors of arts, and orators, and did so gallantly, that he overthrew them and set them all upon their tails. He went afterwards to the Sorbonne, where he maintained arguments against all the theologians [...] and at this were present the greatest part of the lords of the court, the master of requests, presidents, counsellors, those of the accompts, secretaries, advocates and others: as also the sheriffs of the said town, with the physicians and professors of the canon-law [...] he put their backs to the wall, gravelled them in the deepest questions, and made it visibly appear to the world that, compared to him, they were but monkeys and a knot of muffled calves.

In view of such evidence, Pantagruel is called upon to decide the case between my lord Kissbreech and my lord Suckfist, whose complexity has for forty-six weeks held in check "four of the greatest and most learned of all the Parliaments of France, together with the great council and all the principal regents of the universities not only of France, but of England also and Italy." As a condition for accepting the assignment, Pantagruel demands that all the acts of the trial be burnt, and the parties be given the floor directly.

> ... to what a devil ... serve so many paltry heaps, and bundles of papers and copies which you gave me? Is it no better to hear their controversy from their own mouths, while they are face to face before us, then to read these vile fopperies, which are nothing but chicaneries, deceits, diabolical cozenages of Cepola, pernicious sleights, and subversions of equity? For I am sure that you, and all those through whose hands this process hath passed, have by your devices added what you could to it pro & contra; in such sort that, altough their difference perhaps was clear and easy enough to determine at first, you have perplexed and puzzled the cause, by the frivolous, sottish, unreasonable and foolish reasons and opinions of Accursius, Baldus,

62 François Rabelais, *Gargantua & Pantagruel* [1532], trans. Thomas Urquhart and Peter LeMotteux (New York: Dodd, Mead & Co., 1900), 188. On the episode, analyzed from the perspective of the relationship between the rule of substantive law and adversarial rules of litigation, see Giuseppe Rossi, "Contraddittorio processuale e formazione della regola di diritto," in *Audiatur et altera pars. Il contraddittorio tra principio e regola*, ed. Maurizio Manzin and Federico Puppo (Milan: Giuffrè, 2008), 321–341.

> Bartolus de Castro, de Imola ... and those other old mastiffs, who never understood the least law of the pandects: they being but mere blockheads and great tithe-calves, ignorant of all that which was needful for the understanding of the laws.[63]

The understanding of laws, therefore, is different from the mere knowledge of laws: absent the former, no matter how technically refined and perhaps pompous the technical instruments employed may be,[64] still the result shall be disappointing, like the efforts of the learned called upon to resolve the cause finally submitted to Pantagruel. Pantagruel explains that the laws written in Greek and Latin (languages that jurists, in his view, ignore) are "excerpted out of the middle of moral and natural philosophy," and from history; their understanding, therefore, requires knowledge of the past and a moral stature suitable for apprehending and sharing their meaning.

For the law to produce any effect, there must be a shared language, an historical tradition and ethical-moral basis between the rule itself (out of metaphor, the subjects from which it emanates) and the persons called upon to apply it. Otherwise, the rule of law would be inaccessible even if it existed, and the only way to resolve the dispute would be to give the parties the floor directly, in order to recreate *communication*. The inaccessible rule of law, due to the lack of those ele-

---

63 Rabelais, *Gargantua & Pantagruel*, 190. Pantagruel's words are echoed two centuries later in the well-known invective of Ludovico Antonio Muratori: "... in the Jurisprudence of today the least are the laws, the text of which is studied little or nothing by many of the practical Jurists. The most consists of many questions with affirmative or negative doctrines, divisions, subdivisions, exceptions, expansions, limitations, invented and promoted by Interpreters, Treaties, and Consultants; for which all legal knowledge is today full of opinions, that is, full of confusion, to the serious detriment of the public and private" (Ludovico A. Muratori, *Dei difetti della giurisprudenza* (Trento: Stamperia Paroniana, 1743, 13; the first edition is from the previous year [my translation]). The remedies proposed by Muratori are the renewal and improvement of the text of the law through codification. Among the various criticisms, Rapolla objects to Muratori that the new codification would inevitably require interpretation, leading to a return to 'confusion.' Foreseeing the objection, Muratori observes that the certainty guaranteed by codification "will last at least for a while, that is, until the Doctors, with their subtleties and limitations, cheat the new laws, as they did the old ones. When confusion has returned, then some other reform will be made" (letter of August 10, 1741, quoted by Benvenuto Donati, *Lodovico Antonio Muratori e la giurisprudenza del suo tempo* (Modena: Università degli Studi, 1931), 70, n. 4 [my translation]).

64 Maurizio Manzin, "La questione retorica alle origini dell'umanesimo giuridico," in *Retorica, processo, verità*, ed. Francesco Cavalla (Padua: Cedam, 2005), 129: ."... the constant refinement of the scientific instruments adopted by scholastics is beginning to be perceived by some as excessively formalistic, that is, prevalent with respect to the concrete contents of science itself and the ethical orientations that every social discipline (such as law, politics or economics) implies" [my translation].

ments indicated by Pantagruel, is completely ineffective; attempts to access it by inappropriate means are *incongruent* and therefore potentially comical.

In Rabelais' tale, however, the pleadings of the parties, which go on for pages and pages, are themselves completely incomprehensible, as is Pantagruel's final judgment:

> But in that he chargeth the defendant that he was a botcher, a cheese-eater, and trimmer of man's flesh embalmed; which in the arsiversy swagfal tumble was not found true, as by the defendant was very well discussed. The court therefore doth condemn and amerce him in three porringers of curd, well cemented and closed together, shining like pearls, and cod-pieced after the fashion of the country, to be paid unto the said defendant about the middle of August in May: but on the other part, the defendant shall be bound to furnish him with hay and stubble, for stopping the caltrops of his throat, troubled and impulregafixed, with gabardines garbled shuffingly, and friends as before, without costs and for cause.

This ruling achieves the very rare double outcome of reconciling the parties, which "never came to pass since the great rain, nor shall the like occur in thirteen jubilees hereafter," and to raise the enthusiastic cheering of the very learned listeners, who were "so ravished with admiration at the more than human wisdom of Pantagruel" that "they fell into a trance and sudden ecstasy, wherein they stayed for the space of three long hours."[65]

In the story, paradox and comic effect arise from the replacement of communication between the parties, between them and the judge, between the judge and the public, by pretense. Once deprived of the law, which is inaccessible, the trial becomes mere ritual or stage fiction in which each party plays a role. The learned bystanders, for example, do not contradict their own doctrine, revealing their lack of understanding of both the controversy and, above all, the judgment pronounced by a giant with a reputation for learning.

Disappointment

In his reconstruction of what laughter is, Kant rather surprisingly introduces the element of disappointed expectation. Disappointment also appears in Vico, where it is understood as the discovery of the false association from which the disruption of the brain fibers originates, which in turn causes laughter. Kant writes:

> whatever is to arouse lively, convulsive laughter must contain something absurd (hence something that the understanding cannot like for its own sake). Laughter is an affect that arises if a

65 Rabelais, *Gargantua & Pantagruel*, 200–201.

> terse expectation is transformed into nothing. This same transformation certainly does not gladden the understanding, but indirectly it still gladdens us in a very lively way for a moment. So, the cause of this must consist both in the influence that the presentation has on the body and in the body's reciprocal effect on the mind – but not because the presentation is objectively an object of our gratification (for how could an expectation that turned out to be false gratify us?), but solely because it is a mere play of presentations which produces in the body an equilibrium of the vital forces.[66]

The philosopher clarifies that, in order to arouse laughter, the disappointed expectation must turn into nothing, and not into the positive opposite of the expected object, "for this is always something, and may frequently grieve us."[67] Laughter, like hope and sleep, is a relief from the many pains of life; it has nothing to do with the intellect, it is an "animal, that is, bodily sensation." The whimsical manner, for Kant, is the ability to take on

> a certain mental disposition, in which everything is judged in a way quite different from the usual one (even vice-versa), but yet is judged in conformity with certain principles of reason [present] in such a mental attunement. A person who is subject to such changes involuntarily is moody [*launisch*]. But someone who can adopt them at will and purposively (so as to enliven his description of something by means of a contrast arising laughter) is called whimsical [*launig*], as is also the way he conveys [his thoughts].

In short, the "whimsical manner" is connected to the sensation of the absurd, the unreal/irrational,[68] deliberately provoked, in the case of comic art, through the creation of an expectation destined to vanish into thin air, which creates the pleasant

---

66 Immanuel Kant, *Critique of Judgment* [1790], trans. Werner S. Pluhar (Indianapolis/Cambridge: Hackett, 1987), 203.

67 Kant, *Critique of Judgment*, 204. Rosella Prezzo, *Ridere la verità. Scena comica e filosofia* (Milan: Cortina, 1994), 54, observes, with reference to the passage from Kant quoted in the text, that by opening up the nothingness of meaning, laughter reveals "the holes in the net of categories that reason patiently weaves: the first warning of a breakthrough with no guarantee of recovery, which philosophy will not be able to remove and which will subterraneously advance until it visibly gives itself in the age of modernity, marked by nihilism" [my translation].

68 Kant, *Critique of Judgment*, 207. Indeed, not all unreal representations are comic (think of science fiction, or dystopian literature, which tends towards anguish rather than laughter). The spectator's reaction to the representation of unreality would seem, therefore, to be linked to the modality, the style that characterises it (in this sense seems to go the reflection of Luigi Pirandello's essay on humor of 1908 (*L'umorismo*). Consider the famous example of the painted old lady, who can be understood as a comic, humorous or even tragic character depending on the degree of empathy shown by the author describing her.

physical reaction of laughter.[69] The reconstruction is in the groove of the carnivalesque view of laughter, even when this has the law as its object (as much as anything else). By assuming a necessary link between laughter and the absurd, Kant deprives laughter of all descriptive as well as critical value. What is laughed at, therefore, could never be the law, no matter how understood, but something else, something fictitious and absurd which reveals nothing but nothingness.

There is, however, another aspect of laughter, quite distinct from the "humorous manner," which Kant takes into consideration: it is naivete, "the eruption of the sincerity that originally was natural to humanity and which is opposed to the art of dissimulation that has become our second nature. We laugh at such simplicity as does not yet know how to dissemble, and yet we also rejoice in the natural simplicity here thwarting that art of dissimulation."[70]

The transformation into nothingness, in this case, does not concern the object of intellectual expectation, but rather the "beautiful but false illusion," and laughter is only one aspect of the "play of the power of judgment" triggered by naivete. The naive laughter generates "seriousness and esteem" because the naive person demonstrates that "something infinitely better than all accepted custom, viz., integrity and character [*Lauterkeit der Denkungsart*] (or at least the predisposition to it), is after all not wholly extinct in human nature."[71] Finally, laughter and seriousness in the face of naivete are mixed with the sadness generated by regret, which arises from the awareness of the inevitable transience of sincerity, destined to succumb before the immediate restoration of fiction and its primacy.[72]

---

69 "However this manner," Kant adds, "belongs more to agreeable than to fine art, because the object of fine art must always show itself as having some dignity; and so an exhibition of it requires some a certain seriousness, just as taste does when it judges the object" (Kant, *Critique of judgment*, 207).

70 Kant, *Critique of judgment*, 206.

71 Kant, *Critique of judgment*, 206.

72 In Kant's thought, laughter thus takes on a multifaceted connotation with respect to both the feelings on which it grounds and those it arouses; this multifacetedness of laughter almost takes on the structure of a taxonomy (evaluative, of eutrapelia) in Immanuel Kant, *Anthropology from a Pragmatic Point of View* [1798], trans. Mary J. Gregor (The Hague: Nijhoff, 1974), 132, starting from the fundamental bipartition between "good-natured (openhearted) laughter," which "is sociable (insofar as it belongs to the affect of joy)" and "sardonic (sneering) laughter," which "is hostile." Descartes, also starting from a purely physiological reconstruction of laughter, believes in turn that laughter itself finds its origin in a variously mixed plurality of "passions." Although laughter is normally associated with joy, "yet this cannot cause that, but only when that is mean, and that there be some little admiration or hatred mixed with it" (René Descartes, *The Passions of the Soule* [1649], translator unknown (London: Martin & Ridley, 1650), art. 125, 127). In Kant's reconstruction, the naive arouses, precisely, "admiration," and reprobation, if not "hatred," for the pretence it reveals.

The empathetic laughter aroused by the naive or the "art of naivete" differs from the infantile laughter that Baudelaire considers the only example of "non-evil" hilarity, since, according to him, it is the pure fruit of vital joy. In Kant's view the naive laughter has a strong intellectual component, which distinguishes it from the same "ordinary," "animal" laughter, that is the common laughter. Therefore, Kant does not give up on conferring the empathetic laughter aroused by the naive an intellectual, and therefore serious, dimension, which he even logically separates from the purely physiological moment of laughter. The double postulate that laughter is not an intellectual operation, and that judgment must be "serious" in any case, is thus saved. The fact remains that the laughter aroused by the naive is revelatory, or a symptom of intellectual revelation. It is capable, even if only for a brief moment, of disclosing not nothingness, but fiction, in favor of some "infinitely better" aspect of human nature. These passages on laughter and naivete offer interesting insights when compared with the fundamentals of Kantian philosophy of law.

Both Renzo in his encounters with Don Abbondio and Dr. Quibbler, and Pinocchio led before the judge between two gendarmes in the town of Acchiappacitrulli (Trap for Blockheads), are "naive." They evoke laughter, seriousness, and sadness at the same time. The pretence, which they unveil, is represented by the law in its declinations of technical language, statutory interpretation, and trial at court, respectively. Seriousness arises, of course, from solidarity with the naive person who becomes a victim; sadness from the knowledge that, as Kant observes, pretence will prevail in any case. In reality, it will certainly not be the law that ensures Renzo's[73] salvation, but rather faith and trust in Providence. The law shall not ensure

73 The episode of the bread revolt sheds further light on Manzoni's scepticism towards law, through the measure of Chancellor Ferrer, who "fixed the price of bread at the level that would have been right with corn at thirty-three lire per measure. But it was really being sold at up to eighty. Ferrer was behaving like a lady of a certain age, who thinks she can regain her youth by altering the date on her birth certificate." Manzoni adds that "orders much less stupid and unjust than these had ofter remained a dead letter through the sheer resistance of natural forces. But the crowd itself saw to the execution of this order. It had seen its dreams given the force of law, and would not allow them to be turned into a mockery" (Manzoni, *The Bethroted*, 233). Thus, the theme of the expectation of effectiveness generated by the norm is again introduced, which, were it betrayed, could trigger revolutionary action. This, however, is viewed by Manzoni with genuine horror, as demonstrated in the next chapter by Renzo's response to the "debauched looking old man's" proposal to assassinate the vicar of providence. "'For shame!' cried Renzo. He was horrified by the old man's words, and by the faces of the many bystanders who seemed to approve them; but at the same time he was encouraged by others he saw who looked as deeply shocked as himself, though they were keeping quiet about it. 'For shame!' Do we want to do the hangman out of a job? Do we want to kill a fellow Christian? How can we expect God to send us bread, if we do terrible things like that? It's thunderbolts, not bread, that he'd be sending us!" (Manzoni, *The Bethroted*, 250).

Pinocchio's deliverance, which will come out of some kind of moral and personal growth provided by experience. In Kant, positive law, in both its formal and practical dimensions, is based, on the one hand, on coercion and, on the other, on the necessary connection with natural law.[74] Within the framework of the republican constitutional form, such a connection should be guaranteed by the conformity of the institutional decisions to the general will, and thus to reason. The link between law and reason, as understood by the general will, guarantees the moral foundation of the law and its possible universal tendency.[75] Actually, the coercive capacity of law (as shown by the example of the *gride* against the bravoes), the conformity of public decision to the general will and, finally, the correspondence between general will and reason may conceal elements of fiction. Not even law, in other words, is immune from the "art of simulation" that, according to Kant, veils "the sincerity that originally was natural to humanity." Moreover, can we really assume that sincerity belonged to the original condition of humans? Kant himself seems to doubt this, when he argues that, in the absence of freedom guaranteed by law, human freedom would be "wild lawless" and nothing would guarantee that any provisional order would not degenerate into the arbitrariness created by the law of the strongest.[76]

The whimsical manner that provokes laughing at law (as at anything else), leading the intellect to gaze into nothingness, can bring down entire philosophical

---

74 Kant, *The Philosophy of Law* [1797], trans. W. Hastie (Edinburgh: T. &. T. Clark, 1887), 47: "Consequently, if a certain exercise of freedom is itself a hindrance of the Freedom that is according to universal Law, it is wrong; and the compulsion or constraint which is opposed to it is right, as being a hindering of a hindrance of Freedom, and as being in accord with the Freedom which exists in accordance with universal Laws. Hence according to the logical principle of Contradiction, all Right is accompanied with an implied Title or warrant to bring compulsion to bear on any one who may violate it in fact"; moreover, "Now such right is founded, no doubt, upon the consciousness of the Obligation of every individual according to the Law; but if it is to be pure as such, it neither may nor should refer to this consciousness as a motive by which to determine the free act of the Will. For this purpose, however, it founds upon the principle of the possibility of an external Compulsion, such as may co-exist with the Freedom of everyone according to universal Laws" (48).

75 Fabrizio Cattaneo, *L'idea di repubblica da Kant a Habermas* (Turin: Giappichelli, 2013), 58–60; Daniela Falcioni, *Natura e libertà in Kant. Una interpretazione del progetto per la pace perpetua (1795)* (Rome: Bulzoni, 2000), 136.

76 Kant, *The Philosophy of Law*, 169–170: "it is not to be said that the individual in the State has sacrificed a part of his inborn external freedom for a particular purpose; but he has abandoned his wild lawless freedom wholly, in order to find all his proper freedom again entire and undiminished, but in the form of a regulated order of dependence, that is, in a Civil State, regulated by laws of Right, This relation of Dependence thus arises out of his own regulative Law-giving Will." On the same topic see Luigi Ferrajoli, "Garantismo e poteri selvaggi," *Teoria politica* 8.3 (1998): 11.

systems, as Nietzsche will show. But above all, what is most interesting here is that the laughter aroused by the naive person who does not understand the fictions of law and does not participate in them is assimilated, in the eyes of the person who laughs, to the sincerity and straightforwardness of thinking inspired by the phantom of justice or, in the Kantian view, by the "moral law."[77]

Relief: the blessed wandering nature of law

As already mentioned, Kant attributes the ability to generate relief to laughter, but he does not recognize any connection between that and the object of laughter; more generally, just like sleep, laughter is one of the pleasures of living.

Still within the framework of an approach based on the investigation of the physiological origins of laughter, Descartes identifies, instead, one of the causes of laughter in the feeling of deliverance from a danger, provoked by the realization of the fictitious nature of the threat to which the laughing person believed himself to be exposed:

> For that kind of laughter which sometimes accompanies indignation, it is usually artificial and feigned. But when it is natural, it seems to come from the joy a man has to see he cannot be hurt by the evil whereat he is offended, and withal, that he finds himself surprised by the novelty, or the unexpected encounter of this evil. So that joy, hatred, and admiration contribute to it.[78]

The Cartesian passage indicates two different situations in which there is a relationship between laughter and indignation: the first seems to allude to the charac-

---

77 Kant emphasizes the universalism of the 'moral law,' following the fundamental law of practical pure reason: "Act so that the maxim of thy will can always at the same time hold good as a principle of universal legislation," and its corollary "pure reason is practical of itself alone and gives (to man) a universal law which we call the Moral Law" (Immanuel Kant, *Critique of Practical Reason* [1788], trans. T.K. Abbott, New York: Prometheus Books, 1996, 46). Regardless of the universal or historically determined nature of the sense of justice, the problem of the effectiveness of the mechanism of connection between the general will and positive law remains, just like, consequently, the problem of the effectiveness of positive law, with respect to which, according to Kant, the role of coercion is fundamental. Anyway, Kant sees coercion as a beneficial instrument to ensure that opposing arbiters can coexist (Kant, *The Philosophy of Law*, 47; see also 174, where he insists on the necessity of the inscrutability, for the people, of the "origin of supreme power," and the unquestionability of the acts of this power: "The Origin of the Supreme Power is practically inscrutable by the People who are placed under its authority. In other words, the Subject need not reason too curiously in regard to its origin in the practical relation [...]").

78 Descartes, *The Passions of the Soule*, art. 127.

teristic case of satire, in which laughter is the result of the grotesque deformation of facts and people, aimed precisely at provoking laughter, along with indignation. Descartes defines this laughter as artificial and fake because it specifically originates from an artificial operation of deforming reality, which would in itself be apt to cause indignation, and is deformed to provoke a form of exasperation, in which laughter and indignation take on equally extreme forms.

In the second situation, indignation arises from the threat one is exposed to, while laughter, which is this time natural, emerges from the realization of the fictitious quality of this believed danger. There is no artifice whatsoever, but, as in the Kantian case of laughter provoked by the naive, the simple revelation of a pretence. In a fragment dealing with the same theme, Tommaso Campanella dwells on the idea of laughter as the result of a "rejoicing" or "dilatation" of the spirits, deriving from surprise at an "unhoped-for good," but also from the discovery of the fictitious nature of a danger to which one believes oneself to be exposed.[79] One also laughs, Campanella adds, "while others weep over something that they should not weep over," "seeing that the thing about which others grieve and which induces to grief does not really harm."[80] Constituent elements of laughter, therefore, would be surprise and relief. In Campanella's case as well, the emphasis is on the spontaneous and physiological quality of laughter, which does not display the characteristics of an intellectual operation, but rather the pure and simple physical reaction to some external stimulus, which nevertheless possesses a revealing character.

In Kant's view, as well as in those of Descartes and Campanella, what is most interesting is not the "humorous manner," or the "fake and artificial" laughter provoked by those (such as, for example, the satirist) who want to provoke indignation by exasperating the hatred that is inherent in this kind of laughter. The irrational epiphany, that is to say intuitive knowledge, originates from the observation of someone or something that is unconsciously comical, and that may even have a

79 Tommaso Campanella, *La Città del Sole. Scritti scelti* (Nuoro-Soveria Mannelli: Ilisso – Rubbettino, 2006), 82–83. The example of laughter generated by feigning danger is that of laughter induced by tickling, when the spirit "is somewhat sorry for the fear, being there exposed to the insult, and refusing it expands into laughter: while it sees that the scratching does not harm it, and that it can still resist the evil, and it is a great pleasure not to feel the harm of the present evil" [my translation].

80 In this case, Campanella adds, the spirit "after it withdraws bursts into laughter, dilating and despising to cling with the sad clinging of others, and rejoicing in its own valor, that it does not know how to fear what others fear and weep" (Campanella, *La Città del Sole. Scritti scelti*, 83). The theme of laughter as a sign of superiority surfaces.

threatening appearance, to the point of making the observer perceive a danger that is destined to dissolve, and thus to become ridiculous.

The relationship between law and comedy invites one to reflect not so much on the comic representations of law, but on its congenital inconsistencies mentioned above: the ineffectiveness that goes hand in hand with the pomposity and gravity of the threatened evils (sanctions), the seriousness, the tendency to resort to vacuous liturgies. In a single element, the naive, or the delivering laughter show the connatural inability of law to regularly achieve its goals of shaping individuals and societies, that is, the structural characteristic of law to proceed by trial and error.

The most interesting aspect of this line of thought is that it emphasizes relief and deliverance, in addition to indignation, hatred, superiority. Those who laugh discover that the threat is fake, and this is a good thing. From this perspective, the relationship between law and comedy is revealed through the unveiling of the vacuity of law's will to omnipotence. However, such an unveiling generates not only indignation or discouragement, but also relief, for one fundamental reason: it shows that law, like any product of reason (and history), can never totally conform both the individual and social bodies to itself, by completely suffocating intuitive knowledge and irrationality.

As Schopenhauer observes:

> This triumph of knowledge of perception over thought gives us pleasure. For perception is the original kind of knowledge, inseparable from animal nature, in which everything that gives immediate satisfaction to the will presents itself. It is the medium of the present, of enjoyment and cheerfulness; moreover, it is not associated with any exertion. With thinking the opposite holds good: it is the second power of knowledge, whose exercise often requires some, often considerable, exertion; and it is the concepts of thinking that are so often opposed to the satisfaction of our immediate desires, since, as the medium of the past, of the future, and of what is serious, they act as the vehicle of our fears, our regrets, and all our cares. It must therefore be delightful for us to see this strict, untiring, and most troublesome governess, our faculty of reason, for once convicted of inadequacy. Therefore, on this account the mien or appearance of laughter is very closely related to that of joy.[81]

Law, like the strict, tireless and (potentially) oppressive governess, fortunately does not always succeed in its task. Law, in fact, like the "pedant" Schopenhauer talks about,

> with his general maxims almost always comes off badly in life, and shows himself foolish, absurd, and incompetent. ... Even in regard to ethics, the intention to act right or nobly cannot be carried out in all cases in accordance with abstract maxims, since in many instances the

81 Schopenhauer, *Supplements to The World*, 98.

> infinitely nice distinctions in the nature of circumstances necessitate a choice of right, proceeding directly from the character.[82]

The very comedy about law (and especially the unintentional ridiculousness that law sometimes displays) confirms that

> comedy and laughter are, ever since the more remote testimonies of human culture, the self-curative device that humans used in order to preserve the richness of human experiences, and the chance to go on experiencing, from the adaptive flattening of instrumental and discursive rationality about the factualness of the world. Rather, we could say that the human being has a world, and not simply is in the world, properly because he is able to produce this non-adaptive difference.[83]

Not even the historical element, which contributes so significantly to the shaping of law, can lead one to resign oneself to the factualness of the world, as determined in a particular historical moment, in a specific legal experience. Comedy reminds us that there is always the possibility of still being able to have new human experiences, it contributes to relocating law in an eternal becoming, within which today's (legal) error itself can be the premise for both future better experiences and new errors, fruitful or otherwise. In other words, comedy confirms that law does not shy away from the inevitable wandering of the humans, which is, on the contrary, a constituent element of it and a factor of continuous transformation. Vladimir Jankélévitch writes that

> we live in a fleeting world, where things happen but once, just a single time in the whole eternity and then no more … And humor, maybe, is for humans a means to cope with the irreversible, to make life lighter and smooth; humor is made of the same fabric of becoming, it is all mobility and fluidness itself, it adapts so well to the rhythm of irreversibility that the slightest repetition seems to him weirdness and clownish complacency.

Moreover: "if humor is really the elusiveness of temporality, if it is really *ités*, him who goes without ever turning back, we should better say: humor shall forever be

---

82 Schopenhauer, *The World as Will*, 60.

83 Andrea Tagliapietra, "Rido dunque potrei essere. La singolarità e le conseguenze del comico," *Animal Ridens, I castelli di Yale online* 5.2 (2017): 247–264. The author observes that "What prevents the human mind from turning into a simple calculating mechanism, artificially reproducible, the famous 'artificial intelligence' of which science fiction and Silicon Valley computer gurus speak – an expression by which the technological dream of the creation of an intelligent machine conceals the ideological strategy, in place for some time, that pursues the formal reduction of human intelligence to the performance of a machine – lies precisely in the faculty of generating and enduring ineradicable paradoxes" [my translations].

on the road, until the end of times."[84] Laughter brings the law back to the continuous becoming of the world, and re-establishes freedom against a coercive power that, despite Kant's reassurances, contains within itself the germs of repression. An expression of the "elusiveness of temporality," like humor (comedy, and not necessarily the "humorous manner"), is the epiphany of the phantom of justice: it belongs to the "knowledge of intuition," it cannot be "conceptualized" except in a partial and limited manner, it belongs to feeling rather than thinking. Laughing at the law assures us that the phantom of justice will remain as such; it may, at times, "embody" itself in some rule of law or in some "just" judgment, but these will always be partial and, above all, transitory embodiments, which will not change its ectoplasmic nature. The phantom of justice, whatever the law, will fortunately always continue to hover among us.

84 Vladimir Jankélévitch and Béatrice Berlowitz, *Quelques parts dans l'inachevé* (Paris: Gallimard, 1978), 160. [my translation].

Chapter 2
How and why we laugh at law

Law and the elusive nature of humor

If laughing at the seriousness of law depends on the ability of human beings to improve themselves, to the point that they can even conceive the very idea of *law* as being tolerable, who knows what will happen when artificial intelligence enters law offices or even courtrooms. When, at last, millions of sentences and codicils will be processed at a glance, law will become seriously infallible (assuming that an artificial intelligence is exempt from error, or devoid of bias hidden in the folds of the algorithm and its bigdata), and justice will be achieved with such extreme precision that it will even render burdens and statutes of limitations useless. It will happen that, if the rule is only one and incontrovertible, as Horkheimer and Adorno also discuss in their *Dialectics of Enlightenment*,[85] we may be limited in our right to cross-examination, or even deprived of the judge and the court … but "never of the lawyer," say the lawyers! In short, we will most likely be deprived of the *system* as we know it, and also, perhaps, of our personal guarantees. Yet, we will have to give up the fun because we will be thrown into a highly dystopian reality. Today, however, the fallacy of the legal system and its protagonists is a rich source of literary inspiration, although it challenges concepts of fairness and justice.

As suggested in the previous chapter, the *catalog* of the ways in which law is laughed at helps to define a first range of meanings of the comic iconology of the law. However, this catalog can be better understood and formalized through the pragmatic approach offered by literary and non-literary narration, as well as by narratology. But the comic narrative is a highly magmatic subject, and one which is strongly affected by terminological ambiguities. Indeed, there is no real taxonomy of the comic, whereas definitions, species and subspecies have accumulated from classical antiquity to the present day.[86] However, as Pirandello[87] argued,

85 See Max Horkheimer and Theodor W. Adorno, *Dialettica dell'illuminismo* [1947] (Turin: Einaudi, 1966): 24–25: "Guilt and expiation, happiness and misfortune, are […], for mythical justice as for rational justice, the members of an equation. Justice is lost in law" [my translation]. See also Max Horkheimer and Theodor W. Adorno, *Dialectic of Enlightenment* [1947], trans. John Cumming (New York: Seabury Press, 1972).

86 In this regard, we would like to highlight the seminal study by Laura Salmon, who has conducted a meticulous survey on the controversial issue of terminology; Laura Salmon, *I meccanismi dell'umorismo: dalla teoria pirandelliana all'opera di Sergej Dovlatov* (Milan: Feltrinelli, 2018).

https://doi.org/10.1515/9783111286778-004

if the nature of humor could be once and for ever determined, the traditional terms defining it would no longer be so important. In fact, the approaches to comedy can be multiple: we can choose to investigate the way in which one laughs and the quality of the laughter, or rather the role played by laughter in the humorous storytelling of the law. However, those works that provoke laughter lead us to consider *how and why* we have always *questioned* a fundamental aspect of social life, whether these works can be traced back to irony, ridicule, parody, satire, ironic comedy, mockery ... and whatever the ultimate reason for laughter, whether it be morality, a taste for the perverse, the desire to subvert experiential reality, or rather the desire to feel superior, or even the need to confront vices. Considering that literature and the arts play a decisive role in the representation and interpretation of ideologies, the comic narration of the law highlights the latter's real capacity to create order and to reconcile rules with the perception of justice among citizens. From this perspective, narratological studies provide insight into how the mechanisms of comedy are grafted onto recurrent narrative patterns in the literary and cultural tradition of a society. These patterns are in fact also cognitive models, i. e., knowledge that guides individual and collective behavior: in short, the analysis of narrative processes should bring out what the widespread perceptions of jurisdiction actually are.

At first glance, one might say that in our field of interest, laughter is provoked either by astonishment at an absolutely unusual perspective, such as the justifications that the confessed criminals in the musical *Chicago* give for their murders ("I betcha you would have done the same!"), which reveal to what extent we are all potential criminals; or by mockery of *clichés* about the law, most of which corresponds to the gap created between the law of the Book of law and its enforcement, between conformative aspirations of the law and the experience of it. In all these cases, however, we encounter characters who feel they are victims of an oppressive power that limits their autonomy and freedom, whatever the reasons. Yet, it is also often the law itself, as it is regularly enforced, that proves to be absurd and arouse at least a smile, when for example it claims to codify something that seems pointless to codify, such as the size of vegetables or the round shape of the wheel. In this case, it is as if laughter functions as an antibody against the disease of a law that we cannot understand in its legitimacy, precisely because the phantom of justice always hovers over us. Thus, not only in art but also in life, knowledge and understanding of law can pass through laughter.

87 Luigi Pirandello, *L'umorismo* [1908] (Milan: Garzanti, 1995): 19.

Law and comedy

If the places of the law (the courts, the interrogation rooms, the cells ...), the uniforms (of magistrates, lawyers, police ...), the weapons (the service pistols, the judge's gavel ...), the enforcement of the law (from the fine to the pronouncement of sentences ...) are the multiple discourses that create the *narrative* of law, it is interesting to note what Northrop Frye points out about comedy, namely that there is an affinity between the rhetoric of comedy and that of jurisprudence. Comedy consists of opinion (*pistis*) and demonstration (*gnosis*):

> (p)roofs (i.e., the means of bringing about the happier society) are subdivided into oaths, compacts, witnesses, ordeals (or tortures), and laws: in other words, the five forms of material proofs in law cases listed in the *Rhetoric.*[88]

As an example, a Shakespearean play often begins with an absurd, cruel or irrational law which is evaded or broken in the course of action: take *Measure for Measure* (1603–1604), in which Angelo, that is the Duke of Vienna *pro tempore*, imposes a death sentence on Claudius for having had sexual intercourse before marriage, only to be guilty of the same crime himself immediately afterwards. Only the real Duke will bring justice when he wisely and sensibly reveals Angelo's ideological bad faith. The plot of the play builds on and dismantles that sentence. In particular, the title of this play is said to be inspired by the Gospel of Matthew (7:1 and 7:2) which reads: "Judge not, that ye be not judged; for by the judgment wherewith ye judge, ye shall be judged; and by the measure wherewith ye measure, it shall be measured unto you."[89]

In comedy, contracts are the conspiracies organized by the hero's society to make or break the good and right; the witnesses are those who overhear a conversation or are aware of the truth of the facts and intervene in the action which leads to the comic discovery; the ordeals are the touchstones or tests to which

88 Northrope Frye, *Anatomy of Criticism: Four Essays* [1957] (Princeton: Princeton Univ. Press, 1973), 166.

89 A similar narrative structure, whereby the judge becomes the judged, can also be found in Heinrich von Kleist's *The Broken Jug*, a play about the unreliability of human nature and the legal system. The comic plot is mostly set in a courtroom and tells about Judge Adam, who finds himself presiding over a trial in which he will prove to be the guilty party. As written by György Lukács, the author describes the "abuses of patriarchal justice in the countryside, the harassment inflicted on the peasants by the authorities, the peasants' deep distrust of everything that comes "from above," their feeling that one can only protect oneself from the authorities by bribery and deception" (György Lukács, "La tragedia di Heinrich von Kleist," in *Realisti tedeschi del XIX secolo* (Milan: Feltrinelli, 1962): 45 ff. [my translation].

the hero is subjected in order to demonstrate his own character. The story is not just a struggle between good and evil, but it becomes a questioning of a rule of law and of the ritual constraints it imposes, perceived as either fair or unfair by the members of the community. The law is transformed from a legal statute regulating social relations into an obstacle that must be removed for the ultimate achievement of a happier, more inclusive society; law must change and evolve with society in order to emancipate itself from the dominance of the elders. It is not always clear what role the hero plays in this contradictory ideal: the lawyer, the victim ... the judge? It goes without saying that in a court of law, one judges whether a law has been broken or not, but one does not question a law, let alone change it, which is the task of the legislator or the constitutional judge. However, a rule can be constructed through the combination of a set of rules.

In point of fact, in comedy the diegetic structure is dramatic, i. e., the phases of the action are bound by a relationship of cause and effect, and the final achievement is a state different from the initial one – a *better* state that has broken free from domination. In fact, the ending of a comedy consists of a liberation. Frye thus links *survival* and *liberation*, *peripeteia* and *agnition:* where *peripeteia* reverses the point of ritual death into victory, thus achieving survival, *agnition* is the mechanism that brings to light new values, which the consociates will learn to accept, transforming them into their truth and rule. Similarly, in a court of law a judgment should be accepted and shared and, potentially, it should restore peace between the disputants, thus replacing disorder with order. Nevertheless, the rhetorical understanding of the law is based on two opposing approaches: on the one hand, starting from shared *clichés* one should arrive at conclusions that cannot be disproved, except by contradicting the premises due to a *consensus* on the rule that is basically logical; on the other hand, the eristic approach favors a dialectical dispute between the parties. But we mustn't forget the dialectical vicissitudes of lawyers, who wander through the codes, even assuming the role of hero, as the cinema often shows us.[90] Needless to say, the lawyer is often an ambiguous figure. The issue about who the good lawyer is has already been raised: the one who, like Vittorio Gassman in Dino Risi's 1965 film *I mostri*, convinces the court that an honest citizen is an unreliable witness by using lofty and pretentious language, or rather Vincent Gambini, played by Joe Pesci in Jonathan Lynn's *My Cousin Vinny* (1992), who, completely ignoring the rules and procedure, proves with intel-

90 Think in this regard of American cinema and literature where lawyers are protagonists, especially since they can take on the investigative role that other judicial systems allow in a much more limited way.

ligence and courage that his young defendants are in facts innocent?[91] Is the good lawyer the one who knows how to bend the law or the one who does not let the law bend him? To what extent can the law be manipulated by legal discourse and bent to partisan interests? And how can we forget the legislator who, through political intervention, subverts the logical connections of the law to matters of value? Perhaps we could say that talking about law through the lens of comedy also means reflecting on how society strives to overcome its own limitations, i. e., to accept or reject new values. Laughter is in itself a form of liberation because it reveals how we want to experience our responsibility towards reality and social interactions, and thus towards rules and law.[92]

Laughter has the power to unambiguously circumscribe conflict, because those who laugh are aware from the outset of an *incongruity that cannot be tolerated.* As much for comedy as for humor, the rule applies that the spectators know what they want, so the narrative merely formalizes a vice and its cure through the control of aggression or irrationality. Frye calls the final *agnition* of the characters *completion of a design*, a design that the spectators already had in mind from the beginning. If, from a narrative point of view, the pleasure of laughter (however bitter it may be) exhausts itself on its own, the play's happy ending invites the audience to be part of the new society that has been created.[93] It can also be emphasized that if the playwright is writing for a young audience, humor goes beyond the specifics of age and does not include the mocked object, as comedy usually does. The conclusiveness of laughter is found in the sense of superiority towards what is being talked about, in a psychological relief (which often distances a state of aggression), or in the perception of incongruity and thus in the unveiling of social and/or psychological masks.[94] Comedy even helps us to accept that our reality might just be the one we do not like.

Law and the grotesque (Georges Brassens, Victor Hugo)

As pointed out in the previous chapter, in compliance with the principle of *eutrapelia* and in strictly *narratological* terms, challenging the seriousness of law means moving from a *high mimetic* narrative dimension of the legal praxis (comparable

---

91 See also what Giuseppe Rossi says in Carbone and Rossi, "Who is the Monster? Laughing at Friends and Foes," 165.

92 See Beniamino Placido, Preface to Henri Bergson, *Il riso. Saggi sul significato del comico*, trans. A. Cervesato and C. Gallo (Bari: Laterza, 1999), xi.

93 See Frye, *Anatomy of Criticism*, 164.

94 Jerry Palmer, *Taking Humor Seriously* (London: Routledge, 2003), 94.

to epic and tragedy in literature) to a *low-mimetic* dimension of legal experience. It is clear to all that seriousness grants both authoritativeness and authority to the law, so much so that if it were an epic or tragic character it would be considered *above* the common person and/or their environment: in this regard, think about the respectful and decorous behavior that must be maintained in the courtroom, or a certain fear that a uniform or a toga may arouse. Those who wear a uniform place themselves above the community in rank, if not in environment, to the point that the citizen relies on the legal authority conferred by law and finds the idea of a public official committing crimes or assuming immoral attitudes extremely intolerable and reprehensible. On the contrary, through the unhinging[95] of its *mythoi* (discourses), humor lowers the specificity of the supremacy of the law and cancels the distance between the law and the people, thus showing how the law, which is said to be the same *for all*, in practice presents itself different *from all* in form and substance. This tends to give rise to the conflict between what is just, right, fair and what is legal.

We cannot help but mention Georges Brassens' song *Le Gorille* (1952), which tells the story of a gorilla used to living in a cage and performing at fairs, who one day manages to escape and takes advantage of the situation to free itself of its virginity (and says "Today's the day I lose it"). Strangely enough, however, in having to choose between an old woman and a judge with whom to satisfy its cravings, the ape opts to copulate with the latter.

In a world in which everyone is cunning enough to flee at the sight of a wild beast, the only one who does not hurry – because he is convinced that he is *by nature* safe – is the judge. Here Cicero's motto "Cedant arma togae, concedat laurea linguae"[96] ("Let arms give way to civil magistracy and speech") does not seem to have any place: shortly afterwards the judge will have to recognize that the toga he is wearing is not the sign of *high* honor and of the *high* social, intellectual and moral function that makes him – in his opinion – untouchable ("The judge's expressionless thought / "For me to be deemed an ape / That's completely impossible " / The next events proved him wrong. / Beware the gorilla!" [my translation]). And even less his eloquence. The beast, which only follows the law of nature, en-

95 In this case, I consciously do not speak of 'deconstruction' because I no longer feel the need to question master narratives in order to prove that in the folds of language lies the opposite of what is said. We are in a post-postmodern context and instead of the *indeterminacy* of meaning perhaps we should talk about the *contradictory* principle of the contemporary. Comedy in this sense proves to be a harbinger of meaning by opposing two or more positions, especially those that are culturally more widely shared, including the politically or non-politically correct.

96 Marcus Tullius Cicero, *De officiis*, ed. Michael Winterbottom (London: Clarendon Press, 1994), I, 77.

acts a logical process that would be culturally alien to us: the storyteller acknowledges, in fact, that no one would ever mate with a judge, emphasizing that the seriousness and ruthlessness of the law are in no way comparable to pleasure. But the gorilla, which does not shine "in its taste or its intellect" and above all does not feel bound by law, does not care. In this miserable situation, the judge finds himself shouting just like the man he had had decapitated the day before did. In short, remembering Matthew once again, "with the judgment with which you judge, you will be judged." The judge, though still wearing the toga, is deprived of his 'absolute' power (of life and death, in fact) by those who do not recognize the authority of the law. As a consequence, on the one hand the power of law turns out to be a cultural construction, while on the other one, authority is aligned with the citizens and the listener. After all, we would not be laughing if the unpleasant and dark drama had been inflicted on the old woman. We laugh at the comical ridicule (*reductio ad absurdum*) of judicial authority, which for once cannot decide on human destiny. One of the symbols of the law is degraded, according to Bergson,[97] in his most immanent quality, namely the physical body. Here laughter succeeds in ruthlessly doing what Victor Hugo hoped for in the 1832 preface to *The Last Day of a Condemned Man:*

> Happy if, with no other aid than his thoughts, he has mined sufficiently into the subject to make a heart bleed, under the *œs triplex* of a magistrate! Happy if he could render merciful those who consider themselves just! Happy if, penetrating sufficiently deep within the judge, he has sometimes reached the man.[98]

The judge shows a lack of awareness about himself and his role when he believes himself to be superior to everything, to everyone and, even more, superior to a beast. This makes Brassens' character ridiculous, almost bordering on pathetic in some ways. He has a superior self-image because of his power, which he believes to be universal and not limited to the places of jurisdiction.[99] The weakness of his reasoning lies in identifying his body with the symbol he embodies when he wears the robe. He is not pompous like Daumier's lawyers, but he is Hugo's judge: the pitiless individual in triple armor, unable to see the man in front of him. Through the gorilla, the people pass their sentence and abandon the unjust judge to his fate,

---

97 Henri Bergson, *Laughter. An Essay on the Meaning of the Comic* (London: McMillan, 1911), 45–50.
98 Victor Hugo, *The Last Day of a Condemned Man* (Hastings, UK: Delphi Classics, 2015), v. 3. Preface to the 1832 Edition, 2.
99 Konrad Lorenz, "Avowal of Optimism," in *On Aggression* [1963] (London and New York, 2002), 266 ff. Available online: https://monoskop.org/images/d/d0/Lorenz_Konrad_On_Aggression_2002.pdf (last access in February 2023).

since he is insensitive to human suffering.[100] As Freud intended, comedy changes the relationship between the laughter and the object of derision through a process of *comic dis-identification*, since the Other now appears as a gullible fool who cannot stand comparison: the judge was so stupid that he did not run away.

Law and slapstick (Stan Laurel and Oliver Hardy)

A similar situation is developed in the silent film *Do Detectives Think?* directed by Fred Guidol in 1927 and starring Judge Foozle, played by James Finlayson, and the "two worst detectives in the world," Ferdinand Finkleberry and Sherlock Pinkam, interpreted by Stan Laurel and Oliver Hardy.[101] In this film, too, the judge passes a death sentence on a vicious murderer, but at the moment of pronouncing it, he is ostentatiously smug, thus failing to uphold fundamental principles of the legal system such as impartiality and respect for the dignity of the accused. As a counterbalance, the criminal's reaction is to pronounce his own death sentence on the judge, so much so that the latter becomes very frightened. When the criminal manages to escape from prison a few months later, he goes straight to Foozle's house to carry out his revenge.

Far from the places of justice, the small body of the judge-avenger will be shown in all its fragility in the presence of evil: the smug arrogance on his face will vanish when confronted with the chilling image of a vulnerable judge in the bathtub, threatened by the imposing presence of the criminal, who stands alone, armed with a massive knife and clearly not among the guards. The symbol of justice – the judge – has become an ordinary man, but the loss of this man's life would have turned into the loss of Justice if the context had not been comical, and if the two bungling detectives had not intervened to distract the murderer with a ridiculous chase in which they are more prey than hunters.

---

100 In the field of Italian pop music, one can compare what Roberto Vecchioni sings with bitter irony in *Signor Giudice* (1979) in which a condemned man defers to the will of the judge, who at the moment of his arrest is on holiday instead of in court: 'Mr Judge / You come when you want / The longer you make us wait / The better it will be to get out. / Mr Judge, / Buy your trunks, / Eat your arancino / With your tomatoes. / We are many, we are here / Already we call you papa, / Of those daddies who don't know each other. / That day, when it comes, / Judge us mercilessly. / We are so ashamed to be men / This way." The author emphasizes here the power and pettiness of the one who is supposed to practice fairness and justice, but who proves, instead, to be devoid of authority, respect and dignity for the accused, as well as heedless of the value of freedom.

101 For a more extensive discussion of the film see Paola Carbone and Giuseppe Rossi, "Who is the Monster? Laughing at Friends and Foes."

The synthesis of man and justice is found in the mask that Foozle accidentally ends up wearing on the back of his head when he falls down the stairs, tripping over the sheet he's wearing on his way out of the bath, a kind of *himation*. Unaware of this, he has become a two-faced Janus: on the one side, a little man made ridiculous by a sheet, and on the other, a severe but not complacent mask; in other words, a supernatural being who evokes reproach rather than revenge. The mask evokes an ancestral idea of justice and the inevitability of the rule, namely that specific ethical dimension of justice which Foozle did not possess and did not convey in court. Far from an infallible algorithm, paradoxically the judge becomes a wise giant, so much so that he can now fulfill his role: in the end, the criminal is frightened by the image of this strange figure and is captured by the police. In the film, the judge has regained his high-mimetic function thanks to the mask: in fact, the carnival represents the logic of a world in reverse, of an identification with the identity of the other, and the suspension of order and rules. However, the symbolic inversion leads to awareness and the triumph of truth.

It must be emphasized that from the very beginning, the audience sides with Foozle's safety, however reprehensible he may be, because everyone believes the murderer deserves punishment. However, only the comic dimension prevents the story from turning into a tragedy. The judge's death would have called into question not only his way of exercising jurisdiction, but the entire legal system. Laughter is responsible not only for the positive conclusion of the story, but also for the image and principle of law itself. The spectators are able to laugh because they believe they can keep the disorder under control, and because the ethical dimension of law is reaffirmed.[102]

Perhaps we are in the field of the uncanny both in this film and in the song *The Gorilla*, but we must be careful that once the protagonists of the Law are deprived of the comic component, a vindictive attitude towards them does not quickly turn into a social revenge against the person who focuses the ethical interest of the community. Indeed, similar to ironic comedy, laughter becomes a form of liberation from what is unpleasant or terrifying, but it keeps barbarity distinct from the game of sacrifice. It should be noted that laughter possesses its own logic, an autonomous logic with its own rules, which are not simply the outcome of reasoning.[103] Laughter possesses a form of intelligence that exaggerates to the extreme,

102 See Simon Dentith, *Bakhtinian Thought* (London/New York: Routledge, 1995), 76.

103 See Giovanni Bottiroli, "Il comico delle articolazioni," in *Il Comico: approcci semiotici*, eds. Daniele Barbieri, Giovanni Bottiroli, and Alessandro Perissinotto, Documenti di lavoro e prepubblicazioni, 303–304–305 (Urbino: Centro internazionale di Semiotica e Linguistica, 2001), 29. Available online: http://www.giovannibottiroli.it/it/altro/il-comico-delle-articolazioni.html (Last access in

pillorying, mocking, dissolving, and transforming another form of intelligence, namely what we can call *common thinking*, ranging from an institutionalized idea of justice to what is perceived as right, and to political correctness. The role of the narrator is to construct a plurality of logics to be brought into collision within the comic framework. Most of the facts that make us laugh would take on tragic hues outside of a fictitious context, even if the suspension of disbelief, needed in order to avoid mistaking the character for the actor, is always accompanied by critical, analytical, rational thinking, without which the reaction we encode in the very act of laughing would not be activated. However ferocious it may be, humor does not destroy, but it does deconstruct the object of derision by revealing its limits, while at the same time relying precisely on a collective intentionality and on a latent need of the community to bring out a social or individual criticality. Laughter therefore makes us critical, even in its most outrageous form, and its message can easily be controlled by relying on reason. Konrad Lorenz argues that humor is an ally of rational morality.[104]

The whims of law, or the trial as sport (Conan Doyle and Aristophanes)

Even before discussing the capacity of the players of the law to arouse ridicule or laughter, it is worth remembering that it is often the legal system itself that undermines itself when it introduces a paradoxical logic. It can happen that the formal and logical consistency of the law is transformed into a formal rigor or legalism that is just as incapable of guaranteeing social order as it is of creating a serious condition of inequality and injustice. An example of how such a system can be challenged through humor is offered by Arthur Conan Doyle's *The Hound of the Baskervilles,*[105] a novel originally published in serial form in *The Strand Magazine* between 1901 and 1902. In this tale, Sherlock Holmes and Watson are called upon to investigate the mysterious death of Sir Charles Baskerville that occurred on a foggy night on the English moors. Although the circumstances are unusual for a number of reasons, a judge rules that it was a death by natural causes, while the famous detective will prove that it was murder. Thus, from the outset the

June 2020). See also what is said about the subversion in J.D. Gordon, "Introduction: Humor in Legal Education and Scholarship," *BYU Law Review* 2 (1992): 313–323. Available online: https://digitalcommons.law.byu.edu/lawreview/vol1992/iss2/1 (Last access in February 2021).

104 Lorenz, *On Aggression*, 284 ff.

105 Arthur Conan Doyle, *The Hound of the Baskerville* [1901–1902], in *The Complete Sherlock Holmes Long Stories* (London: John Murray and Jonathan Cape, 1973), 130.

law decrees a bogus and non-existent social order that could lead to the ruin of the community if Holmes did not intervene to stop the murderer.

In this work, a comic character – Sir Frankland – emerges from a completely Gothic narrative line: characterized by its darkness, claustrophobic atmosphere, and hints of the supernatural. The tense pace of the story is different from that of comedy, and yet the understanding of the events narrated takes place thanks to this character,[106] whom Watson defines as "a little comic relief where it is badly needed."[107] If, by its very essence, humor does not allow us to be both spontaneous and thoughtful, i. e., inclined to smile and be serious at the same time,[108] in this Gothic and investigative context Frankland's extravagant behavior strikes us even more. This character is the alienating element in the narrative, but also a critical conscience of the relationship between Law and Justice, to the extent that every time he appears we are led to reflect on the ineffectiveness of the latter to guarantee equity and social peace. In the novel, he not only immediately and shrewdly argues against the judge's decision concerning the supposed death by heart attack of his friend Sir Charles, but he is presented to the reader as a rich, quirky, and grumpy old man with an obsessive passion[109] for the "British law":

> This is Mr. Frankland, of Lafter Hall, who lives some four miles to the south of us. He is an elderly man, red-faced, white-haired, and choleric. His passion is for the British law, and he has spent a large fortune in litigation. He fights for the mere pleasure of fighting and is equally ready to take up either side of a question, so that it is no wonder that he has found it a costly amusement. Sometimes he will shut up a right of way and defy the parish to make him open it. At others he will with his own hands tear down some other man's gate and declare that a path has existed there from time immemorial, defying the owner to prosecute him for trespass. He is learned in old manorial and communal rights, and he applies his knowledge sometimes in favor of the villagers of Fernworthy and sometimes against them, so that he is periodically either carried in triumph down the village street or else burned in effigy, according to his latest exploit. He is said to have about seven lawsuits upon his

---

106 He occupies a privileged position also in a literal sense because his house enjoys a panoramic view over the entire moor so that he can see everything that happens. It is also for this reason that he will be able to help Holmes in the investigation. In addition to this, it will eventually become known that the key character in the story is indeed his daughter. See Daniele Barbieri, "Ridere con ritmo. Meccanismi tensivi e iterazione nel testo comico," in *Il Comico: approcci semiotici. Documenti di lavoro e prepubblicazioni*, eds. Daniele Barbieri, Giovanni Bottiroli and Alessandro Perissinotto (Urbino: Centro internazionale di Semiotica e Linguistica, 2001), 6 ff.

107 Doyle, *The Hound of the Baskerville*, 317.

108 See. W.F. Fry, *Sweet Madness: A Study of Humor* (Palo Alto, CA: Pacific Books, 1963), trans. D. Zoletto, *Una dolce follia. L'umorismo e i suoi paradossi* (Milan: Cortina, 2001).

109 Bergson, *Laughter*, 14 ff.

> hands at present, which will probably swallow up the remainder of his fortune and so draw his sting and leave him harmless for the future.[110]

The name "Frankland," hardly chosen at random by Conan Doyle, immediately makes us think of an honest and sincere man, even if his 'frankness' might cause some people discomfort. In fact, contrary to the Platonic ideal, he is an excessive character who fails to govern his passion with common sense; and yet rather than representing an unjust man, Frankland's passion seems to be a form of pathology. We do not see in him a dubious morality or an annoying form of greed (*pleonexia*) marked by dishonesty and selfishness: in reality, he always relies on the judgment of the authorities to decide what is right, which is to say nothing less than the Law. Absurdly, we could say that he does not know how to reasonably measure out his pleasure for arguing.

As can be seen from the brief presentation above, while Sherlock Holmes and Watson manage to bring justice and order to society in contrast to the judge, who proves to be authoritative although his sentence is wrong and empty of value, Frankland does not oppose the law, but rather activates the mechanisms of its functioning in such a paroxysmal way as to undermine the very value of the judicial system. Here it is evident how a vice – I mean the pleasure of arguing and letting the law settle disputes – can activate a comic action with minimum motivation.[111]

Probably, on the one hand he knows his rights very well, but, on the other, he also knows the limits of their correct enforcement. Doyle is very clever in introducing – into a detective story where rationality reigns – a character who takes a paradoxical logic to the limit, thus revealing the irrationality of existence, which has nothing to do with the spiritualism evoked throughout the narrative. Although Watson highlights Frankland's kindness, sympathy and somewhat romantic attitude towards stargazing, he probably embodies the role of the *agroikos*, considering his apparent rusticity and his attachment to the materiality of existence. As with any good comedy, he finds his opposite in Mr. Stapleton, the other neighbor who is educated, kind, extremely sociable and a lover of botany, but also Sir Charles' greedy murderer. Frankland is able to see reality as it is and draw attention to the dangers and fears that the real world hides. Because of his rough (or frank) manners and extravagance, Doyle made him a humorist in spite of himself.

As Salmon explains, humor subverts stereotypes, "conventional morality and uncritical beliefs, i.e., it eliminates the possibility of recognizing oneself in a pre-

---

110 Doyle, *The Hound of the Baskerville*, 316–317.

111 Frye, *Anatomy of Criticism*, 173–174.

conceived script," where a script is defined as "an internalized cognitive structure that provides the speaker with information about how a given element is structured, what its parts and components are, or how a given action is performed [... The script] contains prototypical information about the given element."[112] In the novel, Frankland's humor reveals a cognitive alternative: humor manifests itself in an unpredictable disruption of the rules of jurisprudence and beyond. As can be observed, while the failure of the character to make a *virtuous* use of the law is stigmatized, the law loses its value and vigour when it is nothing more than a strict legalism.[113] By adhering to all the rules that are made available to the citizen, the nobleman conforms to the procedure to such an extent that the judicial system responds every time it is consulted, even for the most extravagant of disputes. Perhaps Frankland misunderstands in an immanent way – and herein lies the essence of the character's comedy – the principle enunciated by St. Paul that the individual must incorporate the law (divine, though!) to the point of making it part of his nature, rather than a mere instrument or objective set of rules to be obeyed.[114] He brings a smile to the scene because he has gone too far in incorporating the very conformative mission of the law: he has so conformed *to* the law that it actually bursts. As is usually the case with humor in which the king is demystified and brought down, while the top and the bottom are reversed, here the law and the legal system are not superseded (no one would say that the law should be replaced or repealed), but the reader is put in a position to criticize them, albeit less violently than Georges Brassens does in his song *The Gorilla.*[115]

---

112 Laura Salmon, *I meccanismi dell'umorismo: dalla teoria pirandelliana all'opera di Sergej Dovlatov* (Milano: F. Angeli, 2018), 72–73 [my translation].

113 Speaking of *King Lear*, Northrop Frye recalls how "transcendental authority" is defined as the power that arises from the knowledge and understanding of the concept of "equity," and that is based on what in the Bible is called the *knowledge of good and evil*. Without this understanding, law becomes nothing more than a form of legalism. See N. Frye, G. Sherbert, and T.Y. Grande, *Northrop Frye's Writings on Shakespeare and the Renaissance* (Toronto: Univ. of Toronto Press, 2010), 583.

114 St Paul, *Letter to the Romans*, Chapter 2. One might perhaps venture to liken adherence to God's law according to St Paul, to the *Sophrosyne* of the ancient Greeks, that is, the mildness of temperament and rationality that the righteous man embodies and which, for this very reason, are a guarantee of fairness and justice in society as well.

115 Although there is no scientific evidence, physiologists believe that there is a close correlation between laughter-smile and the emotional state of aggression. Starting from Hobbes' theory of superiority, numerous approaches to the subject have developed, among them see Gruner's study, *The Game of Humor: A Comprehensive Theory of Why We Laugh* (New Brunswick/London, 2000), according to which comedy is always a game with a winner and a loser, and laughter is a sign of victory.

For the citizens in the village of Fernworty, every lawsuit brought by Frankland requires them to look at the world differently. Their certainties about the place they inhabit are constantly called into question, and with them the scale of values of what is right and what is wrong due to ever-changing justice. It is also worth noting that, at the end of the numerous trials, the villagers either carry Frankland in triumph or burn his effigy (as was ritually done with those condemned *in absentia*). In other words, they symbolically stage (as in a carnival) their consent or dissent as if it were a sentence passed by a more or less disappointed people. Evidently, only the reader is able to laugh at Frankland precisely because they are not directly involved, that is, the reader has managed to inhibit the empathetic component of the relationship between themself and the character. However, not only does this weak manifestation of dissent demonstrate that law cannot please everyone, but it also reveals that the people can do little against the law. After all, the village should be angry at the judicial system rather than at a fellow villager who has formally put his right into effect in a lawful manner. From time to time the law, which is called upon to express its opinion on a great variety of issues, follows a logic and a reason that is not shared by the people, but the people must accept it because it produces the sentence.

In the normal course of life, we tend to think of the law as a personified abstraction capable of understanding, choosing, adapting to situations, but it turns out to be what it is: a set of procedures in the hands of individuals, often professionals, who know what to do with them. For readers, Frankland is the instrument of comic relief, but what is the dividing line between justice and abuse of justice? When does the lawful or ethical use of justice become unlawful? Is temperance, the balance we seek in the virtuous man, also common to law?

Frankland's actions undermine *from below* what is usually looked up to with respect for authority and (supposed) competence: common thinking dictates that the law knows what is right and what must be done. However, Doyle represents a jurisdiction that is willing to protect futility as well as bend to the whims of the bored rich man. Indeed, since Frankland is wealthy and enjoys a privileged social position, he can rely on a judge and on the law for every small matter, which shows that on the one hand the law is open to indiscriminate *use* and, on the other, that it is not for everyone, but only for those who can afford it. Even in the most faithful observance of the law, justice fails itself.

If Frankland were only a humorist to his fellow citizens, as he is to his readers, he would not be a comic hero, but rather a jester, an educator who wants to reveal how the law is a potential monster. Frankland is not aware of his comic nature. Frankland is a literary device in Conan Doyle's hands, and his critique of the legal system is an explicit authorial stance. At the same time, the law does not make itself capable of being a comic hero, as it does not guarantee freedom. But it assumes a highly ambiguous role, due to the fact that, as mentioned in the previous chapter, the law often appears *counter-intuitive.* From a narratological point of view, without his vice Frankland would have been a mere sidekick to the hero-Holmes, but instead he aligns himself with the prototype of the comic hero in his critique of the law's ability to guarantee social order. His message has a great impact on the reader precisely because it is conveyed by a vice that both the inhabitants of Fernworty and we readers do not share: we would not ordinarily behave like Frankland. Implicitly, the reader shares the value attributed to the law by the fictional community, but it is precisely this empathetic detachment that allows us to take a critical stance towards the juridical. Frankland not only helps the hero to solve the case and make justice triumph, but he brings out the rigidity and weakness of the system, which proves to be fallacious insofar as it is governed by a blind procedural rigor that subjects it to human weakness and vanity.[116] In this regard, we cannot fail to remember old Philocleon, the protagonist of Aristophanes' *The Wasps*, who is said to have a craving for the courts: "Thus, to be judging is his hobby, and he groans if he is not sitting on the first seat. [...] If he sees scribbled on some doorway, 'How charming is Demos, the son of Pyrilampes!' he will write beneath it, 'How charming is Cemos!'"[117]

The work is a satire on the Athenian legal system, and although there are many circumstantial references to life at that time, we readers still manage to laugh at what we read, demonstrating how the representation of the exercise and abuse of law still resonates with a contemporary audience. Bringing this work together with a modern detective novel tells us how the feeling towards the law is a pillar of social life across times and cultures, especially when, as in this case, judiciary power is subservient to the political one. In fact, the work was anticipated two years earlier by *Knights*, in which Aristophanes openly takes issue with Cleon, Pericles' successor and demagogue, who governs Athens (also) through an instrumental and unscrupulous use of justice.[118]

The play is presented as a verbal diatribe between a father – Philocleone -, a son – Bdelicleone – and a chorus of judges and jurors who call themselves 'wasps' because of their ability to sting when teased:

116 See Bergson, *Laughter,* 124 ff.

117 Aristophanes, *The Wasps*, ed. Anya Elizabeth Leonard (Classical Wisdom Weekly), 19. Also available online: http://classics.mit.edu/aristophanes/wasps.pl.txt (last accessed in July 2022).

118 See Martina Treu, "Il popolo e i suoi servi," *STRATAGEMMI – Prospettive Teatrali* 038–039.2 (2018) 1 (2019): 97–112, 97 ff. Available online: https://www.stratagemmi.it/wp-content/uploads/2020/03/Stratagemmi-38–39-web.pdf (last accessed in May 2020).

> Look well at us, and you will see that we have all the character and habits of the wasp. Firstly, if roused, no beings are more irascible, more relentless than we are. In all other things, too, we act like wasps. We collect in swarms, in a kind of nests, and some go judging with the Archon, some with the Eleven, others at the Odeon; there are yet others, who hardly move at all, like the grubs in the cells, but remain glued to the walls, and bent double to the ground. We also pay full attention to the discovery of all sorts of means of existing and sting the first who comes, so as to live at his expense.[119]

Philocleon and his colleagues prove from the outset to be less than moderate and guided by reason or even a sense of justice, both in private and public life. As Nikoletta Kanavou points out, these judges (who are popular and paid for the number of their sentences) seem to lack the correctness of thought and action, that in the Greek world would have pleased the gods so much (*Dykaiosine*), as well as the moderate temperament and rationality (*Sophrosyne*) that all together are a guarantee of fairness and justice. Listening to Aristotle, one could say that these judges lack the strong ethical dimension we attribute to the virtuous human, while, like Frankland, the wasps depend on the *extreme* pleasure of arguing (*Philodikia*): they lack a balance that makes them respect the human being even before institutions or the cloak they wear.

As comedy demands, this play stages the clash between the world of the elderly and the world of the youth, but with a different interpretation. In this case it is the son – apparently a righteous, polite and law-abiding man (although in the end he will not prove respectful of *Sophrosyne*) – who takes his father prisoner in his home in order to free him from "going away before dawn basely to calumniate and condemn."[120] Old Philocleone – obstinate, quarrelsome, and obsessed like Frankland with legal disputes, to which everything seems to refer – opposes imprisonment with all his might. He tries to free himself by escaping to the rooftops, by hiding under the belly of a donkey like an Odysseus, by begging his neighbor Lico to help him and promising in return not to 'piss' and 'fart' in his enclosure any more, or by inventing the idea that a curse will fall on him if he does not convict someone that day. When the choir of fellow judges – presented as a single group of indistinct men with no individual identity, and configured as a single character – passes under his windows to call him to go to court he says: "My friends, I have long been pining away while listening to you from my window, but I absolutely know not what to do. I am detained here, because I have long wanted to go

---

119 Aristophanes, *The Wasps*, 59.
120 Aristophanes, *The Wasps*, 36.

with you to the law-court and do all the harm I can."[121] For the court of the Wasps, fairness and the public interest do not seem to take priority.

Like Frankland, Philocleon is therefore an egocentric and extravagant old man with a mania for the law, but instead of suing his fellow citizens, the latter enjoys exercising the power that comes with his office. The Chorus describes him as a harsh judge who will not be persuaded, and when the plaintiffs plead with him, he bows his head and states: "You might just as well try to boil a stone."[122] The other Wasps turn out to be just as vindictive and satisfied with their power of life and death, as well as heedless of the truth. Serving on the jury of the Athenian court gives them the feeling of being nothing less than Zeus: they fear no one, but are feared by all. Here, of course, the law has nothing to do with the divine, but instead with power and corruption. In fact, the demagogue Cleone is the Chorus' privileged interlocutor; it helps to foment antagonism with the deuteragonist, as well as to amplify the play's polemical message.[123] The Chorus first says: "Hence Cleon, our protector, advised us yesterday to come early and with a three days' stock of fiery rage so as to chastise him for his crimes. Let us hurry, comrades, before it is light; come, let us search every nook with our lanterns to see whether those who wish us ill have not set us some trap."[124] And then Philocleon reminds his son that:

> We are the only ones whom Cleon, the great bawler, does not badger. On the contrary, he protects and caresses us; he keeps off the flies, which is what you have never done for your father. Theorus, who is a man not less illustrious than Euphemius, takes the sponge out of the pot and blacks our shoes. See then what good things you deprive and despoil me of. Pray, is this obeying or being a slave, as you pretended to be able to prove?[125]

Aristophanes, in fact, takes issue with Cleon, who controls the legal system through the judges. The judges' lack of respect for their function and for justice is merely a reflection of Cleon's arrogance, who preys on the worst instincts of the citizens for his own purposes. The play demonstrates that the Wasps have no awareness of the power held by political leaders, that is, they lack the capacity for discernment that is proper to *sophrosyne*, but which should be the prerogative of the judge.

---

121 Aristophanes, *The Wasps*, 28.
122 Aristophanes, *The Wasps*, 27.
123 See M. Treu, "'Guidaci a passo di danza' . . . Cori comici sulla scena," in *Συναγωνίζεσθαι. Studies in Honour of Guido Avezzù*, eds. Silvia Bigliazzi, Francesco Lupi, and Gherardo Ugolini (Verona: Skenè. Studies, 2018), 859–881, 861.
124 Aristophanes, *The Wasps*, 26.
125 Aristophanes, *The Wasps*, 39.

Philocleon means 'he who loves Cleon' while Bdelycleon means 'he who hates Cleon'. To understand the positions of the two antagonists, one must remember that in Athens there were no professional magistrates, let alone lawyers, but only judges or jurors selected to judge even if they had no specific legal competence. All this was done in the name of democracy, and every judgment passed was the judgment of the people. Moreover, not only could they not be prosecuted for their mistakes, but they were remunerated according to the number of cases they heard. Cleon was very good at flattering judges with money, so that he could not only control the legal activity of the city but also its enemies. Aristophanes himself was sued by Cleon for attacking him in a play, but as a comedian he enjoyed legal protection – *parrhesia* – and was acquitted.

Although the rules are obeyed (Philocleon and the Wasps operate according to the law just like Frankland), once again the system proves to be fallacious because it fails to prevent 'tyranny' from insinuating itself. Here, the law only appears to be above everyone in the name of justice, because in reality the administration of justice is not autonomous, and of course the people are the first victims as they are deprived of freedom and fair trials. A judge who lacks technical and formal knowledge as well as discernment certainly cannot be the guarantor of justice as we understand it in our legal system. Here, the reaction of the people to the law has nothing to do with that depicted by Conan Doyle or Georges Brassens. In this narrative, the Athenian law represented by Aristophanes does not assume a low mimetic dimension, but is always superior in rank to the citizen. So, what is there to laugh about? One laughs at the logical paradox of making the people believe that they enjoy a fair and democratic legal system – fair in the sense that it is democratic, i. e., governed by the *opinion* of the individual citizen in the name of the *polis.* We cannot fail to emphasize, as Treu states, that Aristophanes speaks to the *polis* of the *polis.* For us, this system goes beyond a principle of fairness and justice since the judgment is not based on strong legal wisdom, although the defendant could have their case pleaded by an orator, *retores,* who was legally responsible for the constitutionality of their statements. It is worth recalling what Seneca wrote in one of his *Letters to Lucilius:*

> For the question is asked, whether the wise man will weigh his opinions, or whether he will apply to others for advice. Now he is compelled to do this when he approaches state and home duties – everything, so to speak, that is mortal. He needs outside advice on such matters, as does the physician, the pilot, the attorney, or the pleader of cases.[126]

---

126 Seneca, *Ad Lucilium, Epistulae morales* (London: William Heinemann and New York: G. P. Putnam's Sons, 1923), trans. Richard M. Gummere. Available online: https://en.wikisource.org/wiki/Moral_letters_to_Lucilius/Letter_109 (last accessed in July 2022).

The wise man needs the lawyer and the judge because, although he has a sense of what is good and fair, he lacks the technical means to guarantee justice in a state of law, let alone in Cleon's Athens. In Aristophanes' portrayal, justice is lacking in Athens because there is a lack of integrity, rectitude, balance, wisdom and judgment, and because, we might add, the system lacks the *technicality* of the law.

As the drama continues, at a certain point the Chorus accuses Bdelycleon of being a demagogue, an enemy of the people and an advocate of monarchy, thus attributing to him, with a skilful logical inversion, the responsibilities that until now have been attributed to Cleon and Philocleon: "CHORUS: It is clear to all the poor that tyranny has attacked us sorely. Proud emulator of Amynias, you, who only take pleasure in doing ill, see how you are preventing us from obeying the laws of the city; you do not even seek a pretext or any plausible excuse, but claim to rule alone."[127] It follows that the son would become a tyrant because he would not allow a legitimately elected juror to use the law as a disposable asset and thus not as an instrument of justice and equity.

On the contrary, in the dialectical confrontation between father and son, the latter will try to make the parent understand how he is actually a servant of power and that the money he earns is nothing but a pittance compared to the earnings of demagogic and populist politicians:

> To those who say: "I shall never betray the interests of the masses; I shall always fight for the people." And it is you, father, who let yourself be caught with their fine talk, who give them all power over yourself. They are the men who extort fifty talents at a time by threat and intimidation from the allies. "Pay tribute to me," they say, "or I shall loose the lightning on your town and destroy it." And you, you are content to gnaw the crumbs of your own might. [...] They want you to be poor, and I will tell you why. It is so that you may know only those who nourish you, and so that, if it pleases them to loose you against one of their foes, you shall leap upon him with fury.[128]

These words convince first the choir and then Philocleon of the young man's common sense and reasons in relation to a legal system that is structured to be used as a whim and is capable of guaranteeing only social disorder, similar to what happens in Conan Doyle's novel.

It is interesting to note that towards the middle of the play, Bdelicleon exclaims: "It is indeed difficult, and requires a wit greater than that of the comic poet, to cure an ancient disease, rooted in our city. But you, our father, son of Cronus..." Aristophanes is well aware that a comedy cannot solve the problem of justice in Athens, but at least comedy serves to conceptualize it thanks to a coherent

---

127 Aristophanes, *The Wasps*, 36.
128 Aristophanes, *The Wasps*, 41–42.

narrative structure and the critical sense stimulated by laughter. As much as Bdelicleon's words are full of irony for an enterprise that he himself doubts he will accomplish, he refers to the importance of laughter in resolving disputes:

> BDELICLEON
> Not if you are with decent people. Either they undertake to appease the offended person or, better still, you say something witty, you tell some comic story, perhaps one of those you have yourself heard at table, either in Aesop's style or in that of Sybaris; everyone laughs and the trouble is ended.[129]

In these words, we find the popular wisdom of resolving disagreements through the sublimation of conflict in laughter and in the unveiling of the absurd. Similarly, Aristophanes stages a fake, home-made trial for the benefit of Philocleon, who realizes that the pleasures his son wants him to get used to are not so awful.

Just as in the beginning Philocleon was inordinately and unreasonably obsessed with the court, in the second half of the play he is excessively busy enjoying himself. The finale is full of scurrilous jokes, which lower the tension and certainly amuse the whole audience. Philocleon develops a habit of eating and drinking excessively at the symposiums, where we know that one of the rules is to behave in moderation in order to allow dialogue between the participants. He also quarrels with everyone he meets, thus passing from judge to potential defendant. Here the character repeats the same lack of balance, moderation and ethics that he showed at the beginning. Following his son's advice, Philocleon tries to resolve all the issues with stories that are amusing to him, but which no one understands: the old man has freed himself from a ritual slavery – the vice of trial – to chain himself to another equally fruitless obsession. Aristophanes depicts an exasperated lack of humor in the disputants, who demonstrate on the contrary a tendency towards aggression that seems to find a solution only in the trial and in the dispute as an end in itself: the people have thus culturally introjected Cleon's will. Once again, people have embraced the legal system. And in any case, the importance of a culture of laughter is implicitly reiterated here, that is, the ability to go beyond the literal meaning to share what Pirandello called the *sentiment of the opposite*, i. e., a form of sympathy/empathy (*sin-patia*).[130]

In a *crescendo* of awareness for the reader, Aristophanes portrays very well the perverse and even sadistic or opportunistic use of law against one's enemies (whether political or not). At the beginning, Philocleon even prefers to give up

129 Aristophanes, *The Wasps*, 66.
130 Salmon, *I meccanismi dell'umorismo*, 58.

the good life that his son can guarantee him, in order to practice his power[131] as a popular judge and see the powerful ones ask for his clemency. Philocleon himself could be a tragic character because of his deleterious obsession, yet we laugh at him because he is *extreme* in our eyes and contains his obsession within himself, just as Molière's Miser contains avarice within himself to the point that we identify the character with the vice. The Wasps are in fact so broken up in their language and behavior that they fail to arouse deference and consideration; they are completely unaware of the importance of the *representation* of their role. Blaise Pascal used to say:

> Which of us would not say that the magistrate, whose venerable gray hair inspires reverence in an entire nation, conducts himself always with pure and lofty reason, judging matters according to their true nature without being swayed by the superficial appearances that only captivate the imagination of weak minds? Look at him as he attends the sermon, brimming with devout zeal, reinforcing the strength of his reasoning with the ardor of charity.[132]

Aristophanes' judges are not concerned with their behavior and the construction of legal *imagery* because authority is conferred on them by *politics.* In centuries much closer to us, many painters and caricaturists have engaged in the humorous representation of the judge. One example of this is William Hogarth's *The Bench* [Fitzwilliam Museum, Cambridge, 1753–1754], where there is a strong contrast between the sumptuousness of the togas and wigs worn by the four judges and their attitudes, which emphasize their indifference to what is happening in the courtroom; to *Un portrait flatté* (1840) by Félicien Rops, published in the satirical magazine *Le Charivari*, where the painter, intent on portraying a judge sleeping on an armchair surrounded by all the classical iconological apparatus, actually draws the image of a woman holding the scales of justice, underlining a visual contrast between the ideal and the reality; or the cartoons by Pino Zac (Giuseppe Zaccaria) which, among the forms of power that are strongly criticized, also present a series of grim, sadistic, sexually-phobic magistrates, always ready to strike the weak in favor of the strong, the poor in favor of the rich; while *Le ventre législatif. Aspect des bancs ministériels de la chambre improstituée* (1834) by Honoré Daumier does not offer a more reassuring picture of legislators. In these cases, as with Aristophanes, criticism of the legal system also becomes a criticism of the political system.

---

131 Aristophanes, *The Wasps*, 28: PHILOCLEON "My friends, he will not have me judge nor do anyone any ill, but he wants me to stay at home and enjoy myself, and I will not."
132 Blaise Pascal, *Pensieri* [1669] (Turin: Einaudi 1997), 116 [my translation].

Readers know well that Aristophanes is denouncing the *real* danger of abusing the exercise of judicial power. It is precisely the character's excessive behavior that weakens our perception of the effect Philocleon might have on society and makes us look at him critically as well as amusedly. If, on the one hand, the author makes us realize how distant jurisdiction and justice are, on the other hand, it is the laughter that Philocleon arouses in us that makes us reaffirm the importance of the law. By *laughing*, Aristophanes states what rules his character is breaking,[133] and thus confronts us with our individual civic responsibility. Mockery acts on the conscience of the addressees to confirm the importance of a principle of 'justice' that does not always go hand in hand with that of the 'legal system'. Sergei Dovlatov defined humor as an "inversion of life," a "smile of the intellect,"[134] which makes us realize that all logic is attackable or there would be no laughter and no logical truths.

Although Frankland and Philocleon are comic characters in *our* eyes, they are very serious in their intentions.[135] Not only do both of them demonstrate that they give voice to their aggressive instincts through the (improper) use of the legal institution, thus transforming the law into a weapon of offense, but they also guarantee us a kind of catharsis through comedy because they shift our attention from the truth of their reasons to the importance of the *correct practice* of law. To refer back to Celsus, an *ius* that is only an *ars*, that is to say an activity governed by rules and techniques, but without the substance seen by Celsus in the *bonum et aequum*, is not Right. Aristophanes and Conan Doyle remind us how the right to fair hearing, once deprived of common sense and intellectual honesty, is a harbinger of chaos and disorder in society. Besides, Frankland's villagers would live more harmoniously by following the rules, but without the imposing and invasive intervention of jurisprudence in their daily lives.

As evidence of how literature mirrors society, it is curious to recall the case of Mrs Giacometti Prodgers, who became famous at the end of the nineteenth century in the pages of the English satirical magazine *Punch* for having obsessed London taxi drivers and judges with her complaints. The story goes that in order to not pay for the whole taxi ride, the woman had found a strategy to be insulted by the drivers so that she could then sue them and ask for compensation. At least fifty disputes reached the courts, but at least as many popular initiatives were taken against the rich woman. Among them, it is worth mentioning that during the Guy Fawkes Night celebration in 1875 a taxi driver was arrested for burning

---

133 See Umberto Eco quoted by Placido in the Preface to Henri Bergson, *Il riso*, xvii.

134 Salmon, *I meccanismi dell'umorismo*, 38.

135 See Bergson, *Laughter*, 16.

the effigy of the lady placed on his car, but the judge acquitted him because he was "acting as a showman for the amusement of the public"; the lady's name spelled backwards – Sregdorpittemmocaig – was used for a character in J.E. Preston's novel *The Sunless City*; but she also appeared in a play by Herbert Campbell. Finally, the year after her death, Mrs Giacometti Prodgers was quoted in yet another satirical article in *Punch*[136] on the occasion of the introduction of the taximeter, which would put an end to the abuses of taxi drivers:

Upon my soul the stingy dodgers
Did ought to be shut up. They're wuss
Than Mrs. JACKERMETTY PRODGERS,
Who earned the 'onest Cabman's cuss.

There are those who believe that the woman could simply be seen as a defender of consumer rights, but in their extravagance Mrs Prodgers, Frankland and Philocleone reveal how the legal system in and of itself is a rigid mechanism, in the Bergsonian sense, and therefore suitable for comic comment.[137] The life (real or fictitious, it matters little) of these characters is not a flow, but a chain of denunciations and trials that deform jurisprudence in our eyes. Legal practice becomes a repetitive gesture, a simple and automatic operation which, precisely because it is exasperatingly repeated, also becomes an object of laughter (for those who are not personally affected, of course!). One of the typical stylistic features of comedy is precisely the periodic repetition of an act or an expression[138] and, in Doyle's novel, thanks to Frankland, the law becomes that puppet that mechanically comes out of the box and amuses the children after frightening them the first time and intriguing them the next. Unlocking the mechanism of the game's reproduction makes the child master of the toy and master of its control. How can this

136 *Punch, Or The London Charivari* 99 (August 23, 1890: "A Autumn-attic happaratus / For measuring off our blooming fares! / Oh, hang it all! They slang and slate us; / They say we crawls, and cheats, and swears. / And we surwives the sneering slaters, / Wot tries our games to circumvent, / But treating us like Try-yer-weighters, / Or chockerlate, or stamps, or scent! / Upon my soul the stingy dodgers / Did ought to be shut up. They're wuss / Than Mrs. JACKERMETTY PRODGERS, / Who earned the 'onest Cabman's cuss. / It's sickening! Ah, I tell yer wot, Sir, / Next they'll stick hup–oh, you may smile– / This:–"Drop a shilling in the slot. Sir, / And the Cab goes for just two mile!"/ Beastly! I ain't no blessed babby, / Thus to be measured off like tape. / Yah! Make a autumn-attic Cabby, / With clock-work whip and a tin cape. / May as well, while you're on the job, Sir. / And then–may rust upset yer works! / The poor man of his beer they'd rob, Sir, / Who'd rob poor Cabby of his perks!"

137 Bergson, *Laughter*, 18 ff.

138 Bergson, *Laughter*, 36.

become fun? It is possible to laugh at the eccentricities of these protagonists because it is true that comedy is born from repetition, but from the repetition of what should not be repeated. Doyle and Aristophanes present us with characters who behave as if they were driven by a cog and who treat the law in the same way. Here the Bergsonian principle of laughter is realized, which undermines the rigidity of life. However, in reality, it is essential that inertia is merely represented and never actualized, it must only be an idea for the imagination.

As a matter of fact, Frankland was not looking for justice, but for litigation: it is Doyle's character that puts justice in danger. At the same time anyway, the law accepts being put in trouble, because it feeds a whole range of professionals, not least lawyers, and thus feeds its *own* power.

Chapter 3
Law vs. Comedy

Leopardi: law and the ambivalent force of laughter

> You laugh openly and loudly about something, even entirely innocently, with one or two people in a café, in a conversation, in a street: everybody who hears or sees you laughing like this will turn and look at you with respect; if they were talking, they will stop, they will seem humbled; they will never dare to laugh at you; if they had previously looked at you boldly or condescendingly, they will lose their boldness or condescension toward you. In the end, simply laughing out loud gives you a definite superiority over all those near and around you, with no exception. The power of laughter is terrible and awful: anyone who has the courage to laugh is master over the other, in the same way as anyone who has the courage to die.

So writes Giacomo Leopardi in a passage from the *Zibaldone*, dated September 23, 1828.[139] This passage, which shows Schopenhauerian influences and assonance with respect to central themes of Nietzsche's philosophy, highlights a clear change of perspective with respect to Hobbes's reconstruction of laughter as a manifestation of superiority: the power of laughter does not arise from judgment, but from the simple act of "laughing loudly." Laughter is a manifestation of power in itself regardless of its object, which may not even be known to those who witness the laughter of others. Yet it produces a reversal of power, transforming the bold or haughty into the defenseless. The power of laughter is "terrible and awful" precisely because it is capable of prevailing over any force, of overcoming any resistance. In any case, unleashing such destructive power requires a courage comparable to that of one who performs the act of self-destruction (and destruction) par excellence, that is to say, suicide. The only way to escape the destructive power of laughter is to "laugh at everything," i. e., the only attitude that is not worthy of laughter.[140] In the same light, an earlier passage in the *Zibaldone* defined laughter as "something that is particularly noticeable in wise men reduced to total despair of life, above all when they have made an extreme decision, one that allows

139 Giacomo Leopardi, *Zibaldone*, ed. Michael Caesar and Franco D'Intino (New York: Farrar, Strauss and Giroux, 2015), par. 4391. The word "awful" is in English in the original text.
140 Leopardi, *Zibaldone*, 1675, par. 3990: "Everything is madness in this world except being mad. Everything is worthy of being laughed at except laughing at everything. Everything is vanity except fine illusions and pleasurable frivolities" (December 17, 1823).

https://doi.org/10.1515/9783111286778-005

them respite precisely in this extremity of horror, and calms them, as though they were already assured of their revenge on fortune and themselves."[141]

Here, too, we recognize clear echoes of suicide. Laughter, therefore, is the result of awareness and personal experimentation of the "total despair of life," of the "extremity of horror," of the misleading character of rationality and of the syllogistic technique that constitutes its expression *par excellence.* Laughter is capable of liberating human beings as a supreme act of revolt against the inescapable destiny to which we are condemned by our own nature and by the universe in which we act. Again, in the *Zibaldone*, Leopardi comments on the fallacy of syllogistic reasoning as follows: "It is very easy to joke about extraordinary things, about bodily defects, etc. The difficult thing is to know how to raise a laugh about ordinary things. A moment's thought will enable you to discover the cause, and you can relate this to your other, analogous, thoughts" (September 23. 1821).[142]

According to Leopardi, however, the power of laughter is ambivalent. In the *Operette morali (Moral Essays)*, Leopardi recognizes that laughter has a consoling "democritean" value, along with the destructive power to cancel rationality (like madness or drunkenness, to which the author refers) or even existence itself, so that those who laugh place themselves in a superior position of dominance over those who have not freed themselves from such forces.[143]

In *In Praise of Birds,* Leopardi reiterates his own conception of laughter as the ultimate manifestation of his awareness of the tragic nature of the human condi-

---

141 Leopardi, *Zibaldone*, 142, par. 188. In the passage, the laughter of the wise men is contrasted with that of the "most desperate and melancholy mad people," in whom "it is very common and natural to hear a stupid and hollow laugh, which simply dies on their lips. They will grasp you by the hand, stare deep into your eyes, and on leaving you, bid you goodbye with a smile that seems even more mad and desperate than madness and despair themselves."

142 Leopardi, *Zibaldone*, 804, par. 1774; he adds: "It is very rare to find anyone who laughs at the truly ridiculous things in society or in individuals. And if anyone does, it is hard to find a friend to back him up, and admit that he is right, or who even understands the reason for his laughter. For the most part men laugh at things that when in effect are anything but ridiculous, and ofter they laugh at them precisely because they are not ridiculous. And they laugh at them all the more the less ridiculous they are" (1239, par. 3000).

143 The reference is to the *Dialogue of Timander ed Eleander:* "By laughing at our woes, I find some comfort; and I seek to bring some to others in the same way. If this is not granted me, I still hold it certain that laughing at our woes is the only profit we can gain from them, and the only remedy to be found in them. The poets say that despair always has a smile on her lips. You must not think that I have no compassion for the unhappiness of humanity. But not being able to cure it by any effort, any art, any labour, any compromise; I consider it far more worthy of man and of magnanimous despair, to laugh at our common woes, than to set myself to sighing, weeping and screeching along with the rest of them, or encouraging others to do likewise" (Leopardi, *Moral Essays*, 184).

tion and of the impossibility of any cause for laughter that is "just and reasonable" (since men are "never satisfied and never truly delighted by anything"). On the other hand, Leopardi adds rather surprisingly that in the present time laughter

> is to be found in a greater dignity and status than it ever was before; having a place and performing an office, in which it supplies to some extent the functions exercised in other times by virtue, justice, honour and suchlike things; and in many cases restraining and scaring men off from evil deeds.[144]

Laughter, therefore, not only has a destructive function, but also a moral function that might appear paradoxical: apparently, laughter might seem to be a substitute for morality, when *de facto* it is the cornerstone of a new morality. The disappearance of virtue, justice, honor and similar moral elements belonging to "other times" has led to the emergence of a new source of rules of behavior, discernment and prevention of "evil deeds," precisely represented by laughter. Laughter thus performs the function that belongs to the law *par excellence.* However, it must be emphasized that for Leopardi, in order to be able to perform its function, law itself must be based on a sharing of moral-ethical principles. The realization of the powerlessness of law is expressed by Leopardi in very clear terms in a passage of the *Discorso sopra lo stato presente dei costumi degl'Italiani* (*Speech on the contemporary morals of the Italians*):

> The constraint and the curb of the laws and of the public force, that nowadays seem the only ones remaining for society, since a very long time have been recognized as mostly inefficient in order to restrain evil, and even more to promote good. Everybody knows, with Horace, that laws without morals are useless, and, on the other hand, that morals are determined and mostly grounded and guaranteed by opinions.[145]

In a passage in the *Zibaldone*, dated September 4, 1823, Leopardi wrote that:

---

144 Leopardi, *Moral Essays*, 166–167. Taking his cue from the Aristotelian-Scholastic definition of man as a "laughable animal," Leopardi again writes in the *Praise of Birds:* "Wondrous also is the use we make of such faculty: for we see many in some cruel mischance, others in great misery of mind, others who scarcely retain any love of life, utterly sure of the vanity of any human good, virtually incapable of any joy, and void of every hope: who nevertheless laugh. Indeed, the better they know the vanity of the aforesaid good, and the unhappiness of life; and the less they hope, and the less they are capable of enjoyment; the more are particular men usually inclined to laughter" (Leopardi, *Moral Essays*, 165–166).

145 Giacomo Leopardi, "Discorso sopra lo stato presente dei costumi degl'Italiani," in Giacomo Leopardi, *Pensieri Moralisti Greci. Volgarizzamenti e scritti vari*, ed. A. Donati (Rome/Bari: Laterza, 1932), 250 [my translation]. On the legal aspects of Leopardi's thought, see the papers collected in Laura Melosi (ed.), *Ius Leopardi. Legge, natura, civiltà* (Florence: Olschki, 2016).

> If no idea of right or wrong, of moral good or evil, exists or is conceived per se in the intellects of men, no law passed by a legislator can render any action or failure to act just or unjust, good or bad. For there can be no reason why obeying any given law is right or wrong, good or bad, and there can be no principle on which to base the right which any one person has to govern another, if the idea of legitimacy, duty, and right is not innate or inspired (as Voltaire would have it, that is naturally and by innate disposition rising in the minds of men, when they reach the age of reason), in human intellects.[146]

On the one hand, the awareness of the end of morality (or rather, of a phase of humanity's moral development based on concepts belonging to antiquity), and therefore of the inanity of law, entails the recognition of the need for a new moral phase. On the other hand, this can only be based on principles and instruments that are completely different from those, by now irretrievable, of the past (a remote past, such as that represented by antiquity, as idealized by Leopardi).

In making birds partake of the capacity for laughter traditionally held to be inherent to humans, the same *Praise of Birds* recognizes the origin of their predisposition to joy in the design of nature that has provided them not only with song, but also with flight, keen hearing, and sight. Constant wandering frees birds from boredom; thanks to their acute senses, they

> all day long enjoy immense and varied spectacles, and from on high perceive, in a single instant, such a vast expanse of land, and distinctly view so many places, as a man, even in his thought, can scarcely comprehend all at once; and we may infer that they must have enormous force and vivacity, and enormous power of imagination.[147]

The liveliness and imagination of the birds, according to Leopardi, are comparable to those of the child: joy arises from the enthusiastic acceptance of dynamism and changeability, from the primacy of sensation and imagination over rationality and experience, which children do not possess and to which birds are insensitive.[148]

According to Leopardi laughter is, therefore, both destroyer and *maieuta*, but (intuitively and not rationally) it reveals an eternal mobility and a constant work of the imagination stimulated by sensation. In this regard, one probably cannot speak of wandering, since no order is rationally conceivable other than that im-

---

146 Leopardi, *Zibaldone*, 1373, par. 3349–3350.

147 Leopardi, *Moral Essays*, 168.

148 "Regarding which we should not fail to mention that birds are equally well-suited to bear the extremes of heat and cold; even without any space of time between the one and the other; for oftentimes we see that from the earth, in little more than an instant, they rise up through the air to a very high altitude, which is to say, to a bitterly cold zone; and many of them, in a brief period, fly through many different climates" (Leopardi, *Moral Essays*, 169).

posed by the human being's innate tragic condition, and thus by the damnation to which the end of morality would condemn him. On the other hand, there remains the possibility for a regeneration of morality, to which laughter is the trigger. In the *Fragment on Suicide* the paradigm is made explicit:

> Either imagination shall return in force, and illusions shall take back their bodies and substance in a mobile and energic life, and life shall turn back to being a lively thing, and not a dead one, and the greatness and beauty of things shall return to look as a substance, and religion shall regain its credit, or this world will become a prison for desperates, and maybe even a desert.[149]

Could there be any role for law, after the "return of the imagination"? What should its nature be, and what kind of relation would it have with the new (phase of) morality precisely founded on the imagination stimulated by sensation? And what relationship would it have to laughter, which is the product of such a new moral phase, and at the same time provides nourishment for it?

In a passage from the *Zibaldone* dated January 17, 1829, Leopardi offers a vision of a possible future law, which is somewhat surprisingly influenced by the rationalism of Enlightenment which grounded the great codes of the nineteenth and early twentieth centuries:

> In this century of such much lawmaking no one has yet thought of making a utopian code of civil and criminal laws, but in due and proper form, such as to serve as a standard of perfection, which should be a model for all other codes, so that their goodness is judged according to the greater or lesser extent to which they resemble it; such also as to make it possible, with few changes or additions required purely by the circumstances of place and time, to be adopted by any nation whatsoever, at least under a given form of government, at least in this century and by civilized nations, etc.[150]

The universalist afflatus is, indeed, limited to the "civilized nations," and this clearly distinguishes Leopardi's position from any philosophy of natural law: in several passages of the *Zibaldone* it is emphasized that natural law does not exist, and that both morality and law are variable in times and places.[151] At the same time, how-

149 Leopardi, "Frammento sul suicidio," in Giacomo Leopardi, *Tutte le opere*, eds. Walter Binni and Enrico Ghidetti (Florence: Sansoni, 1969), I, 199 [my translation].

150 Leopardi, *Zibaldone*, 2005, par. 4439.

151 Leopardi, *Zibaldone*, paragraphs 343, 357, 371, 452: "in nature it has never been believed that there was any other law, or other right of man over man, but that of force" (1880), 2255; moreover: "If we now imagine ourselves in a state of nature, we can see that people feel no repugnance at harming their enemies, in whatever guise they present themselves, any more than animals do, beever, according to the poet from Recanati, humans are animals endowed with instincts, whose main element is individualism.[152] Individualism conceives freedom, and therefore aversion to tyranny, as an inescapable aspect of existence,[153] while it does not necessarily imply, in itself, the perception of harming others as being an act of evil.[154] Moreover, in his creative design that constantly develops over time, God, who pre-exists all morality and the very idea of morality,[155] has gradually given the human being morality, or rather different morals, each of which is 'new' due to the successive transformations of human social living:

> Isolated man had no need for morality, and did not, in fact, have any, natural law being just a dream. He simply had duties of inclination towards himself, the only duties useful and proper to his state. When society became close-knit, morality was propriety, and God gave to man gradually, or rather first one morality then another, according to the successive states of society, and each of these moralities was equally perfect, because it was proper; and isolated man is perfect, without morality.[156]

"Civilization," which is constitutively determined by human behavioral rules, is thus the result of a progressive overcoming of mere instinct, through new manifestations of the moral sense provided by God to humans in the course of the evolu-

cause an enemy is always an enemy, and man is inclined to harm him whenever, wherever, however and as much as he possibly can" (par. 342).

152 Instinct seems to be, in fact, the only "law of nature" that Leopardi contrasts with "civil" or "human" law, pointing out that while the former can be forgotten, or broken "natural laws admit of no such distraction, and it cannot happen that we break them without realizing it, because they are always in our hearts, like an instinct of which we are always aware, and which is not subject to forgetfulness" (Leopardi, *Zibaldone*, 103, par. 118–119).

153 Leopardi, *Zibaldone*, 298, par. 552, where tyranny is defined "a state directly opposed to the nature of all living beings of all species, and hence a sure source of unhappiness."

154 "Natural law varies according to the nature of different creatures. A horse, not being carnivorous, will perhaps judge a wolf that attacks and kills a sheep to be unjust. It will hate it for its blood thirstiness and will feel a sense of horror if it chances to see some examples of its butchery. Not so a lion. Moral good and evil, therefore, have nothing absolute about them. The only wicked acts are those which are repugnant to the inclinations of each kind of operative being, nor are those acts wicked which harm other beings but are not repugnant to the nature of the one who performs them" (Leopardi, *Zibaldone*, 748, par. 1624).

155 Leopardi, *Zibaldone*, 754, par. 1638–1639: "God, therefore, does not have nor can have any morality, something that could only be by admitting Plato's ideas, independent of God, and eternal and necessary models of things; that morality, therefore, is created by him, like everything else, and that he was free to change it in light of the different circumstances of the human race, as he is free to give one that is entirely different, and even opposite, or not give any at all, to a different race of beings whether within the known order of things (such as the inhabitants of other planets), or in others unknown, and equally possible and plausible."

156 Leopardi, *Zibaldone*, 755, par. 1641; see also par. 1712.

tion of social living (which is also determined by God). The social development in "civilized nations" takes place through a constant "contradiction between fact and law," the foundation of which is moral, i. e., through "a contradiction in the order of human affairs, inserting qualities contrary to the intrinsic and essential qualities of man, that is to say, a subjection and inequality contrary to liberty and natural equality."[157]

"Subjection" invokes one of the characteristic elements of law, namely the claim to normativity. "Contradiction," on the other hand, recalls one of the characteristic elements of laughter, namely the rupture, if not the actual overcoming, of rationality. A key element in Leopardi's work is the decline of civilization, from antiquity to his own time. The hypothetical future of law is, therefore, to be traced back to that of civilization,[158] starting from the miserable condition in which it is declining.

In the aforementioned *Discorso*, the residual core of civilization was identified by Leopardi in the reciprocal consideration between people united by the need to "provide for each other's needs, and defend themselves from common harm and danger": the "bon ton," a futile sentiment, because it is based essentially on appearances, starting with those relating to material success.[159]

However, in the work that represents the culmination of his philosophical and poetic journey – *La Ginestra (The Genista)*-, Leopardi expresses himself in different terms, coming to see in the need to unite forces against Nature, "the true culprit, whom we mother name / of men by birth, stepmother in good will" the embryo of a true human brotherhood, within which

> He deems his fellows tied
> In one confederacy against all harms,
> And lovingly enfolds

157 Leopardi, *Zibaldone*, 587.

158 The link between law and civilization is a key element in the thought of a scholar as seemingly distant from Leopardi as Roscoe Pound: see on the subject Giuseppe Rossi, "The Search for the 'Workable Legal Precept' in a Context of Incoherence and Uncertainty: Reflections on Roscoe Pound's Theory of Judicial Empiricism from a European Perspective," *Comparative Law Review* 7 (2017). Available online: http://www.comparativelawreview.unipg.it/index.php/comparative/article/view/131 (last access February 2021).

159 "… the state of opinions and of nations about morals is degraded in this precise misery that is bon ton. This is not only the strongest, but even the only foundation remaining for good morals, and good morals are respected only, generally speaking […] for the very same reasons for which bon ton is respected, and where there is no bon ton, or where bon ton is not respected, there morals lack any foundation and society has no boundaries but force, which may never produce good morals, nor ban bad habits, or keep them afar" (Leopardi, "Discorso," 254 [my translation]).

Them in his arms, and holds
A strong and ready hand to them; no less
He in the shifting chance and change and stress
Of the common war expects.

When this human brotherhood will eventually be recognized,

And justice and religion other root
Acquire once more than proud and vain conceits,
Foundation where is wont to plant its foot
The righteousness of man,
And stands as best what rests on error can.[160]

The rebirth of ethics, of "justice and religion," should find grounds in poetic intuition, of which the laughter of *In Praise of Birds* is the manifestation *par excellence.* In the rediscovered fraternity of humanity united against step-motherly Nature, there may not even be any need for law, just as there was no need for it in "the society that was truly primordial and natural to the human species, as to those of the beasts, in being without supremacy, subjection, inequality, ranks or rules, and could very well answer to the purpose, that is, the common good, just as the society of the ants answers to it."[161] Certainly, the hypothetical new law will no longer be composed of "proud and vain conceits."

Leopardi's thought and the problem of *eutrapelia*

Leopardi's thought presents an undeniable problem of *eutrapelia.* His system is certainly influenced by the political situation in Italy at the time, but it is endowed with universal value. In this system, morality is still possible and can still offer foundation to a claim of normativity of law. The destructive force of laughter is recognized both as having the capacity to generate human dominance over one another, as well as to manifest and nurture poetic intuition: thus, it is evident that laughter cannot always be considered just. The laughter that reveals the bond of brotherhood between humans, in the struggle against Nature and against their own nature (which does not abhor causing suffering, or even death, to another human), is counterpointed by the laughter that destroys this bond, insofar as it is aimed at the pursuit of domination. In both cases laughter has a destructive sig-

160 Giacomo Leopardi, "The Genista, or the Flower of the Desert" [1831], trans. J.M. Morrison, in Giacomo Leopardi, *The Poems (Canti)* (London: Gay and Bird, 1900), 128–140, 133–134.
161 Leopardi, *Zibaldone*, 309–310, par. 587.

nificance, in which illusions and the final revelation of the tragic nature of the human condition in the face of "step-motherly" nature are unveiled, but only in the former is this accompanied by a (mildly) maieutic capacity to stimulate the poetic intuition. As we have said before, whereas rational knowledge would condemn humanity to the final tragedy mentioned in the *Fragment on Suicide*, poetic intuition is capable of laying the foundations for a new morality or, in Leopardi's religious perspective, of constituting the epiphany of a new revelation. The central issue of this revelation should be the acknowledgment of the good-positive quality of life's constant mobility and the imagination's continuous activity.

The human capacity to laugh thus becomes a manifestation of something that constitutes, perhaps, the true *proprium* of humanity, namely the capacity to imagine (like what happens to the "solitary philosopher Amelio" in the *Praise of Birds* when he listens to his favorite creatures, or to the poet himself, "shipwrecked" from the "lonely hill" of the *Infinite*). The foundations of a moral (and potentially juridical) system liberated from the natural instinct and the constraints of rationality could be grounded in imagination. Certainly, this new system is highly undefined. Both the *Zibaldone* and the *Genista* only hint at some very vague sketches of it. However, it certainly appears if not inevitable, certainly possible, and compatible with the human. As mentioned above, indefiniteness is characteristic of the phantom of justice, whose manifestations vary in time and place. If we broaden Leopardi's perspective, the same laughter that unveils the innate errancy of law, restoring it to the flux and recovering spaces of freedom, could constitute the very origin of the phantom of justice. At the very least, it may constitute the instrument of its evocation, or the fruit that is inspired by it. A fruit that possesses only the uncertainty, inconsistency, and unpredictability of imagined things, which may or may not become real.

Far from seeing laughter as a manifestation of superiority and/or a claim of judgment, eutrapelia in the mockery of law is no longer, as was assumed at the beginning of this essay, the result of the intersection of sets of rules, but descends from the *will* of the person laughing and the *effect* of laughter, which could also be independent of the former. The rules of laughter are embryos of rules: they reject rationality in favor of imagination, and its infinite possibilities that open up to found a new morality, and even a new law.

Nietzsche, Don Quixote and eutrapelia

The fundamental point that divides the 'immoralist' Nietzsche from the 'pessimist' Leopardi is the affirmation of the mystifying nature of morality, and thus the need for its ultimate overcoming through laughter.[162] By breaking the link between law and morality through laughter (together, it may be said, with every other 'certainty'), Nietzsche opens up an idea of law as a mere act of force that will constitute, even more than Hobbesian conceptions, the focal point of legal positivism. This idea is only minimally undermined (perhaps as a side effect) by the "pure' doctrines of law, with their exaltation of the inescapability of the logical foundation of law itself, which in turn see in Nietzsche their point of origin.[163]

In early works such as *The Birth of Tragedy* and *Richard Wagner in Bayreuth*, Nietzsche saw an antidote against the deceptions of rational speculation in the rediscovery of the Dionysian made possible by art. Later, these positions would be replaced by the denunciation of falsifications of art, of which the fierce polemic waged against Wagner is an emblematic example. In aphorism No. 459 of *Human, All Too Human*, Nietzsche contrasts "arbitrary" law with "traditional" law, to arrive at the conclusion of the "necessity" of the former:

> Arbitrary law necessary. Lawyers argue whether that law which is most thoroughly thought out, or that which is easiest to understand should prevail in a people. The first type, whose greatest model is Roman law, seems incomprehensible to the layman and therefore no expression of his sense of justice. Popular laws, like the Germanic, for example, were crude, superstitious, illogical, in part silly, but they reflected quite specific inherited customs and feelings. But when law is no longer a tradition, as in our case, it can only be commanded, or forced; none of us has a traditional sense of justice any longer; therefore we must content ourselves with arbitrary laws, which express the necessity of having to have a law. Then, the most logical law is the most acceptable, because it is the most impartial, even admitting that, in the relationship of crime and punishment, the smallest unit of measure is always set arbitrarily.[164]

Nevertheless, according to Nietzsche "sense of justice" (morality), "tradition," and, even more so, logic are nothing but mystifications, the results of innate human cruelty, regarding which the philosopher places himself in a non-evaluative position. The very "necessity of having to have a law" originates from a clash of forces which cannot be eliminated. Even if one assumes the primacy of logic as the source of law, by virtue of its aseptic nature there will always exist a margin of discretion, which will maintain space for the use of force.

Nietzsche starts precisely with an analysis of the debtor-creditor relationship in order to conduct his own demolishing critique of one of the cornerstones of any

---

162 Nietzsche's fragments on Leopardi, alongside various essays, are published in Friedrich Nietzsche, *Intorno a Leopardi*, ed. C. Galimberti (Genoa: Il Melangolo, 1999).

163 Through Kelsen's "anti-metaphysical" reading of Nietzsche: see below in the text.

164 Friedrich Nietzsche, *Human, All Too Human. A Book for Free Spirits* [1878], trans. Marion Faber and Stephen Lehmann (Lincoln: Univ. of Nebraska Press, 1996), 219.

morality, namely the concept of guilt. In the very moment when the law recognizes the creditor's possibility to gain satisfaction from the debtor's assets, or even, in archaic forms, from the debtor's person (or freedom), it legitimizes a connection between the 'damage' suffered by the creditor and the 'pain' that the latter can legally inflict on the debtor. The pleasure derived from the exercise of cruelty is thus institutionalized. The mutilation of the debtor's body as an archaic and cruel form of satisfaction of the creditor is an example:

> [...] the creditor could inflict any kind of indignity and torture upon the body of the debtor; for example, cut from it as much as seemed commesurate with the size of the debt – and everywhere and from early times one had exact evaluations, legal evaluations, of the individual limbs and parts of the body from this point of view, some of them going into horrible and minute detail.[165]

Among the representations of this pleasure – along with the "executions, torturings, or perhaps and auto-da-fè" that accompanied "princely weddings" and "public festivals of the most magnificent kind" – Nietzsche recalls that "no noble household was without creatures upon whom one could heedlessly vent one's malice and cruel jokes," as in the case of Don Quixote at the Duchess's Court. The philosopher adds that:

> Today we read Don Quixote with a bitter taste in our mouth, almost with a feeling of torment, and would thus seem very strange and incomprehensible to its author and his contemporaries: they read it with the clearest conscience in the world as the most cheerful of books, they laughed themselves almost to death over it.[166]

---

165 Friedrich Nietzsche, "On the Genealogy of Morals" [1887], trans. W. Kaufmann and R.J. Hollingdale, in Friedrich Nietzsche, *On the Genealogy of Morals and Ecce Homo* (New York: Vintage Books Random House, 1989), 24–166, 64. The Shakespearean example of *The Merchant of Venice* shows, however, that law can contain within itself both the abstract recognition of such a claim and the technical means to disarm it. In the case of Portia's argument, it is a question of *interpretation:* "Portia's argumentation does nothing but poetically pose the constant problem of interpretation, the subtle determination of the exact scope of the norm in the face of the concrete case, which is then an inescapable path of its very applicability, and therefore of its very positivity" (Tullio Ascarelli, "Antigone e Porzia," in Tullio Ascarelli, *Problemi giuridici* (Milan: Giuffrè, 1959), I, 11 [my translation]); in a similar sense Eugenio Ripepe, "Ogni persona è più persone in una. Il mercante di Venezia, l'identità individuale come identituà plurale e l'impossibilità di ri(con)durre il diritto alla giustizia o la giustizia al diritto," in *Dei confini, dell'identità e di altri demoni. La diversità tra letteratura e diritto*, eds. Daniele M. Cananzi and Andrea Salvati (Turin: Giappichelli, 2018), 48.
166 Nietzsche, "On the Genealogy," 66. See also the fragment quoted by Walter A. Kaufmann, *Nietzsche: Philosopher, Psychologist, Antichrist* (Princeton: Princeton Univ. Press, 2013), 71, footnote 40, alongside further similar fragments: "Cervantes could have fought the Inquisition, but he preferred to make its victims, i.e., the heretics and idealists of all kinds, look ridiculous ..."

It is surprising, at least at first glance, this mention of eutrapelia and the chronological and geographical variability of the comedy, on the part of the "immoralist" philosopher who wrote: "I do not want to be a holy man; sooner even a buffoon. – Perhaps, I am a buffoon. – Yet, in spite of that – or rather not in spite of it, because so far nobody has been more mendacious than holy men – the truth speaks out of me." Nietzsche claimed "revaluation of all values," the "formula for an act of supreme self-examination on the part of humanity", which "become flesh and genius in me."[167] Criticizing the maxim, attributed to Spinoza, "non ridere, non lugere, neque detestari, sed intelligere" (not to laugh, not to lament, not to detest, but to understand), Nietzsche argues that knowledge, which is always accidental and transitory, is the result of the unconscious, inner struggle between conflicting impulses "to laugh, lament, and curse."[168] According to the philosopher, laughter, lament, and execration are irreconcilable, irreducible to any kind of "justice" or "contract." They must necessarily clash, and from the clash arises – like "the spark from the clash of two swords" – knowledge, having the same suddenness, unpredictability and impermanence.

On the one hand, according to Nietzsche's thought laughter is an instrument of destruction of false certainties, rational or otherwise, and thus a tool to liberate

---

167 Friedrich Nietzsche, "Ecce homo," trans. W. A. Kaufmann, in Friedrich Nietzsche, *On the Genealogy of Morals and Ecce Homo*, 217–338, 325.

168 Friedrich Nietzsche, *The Gay Science*, trans. W.A. Kaufmann (New York: Vintage Books Random House, 1974), 261–262, par. 333; the reference goes to the third part of the *Ethica*, where Spinoza criticizes those who "qui hominum Affectus, et actiones detestari, vel ridere malunt, quam intelligere" ("those who prefer rather to abuse and ridicule the emotions and actions of men than to understand them"). Indeed, the execration or derision of human feelings and actions would prevent one from grasping the universal laws of nature that necessarily govern human feeling and action. According to Spinoza: "Nothing happens in nature: for nature is always the same and one everywhere, and its ability and power of acting, that is, the laws and rules of nature according to which all things are made and changed from one into another, are everywhere and always the same, and therefore one and the same manner must there be to understand the nature of all things, that is, by means of the universal laws and rules of nature." Baruch Spinoza, *Ethics*, trans. A. Boyle (London: Dent & Sons, 1941), 83–84. Nietzsche's position is the opposite: nature escapes any predefined law intelligible to man, whose knowledge is always merely accidental and transitory. On Nietzsche's passage, Michel Foucault, "Truth and Juridical Forms," in Michel Foucault, *Power*, ed. James D. Faubion, trans. R. Hurley (New York: New Press, 2000), 1–89, 12 observes: "If these three drives – laughing, lamenting, hating – manage to produce knowledge, this is not, according to Nietzsche, because they have subsided, as in Spinoza, or made peace, or because they have attained a unity. On the contrary, it's because they have tried, as Nietzsche says, to harm one another, it's because they are in a state of war – in a momentary stabilization of this state of war, they reach a kind of state, a kind of hiatus, in which knowledge will finally appear as the spark between two swords."

humankind through the killing of the "spirit of gravity,"[169] of which "the prejudice of this serious beast against all gay science" constitutes fruit.[170] On the other hand, execration is reserved for the lies of reason, morality, religion, and so on, destined to be swept away by the power of laughter, which seems to stand beyond execration.

In the quoted passage on Don Quixote, however, laughter also seems to become part of the spirit of gravity. Nietzsche seems to suggest a re-evaluation of the value of laughter, whose variability is revealed (whereas in the German thinker's work laughter is identified as perhaps the only constant in the entire philosophical system). Laughter shows a potential lying nature. It appears to share exactly the same misleading capacity which, according to Nietzsche, would characterize any other human cognitive or evaluative instrument.

Nietzsche blames not only the ridiculousness into which the Duchess and Cervantes have plunged Don Quixote, whose figure is notoriously sorrowful, but also the final return to sanity that precedes the hero's 'second death' at the end of the second part of the work. The latter is so different from the first death, which closes the previous part, shrouded in mystery and celebrated by the epitaphs of the "Academicians of the Argamasilla." For the philosopher, Don Quixote's regaining of consciousness is emblematic of the greatest threat to mankind: self-denial.[171] The opposite, one might say, of the free death preached by Zarathustra: "in your death, your spirit and your virtue Should still glow like a sunset glow around the earth: otherwise yours is a bad death."[172]

Ridicule is as unjust as the deprivation of the Knight of La Mancha's virtue. In Nietzsche's view, his virtue is *truer* than ever because it is deprived of any expectation of reward[173] other than the eternal fame of being the greatest knight-errant of all time. Don Quixote's coming to his senses is a disgrace because, unlike the "first death" and the various segregations and attempts to "cure" that the hero un-

169 Friedrich Nietzsche, *Thus Spoke Zarathustra. A Book for Everyone and No One*, trans. R.J Hollingdale (London: Penguin, 1969), 210.

170 Nietzsche, *The Gay Science*, 257, par. 327.

171 Friedrich Nietzsche, "Schopenhauer as Educator" [1874], trans. R.J Hollingdale, in Friedrich Nietzsche, *Untimely Meditations* (Cambridge: Cambridge Univ. Press, 1983), 125–194, 155: "This eternal becoming is a lying puppet-play in beholding which man forgets himself, the actual distraction which disperses the individual to the four winds, the endless stupid game which the great child, time, plays before us and with us. That heroism of truthfulness consists in one day ceasing to be the toy it plays with."

172 Nietzsche, *Thus Spoke Zarathustra*, 99.

173 Nietzsche, *Thus Spoke Zarathustra*, 117: "My beauty laughed at you, you virtuous, today. And thus came its voice to me: 'They want to be – paid as well! Do you want reward for virtue and heaven for earth, and eternity for your today?"

dergoes in the course of the novel, it definitively breaks the "eternal return" of time,[174] and irretrievably frustrates the only real hope of eternity.

According to Nietzsche, Don Quixote, is one of the proudest bearers of a moral system, that of chivalry (an expression of an "ethical will to power"?[175]), which he himself, almost as a "superman" defines as superior to any other science, value or human institution – including, it goes without saying – legal ones. The *hidalgo*'s decision to free the convicts, which is perhaps the most significant example of this among the many cases scattered throughout the book, originates from a judgment derived from a "trial" that he himself holds, interrogating the convicts as an inquisitor. The answers that Don Quixote receives from the convicts are ironic, but he does not grasp this nature.[176] After being assaulted and robbed by the convicts he freed, Don Quixote admits his "mistake" to Sancho.[177] However, in the "eternal return" of history, when the gendarmes of the Holy Brotherhood attempt to arrest him on the basis of a special warrant for having freed the convicts, the hidalgo as-

---

174 "This life as you now live it and you have lived it, you will have to live once more and innumerable times more; and there will be nothing new in it, but every pain and every joy and every thought and sigh and everything unutterably small or great in your life will have to return to you, all in the same succession and sequence – even this spider and this moonlight between the trees, and even this moment and I myself. The eternal hourglass of existence is turned upside down again and again, and you with it, speck of dust!" (Nietzsche, *The Gay Science*, 273, par. 341)

175 Michel Foucault, *The Order of Things. An Archaeology of the Human Sciences* [1966] (New York: Pantheon Books – Random House, 1970), 46 identifies instead in Don Quixote the symbol of the normativity of language ("in his reality as an impoverished hidalgo he can become a knight only by listening from afar to the age-old epic that gives its form to the Law"), and of its boundaries (in the work, "language breaks off its old kinship with things and enters into that lonely sovereignty from which it will reappear, in its separated state, only as literature; because it marks the point where resemblance enters an age which is, from the point of view of resemblance, one of madness and imagination": 49). From this perspective, Don Quixote's final coming to his senses seems a vain attempt to restore the link between language and reality, which can only be destined to be broken again.

176 The prisoner who claims to find himself in chains for love, for example, points out that "it was not such love as your worship imagines ... mine was a strong affection for a basket of fine linen, which I embraced so closely that, if justice had not taken it from me by force, I should not have parted with it by my own good-will even to the present day" (Miguel de Cervantes, *Adventures of Don Quixote de La Mancha* [1605], trans. Charles Jarvis (New York: Crowell & Co., without year), 148). The responses of the convicts, moreover, reveal, through irony, the arbitrariness of a judicial system based on torture and the imposition of exemplary punishments, totally disproportionate to the extent of the crime.

177 "Sancho, I have always heard it said that to do good to the vulgar is to throw water into the sea. Had I believed what you said to me, I might have prevented this trouble: but it is done – I must have patience, and henceforth take warning" (Cervantes, *The Adventures of Don Quixote*, 156). The "sage" Don Quixote, following Sancho's style, quotes proverbs ...

serts himself as the holder of a true right to the transmutation of values, which prevails over any legal rule:

> who was the blockhead that signed the warrant for apprehending such a knight as I am? Who was he that knew not that knights-errant are exempt from all judicial authority, that their sword is their law, valor their privilege, and their own will their edicts? Who was the madman, I say again, who knew not that there is no patent of gentility which contains so many privileges and exemptions as are required by the knight-errant on the day he devotes himself to the rigorous exercise of chivalry? What knight-errant ever paid custom, poll tax, subsidy, quit-rent, porterage, of ferryboat? What tailor ever brought in a bill for making his clothes? What governor that lodged him in his castle ever made him pay for his entertainment?[178]

Don Quixote's peroration obviously sounds ridiculous, but laughter produces an effect opposite to the one that Nietzsche attributes to it: it restores the value of law and one of its characteristic institutions – the obligatory relationship (*obligatio*) – which for Nietzsche represents "a great deal of severity, cruelty, and pain."[179] Laughter operates a kind of counter-transmutation, which generates a restoration of the lie.[180] In other words, following Zarathustra's approach, Don Quixote is telling the truth, while the reader who laughs at his speech is cheated by his own laughter into believing that the law and its underlying values are actually truthful. The episode continues in an equally significant vein. The curate seeks to persuade the officers that "the knight, as they might easily perceive, was deranged in his mind, it was useless for them to proceed further in the affair; for if they were to apprehend him, he would soon be released as insane." And finally: "the priest said so much, and Don Quixote acted so extravagantly, that the officers would have been more crazy than himself, had they not desisted after such evidence of his infirmity. They judged it best, therefore, to be quiet ..."[181] The curate's intervention,

---

178 Cervantes, *Adventures of Don Quixote*, 340.

179 Nietzsche, "On the Genealogy," 64.

180 In an episode of Mario Monicelli's movie *Il Marchese del Grillo* (The Marquis del Grillo – 1981), the protagonist, played by Alberto Sordi, arbitrarily refuses to pay a Jewish cabinetmaker for work he has done, and obtains through bribery an unjust favorable sentence; he then commissions solemn funeral masses for all the churches in Rome, and when called upon by the Pope to explain, he replies that he intended to demonstrate (and mourn) the death of justice. Pius VII's reply is that "justice is not of this world, but of the other" and that, in any case, the order of institutions must be preserved. In contrast to Cervantes' tale, here laughter achieves the full subversion of the juridical rule: the rich aristocrat can refuse the poor craftsman payment of his due, with the approval of the jurisdiction, in the knowledge of the necessity of injustice in the supreme power.

181 Cervantes, *Adventure of Don Quixote*, 341.

seemingly benevolent towards the hidalgo, actually anticipates Don Quixote's 'second death': it propitiates the recognition of his madness and gives rise to a sort of symbolic murder of the knight. Thus, laughter can lead to the transmutation of values, but also to their restoration; to the triumph of truth as indicated by Nietzsche, or to the triumph of lies. The distinction between the two types of laughter ultimately poses a problem of justice. The emergence of the issue of eutrapelia in Nietzsche's thought no longer seems surprising at this point.

The return of law to the becoming and the revenge of the phantom of justice

Nietzsche's perhaps most famous passage on laughter reads: "This laugher's crown, this rose-wreath crown: I myself have set this crown on my head, I myself have canonized my laughter [...] to you, my brothers, do I throw this crown! I have canonized laughter; you, Higher Men, learn – to laugh."[182] Laughter, therefore, as in Leopardi, is not in itself a herald of positive values; it requires an operation of "sanctification," which is the work of the philosopher, and it is also necessary for "superior men," who are free from the deceptions of the past, to learn how to laugh, i. e., to use laughter in the *right way:* in other words, to possess eutrapelia. In another famous passage, Nietzsche states "I should actually risk an order of rank among philosophers depending of their laughter – all the way up to those capable of golden laughter."[183] There is, therefore, a dignity of laughter, a kind of true scale of value structuring a philosophical "new thought," that is aware of the (poly) valence of laughter itself, and which culminates with the "golden laughter," that frees us from falsehood: the laughter of Zarathustra, who longs for the laughter of "a transformed being, surrounded with the light, laughing. Never yet on earth any man laughed as he laughed."[184]

The premise for the emergence of the "gay science" is the alliance between laughter and wisdom, rooted in the awareness that "the species is everything, one is always none," and in the renunciation of the claim to identify a purpose for existence, and with it any rules functional to its attainment.[185]

Since wisdom is disengaged as much from any consideration of an end as from any individual connotation, it is expressed in the ability to laugh in the right way,

182 Nietzsche, *Thus Spoke Zarathustra*, 305–306.

183 Friedrich Nietzsche, *Beyond Good and Evil. Prelude to a Philosophy of the Future* [1886], trans. W. Kaufmann (New York: Vintage Books – Random House, 1989), 232.

184 Nietzsche, *Thus Spoke Zarathustra*, 180.

185 Nietzsche, *The Gay Science*, 74.

giving the quality of science to gaiety, and vice versa, giving science the attribute of "gaiety." It is precisely eutrapelia, the quality of laughter, that seems to represent the hinge between the two elements.

The philosopher's entire oeuvre is permeated, moreover, by constant indignation (the execration evoked in the criticism towards Spinoza) against lies and an equally constant aspiration to discover the truth against the oppression generated by the unjust deceptions of the past, of which morality is the most conspicuous part.

The passage from *Zarathustra* that concludes with the exhortation to learn how to laugh includes an evocation of one of the concepts to which Nietzsche is most averse, that of guilt/sin, the nucleus of every hypothesis of morality: "What has been the greatest sin here on earth? Was it not the saying of him who said 'Woe to those who laugh'"?[186] The same indignation transpires with regard to, for example, Schopenhauer's attitude towards ethics:

> Listen, for example, with what almost venerable innocence Schopenhauer still described his task, and then draw your conclusion about the scientific standing of a 'science' whose ultimate masters still talk like children and little old women: 'The principle' he says (p. 136 of Grundprobleme der Moral), 'the fundamental proposition on whose content all moral philosophers are really agreed – neminem laede, immo omnes, quantum potes, juva' – that is really the proposition for which all moralist endeavor to find the rational foundation ... the real basis of ethics which one has been looking for thousands of years as for the philosopher's stone.' – The difficulty of providing a rational foundation for the principle cited may indeed be great – As it is well-known, Schopenhauer did not succeed either; – and whoever has once felt deeply how insipidly false and sentimental this principle is in a world whose essence is will to power, may allow himself to be reminded that Schopenhauer, though a pessimist, really – played the flute. Every day, after dinner: one should read his biography on that. And incidentally: a pessimist, one who denies God and the world but comes to a stop before morality – who affirms morality and plays the flute, the 'laede neminem' morality– what? Is that really – a pessimist?[187]

The rupture of the postulate of human beings' moral nature, and the opposing affirmation of a connatural contradiction between the "will to power" and a fundamental moral principle, which the entire legal tradition of Roman basis has made its own as the *neminem laedere*, is finally based on judgments of a paradoxically moral nature. Philosophers weakly withdraw from coming to terms with the defining element of the human being represented by the will to power, and resort to hypocritical and reassuring stratagems.

---

186 Nietzsche, *Thus Spoke Zarathustra*, 304.
187 Nietzsche, *Beyond Good and Evil*, 98.

Therefore, the transmutation of values brought about by laughter does not seem to announce the impossibility of morality, but, on the contrary, the subversion of recognized morality for the benefit of a new morality, just as, in general, the destruction of false certainties originating from the lies of the past announces a new truth, of which Nietzsche proclaims himself the standard-bearer on several occasions. The "new truth" announced by Nietzsche, however, is different from all previous truths not only in content, but in its very nature. It is the fruit of the "suspension" and "non-affirmation" characteristic of laughter, and it takes as its central element the awareness of not knowing (of something which is not "thinkable" rationally, nor expressible through language). This no longer constitutes a Socratic premise for a maieutic path destined to lead to its opposite (knowledge), but represents an ineliminable datum.[188] Nonetheless, it is necessary to continue attempting to think, even to think the unthinkable, with tools other than the usual rational thought (the Cartesian *cogito*), and to express ourselves with words that are necessarily different from those of the usual philosophical language and that are obviously far less precise (Bataille's *mots glissants?*[189]).

Horkheimer and Adorno point out that names carry with themselves the same duplicity as laughter, that is a symbol of natural destructive forces, but at the same time of "blind nature's" capacity to perceive itself as such, and to get rid of its ruinous violence ("... perhaps names are no more than frozen laughter, as it is evident nowadays in nicknames – the only ones that retain something of the original action of name-giving").[190] Michel Foucault writes in *The Order of Things:*

> For modern thought, no morality is possible. Thought had already left itself in its own being as early as the nineteenth century; it is no longer theoretical. As soon as it functions it offends or reconciles, attracts or repels, breaks, dissociates, unites or reunites; it cannot help but liberate and enslave.

---

188 Donà, *Filosofia dell'errore*, 185–186: ."".. the laughter provoked by humor is an essentially tragic laughter; precisely because it does not tell of our simply feeling at a safe distance from the nonsense of this or that narrative ... but of our being hopelessly involved in a nonsense that, precisely because it is always ours too, can only tell us this: that we have in truth very little to laugh at ... that which makes us laugh so irresistibly anyway" [my translation].

189 The word "silence," which, when pronounced, announces its own death, substituting silence with sound, and thus encompassing in itself its own opposite ("Je ne donnerai qu'un exemple de mot glissant. Je dis mot: ce peut être aussi bien la phrase où l'on insère le mot, mais je me borne au mot silence. Du mot il est déjà, je l'ai dit, l'abolition du bruit qu'est le mot; entre tous les mots c'est le plus pervers, ou le plus poétique: il est lui-même gage de sa mort": Georges Bataille, "L'expérience interieure" [1943], in Georges Bataille, *Oeuvres complètes* (Paris: Gallimard, 1973), VII, 393.

190 Max Horkheimer and Theodor W. Adorno, *Dialectic of Enlightenment* [1947], trans. John Cumming (New York: Seabury Press, 1972), 77.

According to the French philosopher, the "old" ethical form "was articulated upon the order of the world," while "the modern one ... formulates no morality, since any imperative is lodged within thought and its movement, towards the apprehension of the unthought." A footnote adds that "the Kantian moment is the link between the two: it is the discovery that the subject, in so far as he is reasonable, applies to himself his own law, which is the universal law."[191]

The cognition of not-knowing and the overcoming of the *cogito* lead, therefore, to the emergence of a "new imperative," represented by the necessity to continue to think (to speak and write) and accepting not knowing as a constitutive element of knowledge, rather than in Cartesian terms as an error to be corrected. As was already the case for Nietzsche, the "new thought" is no longer theory but experience, starting with the experience of laughter, which arises from life and society, and which inevitably affects them. In the quoted footnote, the attribute "reasonable" gives way to doubts on the source and content of "reasonableness," and thus on the very source of the new "imperative" aimed at the recovery of the unthought, or rather at continuing to think, to avoid the renunciation of thought as a consequence of the awareness of its limits. Similarly, although Nietzsche's "immoralism" seems to display the traits of an inverted morality, it arguably goes further, taking on the traits not so much of the a-moral as of the non-moral. Nietzsche pursues a principle of justice, which is *not moral*, hinging on the primacy of the truth revealed by laughter, just as this same new truth distinguishes itself from any rational idea of knowledge, in order to go as far as the boundaries of the unthinkable, and the non-expressible through language, and the attempt to "apprehend the unthought." The core of non-morality is the awareness of the non-existence of a moral foundation, i.e., a definite and stable value framework, which cannot be overcome through the process of destruction and transformation-transmutation triggered by laughter. Unlike morality, non-morality is iridescent, in its foundations and consequences; it hinges on laughter but, as we see from Nietzsche's approach to Don Quixote, laughter itself is iridescent, multifarious, and broad-spectrum by definition. The non-morality of which Nietzsche implicitly posits the premises, and of which eutrapelia is an integral, if not a key factor, goes to the limits of any rule of behavior, be it legal, religious, ethical or of any other nature, casting doubt on its foundations and application. Nonetheless, it does not eliminate the thinkability of a rule, even if, paradoxically, it is the prohibition of any rule at all: a 1968-style "Il est interdit d'interdire." Just as an awareness of the limits of thought, and the questioning of the very identity of the thinking "I" do not eliminate, but reinforce, the need to continue thinking.

191 Foucault, *The Order of Things*, 327–328.

If, following Leopardi's thought, the phantom of justice wanders wherever someone laughs, on the boundary between reality and poetic imagination, following Nietzsche's thought it lies on the extreme border of the thinkable, where the individual becomes aware, by laughing, of the incapacity of thought, of the fictitious nature of the ego, of the finiteness of existence, of the irrelevance of the individual in the universe, of the absence of an end (in the eternal return of time), of the will to power as the source of every moral conception of good and evil.[192] However, at the same time, the individual cannot escape the dialectic between good and evil, and the continuous creative destruction that this brings about, until there is a final synthesis that is probably unrealizable and only expressible in a very confused way:

> Truly, I say to you: Unchanging good and evil does not exist! From out of themselves they must overcome themselves again and again ... And he who has to be a creator in good and evil, truly, has first to be a destroyer and break values. Thus the greatest evil belongs with the greatest good: this, however, is the creative good.[193]

Law can be conceived as a rational discourse, carried out through a very ambitious technical language, with claims to conform reality to itself and, above all, to stability (in the sense that it will be very shortly specified). Nietzsche's approach challenges this view profoundly. The very possibility of imagining a descriptive discourse of reality and, all the more so, a conformative one is weakened alongside any claim to normativity thought out rationally and expressed through language.[194] The connection between Nietzsche and legal positivism lies in Kelsen's attempt to criticize Heidegger's metaphysical reading of Nietzsche, to trace back exclusively to

---

192 Nietzsche, *Thus Spoke Zarathustra*, 139.

193 Nietzsche, *Thus Spoke Zarathustra*, 140; See also, among the many passages on the subject, the *Genealogy of Morals*, where Nietzsche invokes "the man of the future, who will redeem us not only from the hitherto reigning ideal but also from that which was bound to grow out of it, the great nausea, the will to nothingness, nihilism ... this Antichrist and antinichilist, this victor over God and nothingness – he must come one day." (Nietzsche, "On the Genealogy," 96).

194 As Prezzo, *Ridere la verità*, 46–47 recalls, Foucault himself, in the introduction to *The Order of Things*, reports that the book was born from the laughter aroused by reading a text by Borges. It is *The Analytical Language of John Wilkins* of 1952 – in Jorge Luis Borges, *Other Inquisitions*, trans. Ruth LC. Simms (Austin – London: Univ. of Texas Press, 1964), 101–105, in which the Argentinean writer ironizes the human aspiration to classify, and to express the real through language, which he defines, quoting Chesterton, as "an arbitrary system of grunts and squeals." "Obviously," Borges concludes, "there is no classification of the universe that is not arbitrary and conjectural. The reason is very simple: we do not know what the universe is." However, "the impossibility of penetrating the divine scheme of the universe cannot dissuade us from outlining human schemes, even though we are aware that they are provisional."

human choices – and hence to statutory decisions – the value-related foundations of law: "the values established by the will to power are definitively not metaphysical but empirical values, established by the will of man."[195] The conceptual heart of Kelsenian positivism lies, in fact, precisely in the idea that it is the law itself that lays its own foundation, through the *Grundnorm*, and establishes the ways and limits of its own transformation. It is the law itself that perennially defines the notion of the juridical and regulates its own changes. Only the legal rule can determine how it will be changed, and how new juridical rules will be produced. Indeed, historical experience teaches us that no system, no conception of law, no mode of changing law or producing new law has lasted forever, although traces of it may have survived through even radical transformations.[196]

In fact, one of the characterizing aspects of Nietzsche's anti-metaphysics is the rediscovery of the Dionysian against "the illusion of Apollo": the eternity of the beautiful form. The same "eternal return of time" does not express stability but, as has recently been observed, the "constant renewal of an agonal scenario, where multiple forces clash, thus showing the absence of a stable foundation, of a *Grund*."[197]

Until he comes to his senses, Don Quixote perennially relives his exploits in an agonal scenario, where everything is in competition, starting with different and contrasting being of entities: giants against windmills, Mambrino's helmet versus a barber's basin, Dulcinea del Toboso versus Aldonza Lorenzo.

Nietzsche's immoralism/non-moralism obliges juridical thought to be aware of the continuous repetition, in an "eternal return," of dilemmas that require choices in terms of justice, on the basis of necessarily indefinite and constantly changing criteria, which derive from the "pressing on" and "continuous overcoming" of good and evil in relation to which the law can only play a limited and transient role.

The very idea of subtracting from this continual return of the unstable a perennial idea of law, or a pre-established mode of producing law, and thus a given idea and legitimization of the power of individuals over others, is unrealistic. Law, like any other knowledge or human production, will not escape the state of suspension that is, by its own nature, a characteristic of laughter, and of competition that constantly returns.

---

195 Hans Kelsen, *Secular Religion. A Polemic against the Misinterpretation of Modern Social Philosophy, Science and Politics as "New Religions"* [1964] (Vienna/New York: Springer, 2012), 242.

196 See Rodolfo Sacco, "Il sustrato romanistico del diritto civile dei Paesi socialisti," *Rivista di diritto civile* 15 (1969), II: 115–131 on the survival of Romanist models in the law of socialist countries, despite the claims of absolute novelty that characterised that legal experiences.

197 See Cosimo Nicolini Coen, *"Heidegger e Kelsen lettori di Nietzsche: il nodo del rapporto tra metafisica e umanismo," Poli-Femo* 8 (2017): 165.

On the other hand, as Horkheimer and Adorno observe, taking hints from Tiresias' prophecy to Ulysses in the Hades, "laughter is marked by the guilt of subjectivity, but in the suspension of law which it indicates it also points beyond thralldom. It is a promise of the way home." Laughter, therefore, resolves the aspiration to return, it relieves homesickness. If the latter grows out of the loss of the "primal state of man," the nomadism broken by "the fixed order of property dependent on the settled life," "it is nevertheless the settled life and fixed property (only in which the notion of a homeland can appear) to which all longing and all homesickness are directed." "Homeland is the state of having escaped"[198]: laughter which opens the way to the homeland is destruction, a symbolic restoration of nomadic life, of errancy, but at the same time it is a promise of future stability, of "having escaped," of final deliverance. The "settled life," even if it existed or had ever existed, could not but trigger the return of homesickness.

The only constant element is the indefinite, indefinable justice: the ectoplasm that has always hovered, and will always hover, over every provisional morality, over every unstable ethical agreement and, more than ever, over every legal rule or institution. The restitution of law to the eternal return of becoming through laughter is the nemesis of the phantom of justice.

The force of laughter versus the force of law: satire

"Fantasy will destroy power and laughter will bury you!" So goes a youth protest slogan, which may or may not come from nineteenth-century anarchism. Satire is the form of comedy that exalts the critical or even destructive – subversive power of laughter. The law and its actors, including the institutions, are notoriously one of the most frequent targets of satire. This is not surprising, both because of the transformative claim they carry, which exposes them to comparison with other claims of judgment and other possible sources of normativity, and because of the expectation of justice they generate in the community, which is often destined to be disappointed. The relationship between satire and law thus takes on the connotation of a clash between claims to judgment/normativity, or even of a real clash of forces. Satire can often denounce the ineffectiveness of a law that is abstractly "just," such as the vacuity of its claim to shape society and determine human behaviors. Satire can question the very normativity of law, opposing it to a different system of moral / ethical rules. By mocking the juridical rules and their enforcers, satire shows their low moral quality. Satire, therefore, mocks the juridical and its actors in

198 Horkheimer, Adorno, *Dialectic of the Enlightenment*, 78.

order to bring about an awareness of the need for moral/value renewal through laughter.

All these aspects can be found, for instance, in the image of the madman blindfolding Justice, which is included among the illustrations (attributed to Dürer) accompanying the *Ship of Fools.* This poem was published in 1494 by the Alsatian jurist Sebastian Brant, and it is considered the first satire of the modern era.

In Brant's text, satire is a moral denunciation against a particular "madness" – one of the many stigmatized in the work – which consists in the deliberate perversion (blinding) of Justice by corrupt and greedy judges and lawyers. Evoking a theme that recurs both in the aforementioned Rabelaisian episode in which Pantagruel is called upon to settle a complex legal dispute and in Leopardi's own reflections on morality, the poet praises the quality of the law of antiquity and laments its corruption by his contemporaries, thus hoping for a return to lost purity.[199] In the commentary in verse by the English translator-adapter Alexander Barclay, the denunciation of the "mad" corrupters of justice is accompanied by an exhortation to the young "Studentes of the Chauncery" (the elderly are now considered irredeemable) to

> Remember that Justyce longe hath in bondage be
> Reduce ye hir nowe vnto lybertye at the last.

Nevertheless

> But certaynly I fere lyst she hath lost hir name
> Or by longe prysonment shall after euer be lame

therefore, corruption may now be irreversible, and Justice definitively irretrievable.[200]

In the *Constitutio criminalis Bambergensis* of 1507, the (satirical) image of an entire panel of blindfolded judges, with the same rattled cap worn by the "mad-

---

199 "Whan noble Rome all the worlde dyd goueme / Theyr councellers were olde men iust and prudent / Whiche egally dyd euery thynge desceme / Wherby theyr Empyre became so excellent / But nowe a dayes he shall haue his intent / That hath most golde, and so it is befall / That aungels worke wonders in westmynster hall": Sebastian Brant, *The Ship of Fools*, trans. Alexander Barclay (Edinburgh, 1874), I, 25; the translation – adaptation was first published in 1509. The lines are included in the part of the poem dealing with "euyl Counsellors, Juges and men of lawe." Both this passage and the subsequent one, dedicated to "great struyers in the lawe for thynges of nought" (which opens with the picture of the blindfolded Justice) evoke the threat of the divine punishment on those who subvert justice (Brant, *The Ship*, II, 48).

200 Alexander Barclay, in Brant, *The Ship of Fools*, I, 28.

man" who blindfolds Justice, will be used to stigmatize the attitude of the "blind fools" who judge on the basis of bad customs and are opposed to law, understood in the sense of legislation.[201] Drawing from Brant's satire and the image attributed to Dürer, Barclay finds a cue to rely on the moral renewal associated with the generational change of the forensic class, though not without some skepticism. The prince of Bamberg, soon followed by other sovereigns as it is well known, preferred to attribute to the statutory law, and thus to himself, the task of restoring the sight of Justice. Thanks to the removal of the image of the "madman" and thus of the corrupter (and of corruptibility), the blindfolded Justice was gradually transformed into a symbol of impartiality,[202] ensured first and foremost by the pre-existence, in the law, of the rule to be applied to concrete cases. Not by chance, in this new context the law is symbolically represented by a wide-open eye that is capable of total vision.[203] The satirical image of the "madman" blindfolding Justice does not only lead to the idea of deprivation of sight. In a poem included in the *Spoon River Anthology*, Masters, who practiced law for a long time,[204] imagines that on the day after the hanging of "two anarchists in Chicago," a "young man in a red cap" suddenly removes the blindfold from the statue of Justice placed in front of the steps of the Court House; an unjust Justice, who strikes at random with his sword, and lets the scales fall on the side that has been filled with gold:

201 See Adriano Prosperi, *Giustizia bendata. Percorsi storici di un'immagine* (Turin: Einaudi, 2009), 37; Mario Sbriccoli, "La benda della giustizia. Iconografia e leggi penali dal Medioevo all'età moderna," in Mario Sbriccoli, *Storia del diritto penale e della giustizia* (Milan: Giuffrè, 2008), 155–208, 191; Dennis E. Curtis and Judith Resnik, "Images of Justice," *Yale Law Journal* 96 (1987): 1727–1772; Judith Resnik and Dennis E. Curtis, *Representing Justice: Invention, Controversy and Rights in City – States and Democratic Courtrooms* (New Haven/London: Yale Univ. Press, 2011).
202 See Sbriccoli, "La benda della giustizia," 195: "with an unexpected and theatrical inversion of the polarity of the message, Power reverses its communicative value and puts a blindfold over the attentive and penetrating eyes of 'its' Justice ... and 'claims' the blindfold" [my translation]; Anna Simone, *Rappresentare il diritto e la giustizia nella modernità. Universi simbolici, iconografia, mutamento sociale* (Milan: Mimesis, 2015), 56–57; Marcilio Franca, "The Blindness of Justice: An Iconographic Dialogue between Art and Law," in *Law and the Senses*, eds. Andrea Pavoni, Danilo Mandic, Caterina Nirta and Andrea Philippopoulos-Mihalopoulos, (London: Univ. of Westminster Press, 2018), 159–196, 180.
203 On the subject Michael Stolleis, *The Eye of the Law. Two Essays on Legal History* (Abingdon: Birkbeck Law Press, 2009); Simone, *Rappresentare il diritto*, 76: "The prince and the sovereign become the very representatives of God on earth who watch over their subjects through the iconography of the eye of the law" [my translation].
204 On Masters' forensic activities and the connections with American realist legal thought, Steven Richman, "Edgar Lee Masters and the Poetics of Legal Realism," *California Western Law Review* 31 (1994): 103–126.

> And lo, the lashes had been eaten away
> From the oozy eye-lids;
> The eye-balls were seared with a milky mucus;
> The madness of a dying soul
> Was written on her face
> But the multitude saw why she wore the bandage.[205]

Thus the "madman" who blindfolds Justice might not blind her, but prevent the beholder from grasping her congenital blindness. Not only that: the gesture of the "madman" could be a revelation of the fact that Justice, apparently endowed with acute sight[206], is actually blind, or at least myopic. Precisely in this vein, Horkheimer and Adorno, in the *Dialectic of Enlightenment*, observe that

> the balance held by Zeus, which symbolizes the justice of the entire patriarchal world, refers back to mere nature. The step from chaos to civilization, in which natural conditions exert their power no longer directly but through the medium of the human consciousness, has not changed the principle of equivalence. Indeed, men paid for this very step by worshipping what they were once in thrall to only in the same way as all other creatures. Before, the fetishes were subject to the law of equivalence. Now equivalence itself has become a fetish. The blindfold over Justitia's eyes does not only mean that there should be no assault upon justice, but that justice does not originate in freedom.[207]

Thus, Justice's inability to see, due to the blindfold, shows the artificial nature of law as a product of the passage from fact to rule based on the conceptual assumption of the assimilability of different facts within the same paradigm, with the consequent loss of the uniqueness of each of these facts.

---

205 Edgar Lee Masters, "Carl Hamblin," in Edgar Lee Masters, *Spoon River Anthology* [1914–1915] (New York: 1916), 130.

206 In accordance with classical representations: see Michael Jay, "Must Justice Be Blind? The Challenge of Images to the Law," *Filozofski vestnik* 17 (1996): 65–81; in the sixteenth century Vincenzo Cartari, *Le imagini de i dei de gli antichi* [1571], 466–467 (available online: https://gallica.bnf.fr/ark:/12148/bpt6k59561r/f495.item; last access in March 2021): "according to Aulus Gellius, in the form of a beautiful virgin [...] with eyes of the sharpest sight, from which Plato said that Justice sees everything [...]. And Apuleius swears by the eye of the Sun and Justice together, as not seeing this less than that. We have to understand that these things must be in the ministers of justice, because it is necessary for them to penetrate to the hidden and occult truth with the sharpest sight" [my translation].

207 Horkheimer, Adorno, *Dialectic of the Enlightenment*, 16–17. M. Jay, "Must Justice Be Blind?," 71 observes that "The freedom of which Horkheimer and Adorno speak is thus the ability of the particular, the unique, the incommensurable, the improper to escape from the dominating power of the exchange principle that is manifested in universalizing concepts and in the reduction of justice to the law of equivalents."

If the idea of the madman blindfolding Justice, or the panel of blindfolded judges in rattlesnake hats, makes one laugh, this laughter may not only be one of outrage, but also of relief: fortunately, Justice does not see everything, the law is not omnipotent, it cannot provide the measure of the world, nor impose a definitive form, or morality on it.[208]

Satire on law or against law can push towards Nietzschean a-moralism. It challenges spectators-readers to confront not only the value assumptions of the rules of law and institutions, but to use their own moral sense, and the moral sense of the community to which they belong – or even that of humanity – to wonder whether there really is anything definitively just or unjust, and how that can be expressed. Satire can advocate the need for new law, new moral values, new ethics, the impossibility of any law, the changing nature of any (non-moral) morality. It has a subversive role in all cases, and faced with satire law, aspiring above all to its own preservation (even through change, where necessary: every legal system contains, perhaps more than any other, rules on the production of new law), cannot help but react.

Law, fear, and laughter: satire and dictatorships

In *Human, All Too Human*, Nietzsche echoes the idea of laughter as relief and sees a connection between laughter and (momentary) liberation from fear. Humanity was accustomed for hundreds of thousands of years to reacting with fear to the unexpected, and social relations were governed by the idea that "all security rested on the expected, on tradition in meaning and activity." Therefore,

> at every sudden, unexpected word or deed, if it comes without danger or harm, man is released and experiences instead the opposite of fright. The cringing creature, trembling in fear, springs up, expands wide – man laughs. This transition from momentary fear to short-lived exuberance is called the comic.[209]

Unlike Descartes and Campanella, as well as, of course, Kant,[210] Nietzsche, in the passage above, identifies fear linked to anthropological factors as the most fre-

208 Awareness of the limits of law, as of every instrument of knowledge and every work of human creation, does not necessarily generate melancholy, as the symbolism of Dürer's famous engraving suggests.

209 Nietzsche, *Human, All Too Human*, 115.

210 The same "balance of vital forces" that closes the Kant passage examined in a previous chapter would, in fact, also seem to refer, in a very different context, to the idea of laughter as an outburst, or self-defense.

quent emotional state in humans, and laughter as a transitory moment of liberation and courage.

In his 1927 essay on *Humor*[211] Freud, who had already emphasized the liberating function of laughter in his extensive 1905 study on the *Joke and Its Relation to the Unconscious*[212] (favoring, however, the aspect of the liberation of emotional energy, and thus a physiological-economic view of laughter[213]), reflects in turn on the relationship between laughter and fear: the ego "refuses to be hurt by the arrows of reality or to be compelled to suffer. It insists that it is impervious to wounds dealt by the outside world, in fact, that these are merely occasions for affording it pleasure."[214]

Freud finds "something fine and elevating" in humor's ability to lead to the "triumph of narcissism," to the "victorious assertion of the invulnerability of the ego". Humor thus becomes "unlike the comic," "not ... absence or inexperience of pain, but the ability to escape its petrification."[215] In the example from which Freud takes his cue, the state of fear and suffering is caused by the exercise, in its highest degree (the execution of capital punishment), of the punitive claim of law. A man condemned to death, escorted to the gallows, observes the clear morning sky and comments "Well, this is a good beginning to a week!"

The more the effectiveness of a rule or of an entire legal system is based on mere force, the more this system will tend to lose its sense of humor, its tolerance for comedy or, even more so, for the more uncovered and aggressive forms of criticism that are typical of satire. Dictatorships of all forms and religious fundamentalisms do not accept mockery, even in the most apparently innocent ways. As Giovannino Guareschi wrote: "humor forbids rhetoric, and dictatorships are the living denial of humor. Dictatorships do not understand humor and despise it, like any of

211 Sigmund Freud, "humor" [1927], in Sigmund Freud, *Collected Papers*, ed. James Strachey (London: Hogarth Press, 1950), V, 215–221.

212 Sigmund Freud, *The Joke and Its Relation to the Unconscious* [1905], trans. John Carey (London: Penguin, 2003).

213 Morreal, *Philosophy of Humor*, 43.

214 According to Freud, this is made possible by the action of the superego, which performs a parental function vis-à-vis the ego, transforming, in the case of humor, a real threat into a feigned danger: the humorous attitude consists in "the subject's removing the accent from his own ego and transferring it to his super-ego. To the super-ego, thus inflated, the ego can appear tiny and all interests trivial, and with this fresh distribution of energy it may be an easy matter for it to suppress the potential reactions of the ego" (Freud, "humor," 218–219).

215 See Maria Felicia Schepis, *Colui che ride. Per una ricreazione dello spazio politico* (Milan: Angeli, 2011), 62, who perceives in Freud's essay "a gloomy foreboding of the impending doom that will befall the world within a few years of its publication" [my translation]; see also Ercoli, *Filosofia dell'umorismo*, 63.

the too many things they cannot understand. Since they deny humor, dictatorships are therefore the triumph of rhetoric, and to fight rhetoric is to fight dictatorship."[216]

In these contexts, laughing at the law, that has been reduced to a mere instrument of oppression through the spread of fear and the use of force, becomes a clandestine act and a form of resistance. The human capacity to laugh cannot be suppressed. When laughter is countered by the repressive force of law turned into an instrument of mere coercion, laughing clandestinely at this unjust, arbitrary, and violent legal system can become a means of preserving the push towards what is righteous, despite the degradation of law – and at the expense of it.

Scholars have proven that humor during the Third Reich took on different functions: a critical function (from inside and outside the system, as shown in Chaplin's famous film) aimed at creating cohesion and solidarity between the victims and/or opponents, but also a reach for survival, by helping the oppressed to go through suffering without losing their minds,[217] by refusing to surrender to tragedy, as Freud well pointed out.

Laughter is not only an instrument of resistance, but also a source of hope, as it is a constant reminder of the impossibility for totalitarianisms to achieve their ultimate goal, i. e., the annihilation of the individual within a completely regulated society-state. The coercive tools of total institutions, as potent and brutal as they may be, do find some intrinsic limits. The most consistent of these is probably found in the paradox that is often generated by the incompressibility of the human being within the rigid forms of the ideology to which the dictator aspires. On this point, I find this episode of life in the Gulag narrated by Aleksandr Solženicyn, in *A Day in the Life of Ivan Denisovič* [218] quite emblematic:

> At one time the Commandant had issued an order that no prisoner was to walk along the camp alone ... The Commandant had been very firm about this order, and nobody had dared to oppose him. The warders seized prisoners walking on their own, recorded their numbers, and shoved them in the cells. But the order collapsed, quietly and gradually, as many high-sounding orders had the habit of doing. Say someone was summoned by the security people – did he have to go in a group of other people? Or if you had to get something from the stores – 'Why should I go along with you?' Or if someone had the idea of going to the CES to read the newspapers, who would he get to go with him? One man wants to get his felt boots

216 The quotation is taken from an article in the Italian satirical periodical *Candido* of October 12, 1946, II, 41, republished in Giovanni Guareschi, *Italia provvisoria: album del dopoguerra* (Milan: Rizzoli, 2012), 43–44 [my translation].

217 Morreal, *Philosophy of Humor*, 1à94 ff., and further readings and examples cited therein.

218 Aleksandr Solženicyn, *One Day in the Life of Ivan Denisovich* [1962], trans. Gillon Aitken (Frogmore St. Albans: Triad/Panther, 1978), 137–138.

> repaired, another to go the drying-room, a third simply to go from one hut to another (although this was forbidden above anything else!) – well, how can you prevent them? With his order, the Commandant had wanted to take away from the prisoners the last vestiges of freedom they possessed, but it didn't work out like that, the pot-bellied old fool.

Finally, it is the camp commandant who is ridiculous, not only because he is a "pot-bellied old man," but also because he is completely powerless, even though he is the head of a total institution, in the face of the infinite possible occurrences of existence, even the smallest ones (such as repairing a pair of felt boots, or the sudden interest of a prisoner in the newspapers of the Cultural Educational Service – CES). The impotence of the camp commandant, the "quiet and gradual" fiascos into which the "high-sounding orders" are often resolved, represent the insurmountable frontier set by the comedy for totalitarianism.

Satire and the liberal position of US case law

In liberal systems, the cultural and political debate is primarily inspired by the theory of the "free marketplace of ideas." They tend to assume that the just, i. e., the idea that conforms to the social pact that founds the constitutional order, shall prevail by its very nature.[219] Therefore, such systems tend to tolerate the derision of the law, of institutions and of those who embody them, just like they more generally tolerate the bitterly disrespectful derision of any public figure. US First Amendment case law is emblematic. Let us consider the case involving the conservative preacher and political leader Jerry Falwell vs. the publisher of the pornographic magazine "Hustler," who published a parody of a Campari advertising campaign in the November 1983 issue. In the form of a mock interview, the publisher recounted Falwell's sexual initiation through an incestuous experience in a brothel. On this occasion, the plaintiff's lawyers thought to circumvent the strict limits set by federal case law to defamation actions brought by public figures,[220]

---

219 See Justice Holmes' dissent in *Abrams v. United States*, 250 U.S. 616, 630 (1919): "when men have realized that time has upset many fighting faiths, they may come to believe even more than they believe the very foundations of their own conduct that the ultimate good desired is better reached by free trade in ideas — that the best test of truth is the power of the thought to get itself accepted in the competition of the market" and all the following decisions, including *New York Times Co. v. Sullivan*, 376 U.S. 254 (1964), *Gertz v. Robert Welch, Inc.*, 418 U.S. 323, 339 (1974); *Bose Corp. v. Consumers Union of United States, Inc.*, 466 U.S. 485, 503–504 (1984).

220 See, in particular, *New York Times v. Sullivan*, cited above, where the Court imposed on the defamation plaintiff who is a public figure the burden of proof of actual malice (awareness of fal-

invoking profiles of damage not to reputation, but to the person (the tort of emotional distress), in relation to the suffering caused by false and outrageous statements.[221] The Supreme Court,[222] while not appreciating the coarse mockery of "Hustler" and clearly distinguishing it from much more refined forms of political satire in the past, made a clear rejection. "The political cartoon," argued Chief Justice Rhenquist on behalf of an almost unanimous Court,[223] "is a weapon of attack, of scorn and ridicule and satire; it is least effective when it tries to pat some politician on the back. It is usually as welcome as a bee sting, and is always controversial in some quarters." About outrageousness:

> Outrageousness in the area of political and social discourse has an inherent subjectiveness about it which would allow a jury to impose liability on the basis of the jurors' tastes or views, or perhaps on the basis of their dislike of a particular expression. An outrageousness standard thus runs afoul of our longstanding refusal to allow damages to be awarded because the speech in question may have an adverse emotional impact on the audience.

The *opinion of the Court* in *Falwell* also maintains:

> [T]he fact that society may find speech offensive is not a sufficient reason for suppressing it. Indeed, if it is the speaker's opinion that gives offense, that consequence is a reason for according it constitutional protection. For it is a central tenet of the First Amendment that the government must remain neutral in the marketplace of ideas.[224]

---

sity and intent to harm) on the person who has disseminated false information injurious to another's reputation.

221 A detailed analysis of the case, including the facts and arguments of the parties, in Rodney A. Smolla, "Emotional Distress and the First Amendment: An Analysis of Hustler v. Falwell," *Arizona State Law Journal* 20 (1988): 423–474.

222 *Hustler Magazine, Inc. v. Falwell*, 485 US 46 (1988)

223 Elizabeth Blanks Hindman, *Rights v. Responsibilities: The Supreme Court and the Media* (Westport: Greenwood, 1997), 134: "Chief Justice Rhenquist [...] in a surprising move for a conservative, refused Falwell's request to bring into law a specific conception of the good." There is a brief concurring opinion by Justice White, who merely emphasizes the irrelevance, in his view, of the precedent *New York Times v. Sullivan*, because in Falwell's case there were conspicuously false statements. In fact, what is relevant is the incompatibility between the tort of emotional distress, as applied to the suffering caused to public figures by a thought-provoking activity, and the critical function that the First Amendment assigns to freedom of expression: see Mark A. Fisher, E. Gabriel Perle, John Taylor Williams, *Perle, Williams and Fisher on Publishing Law* (Boston: Aspen, 2015) supp., 8–11.

224 The decision shows a sort of logical short-circuit when, on the one hand, it reaffirms the need for proof of "actual malice" on the part of the plaintiff, in line with *New York Times v. Sullivan*, while, on the other hand, it notes that in the present case the statements of "Hustler" could not have been taken seriously by anyone, and were therefore notoriously false, and spread by the periodical with a clear intent to denigrate Falwell, accused, in essence, of being a hypocritical moral-

Moreover, as early as 1952 the Supreme Court had already ruled out that the "sacrilegious" nature of a manifestation of thought could justify, in light of the First Amendment, repressive measures provided for by state legislation, primarily because of the vagueness and relativity of the notion of "sacrilege":

> In seeking to apply the broad and all-inclusive definition of *sacrilegious* given by the New York courts, the censor is set adrift upon a boundless sea amid a myriad of conflicting currents of religious views, with no charts but those provided by the most vocal and powerful orthodoxies [...] Under such a standard the most careful and tolerant censor would find it virtually impossible to avoid favoring one religion over another, and he would be subject to an inevitable tendency to ban the expression of unpopular sentiments sacred to a religious minority [...] It is not the business of government in our nation to suppress real or imagined attacks upon a particular religious doctrine, whether they appear in publications, speeches, or motion pictures.[225]

The middle way: satire and the European legal systems

The Italian legal system and various European ones take middle-ground positions regarding the freedom to mock the legal system, institutions, and their exponents (and public figures in general). The approach ascribable to the combined provisions of Articles 4 and 11 of the 1789 Declaration shows a model, shared by Articles 21(1) and (6) of the Italian Constitution, in which the freedom of expression does not have an absolute nature (as in the First Amendment). Rather, it represents a right/value that the interpreter, in particular the judiciary, must balance against conflicting rights/values. In comparison with the previously mentioned 1952 ruling by the Supreme Court, what was affirmed by the French *Cour de Cassation*, on the occasion of the protests concerning the screening of Martin Scorsese's film *Last Temptation of Christ*, is quite emblematic. The court shared the position of the

---

ist. Indeed, the decision rejects Falwell's claim despite the defendant's "actual malice," based on the mere assertion of the prevalence of the general interest in free speech about persons of public interest over the interest of the latter in the protection of their personal sphere, narrowly understood. This strongly liberal approach has not failed to raise even radical criticism: see Robert C. Post, "The Constitutional Concept of Public Discourse: Outrageous Opinion, Democratic Deliberation, and Hustler Magazine v. Falwell," *Harvard Law Review* 103 (1990): 601–686, 643, according to which "in the heterogeneity of contemporary culture only the law can authoritatively speak for norms that define a common ideal of rational deliberation."

225 *Joseph Burstyn, Inc. v. Wilson* 343 US 495 (1952); the case concerned the censorship in New York State of the episode "The Miracle" from Roberto Rossellini's film "Amore" (1948), which told the story of a shepherdess with a strong religious faith, who is convinced that she is the bearer of a miraculous pregnancy after being seduced, while drunk, by a shepherd resembling St. Joseph.

lower judges, that had imposed a warning on the film's promotional material and its potential harm to religious sensibilities, by stating that:

> the principle of freedom of expression, particularly with reference to artistic creations, on one side, like, on the other side, that of the respect due to beliefs and the right to practice one's own religion, being of equal value, it belongs to the judge of the merits to decide measures apt at granting that this necessary balance is respected; without denying the possibility of abuses of right in peer areas, which would constitute clearly wrongful behaviors, the court of appeal, which decided that it was necessary to avoid that 'anyone may find himself, not being previously warned, in a situation of being hurt in his deepest beliefs,' as well as to avoid any infringement of freedom of expression, could estimate that there were not, in the case at stake, clearly wrongful behaviors, and it could decide, in its discretion, the most appropriate measures in order to safeguard the right balance of rights and liberties at stake; in thus doing, it did not consider the personal sensitivity of one or another spectator, and it answered, with the generality of the measures granted, to the worries expressed in the claims.[226]

The basic features of the model can be found in case law on the right of satire. For example, in a 2016 judgment,[227] the Italian Supreme Court reconstructs its precedents on the subject as follows:

> The right to satire, unlike the right to report news, is exempt from the parameter of the truth of the fact, insofar as it expresses, by means of paradox and surreal metaphor, an ironic judgment on a fact, provided that the fact is expressed in a manner that is openly different from reality, so much so that its improbability and hyperbolic character can be immediately appreciated: otherwise, not even satire escapes the limit of correctness and continence of the expressions or images used, representing in any case a form of criticism characterised by the corrosive nature of the particular means of expression (Cass. 19 August 2015, no. 16899, where reference is made to Cass. 4 September 2012, no. 14822 and Cass. no. 28411/08 and 23314/07). Obviously, no exemption can be admitted when satire becomes a pure form of mockery, contempt and destruction of personal dignity (Court of Cassation 24 March 2015, no. 5851), or when it entails the use of gratuitous, vulgar, humiliating or mocking expressions that are not necessary for the exercise of the right (Court of Cassation 11 September 2014, no. 19178), entailing vulgar or repugnant juxtapositions or such as to entail the deformation of the public image of the target subject and to arouse contempt of the person or the ridicule of his public image (Cass, ord. 17 September 2013, no. 21235).

---

226 Cass., Ch. Civ. I, October 29, 1990, 88–19366, *Bulletin* 1990 I N° 226 p. 161 [my translation]. French case law, on the other hand, rejected various claims against Charlie Hebdo's vignettes satirizing Prophet Muhammad: see Trib. Paris, 17me chambre, 22 mars 2007, affirmed by C. App. Paris, 12 mars 2008, *Val*, available at the URL http://www.guglielmi.fr/IMG/pdf/CA_Paris_12_mars_2008.pdf (last access March 2021).

227 Cass. Civ., sez. III, April 7, 2016, n. 6787, *F.R. v. Gruppo Editoriale L'Espresso*, in *Diritto & Giustizia* 18 (2016), 53, with a note by Attilio Ievolella [my translation].

At the declamatory level, freedom of satire is constantly expressed: in practice, it is conditioned by many ifs and buts, starting from the actual identification of which specific ways of expressing thought can be defined as satire,[228] and by the subjective or institutional interests, with respect to which freedom of satire may be recessive. This includes the interests of the victim, a public figure, to not suffer "the ridicule of his public image." French case law shows similar caution.[229] Thus it is reasonable to suppose that Jerry Falwell's case would have had better luck if it had been made before an Italian or French judge, even in the pure and simple form of a civil or criminal action for libel/defamation, without any need for attempts to circumvent rules favouring the freedom of expression. Moreover, the limits to the right of satire in Europe may also originate from reasons different from the protection of the person, or of religious convictions, which relate directly to the protection of national or foreign institutions.[230]

The maieutic capacity of laughter and its limits: laughing is not always "just"

Plato, well before Leopardi and Nietzsche, had already sensed the power of laughter; however, he was struck far more by its capacity to destabilize a social order and to undermine any ethics than by its maieutic value. In the *Laws*, the philosopher wonders whether the law should

---

228 According to Cass. Civ. Sec. III, November 8, 2007, no. 23314, *A. Mondadori Editore S.p.A.* v. G.C.C., *Giustizia civile* (2008), 651, with a note by Gianni Ballarani: "Satire is an artistic expression to the extent that it operates a symbolic representation that, particularly in the case of a cartoon, presents itself as a caricature metaphor. The peculiarity of satire, which expresses itself through paradox and surreal metaphor, removes it from the parameter of truth and makes it heterogeneous with respect to the chronicle; unlike the chronicle which, having the purpose of providing information on facts and people, is subject to the scrutiny of historical evidence, satire takes on the connotations of improbability and hyperbole to arouse laughter and lash out at customs. In short, satire is an ironic reproduction and not a chronicle of a fact; it expresses a judgment that necessarily takes on subjective and debatable connotations, eschewing a demonstration of truthfulness".

229 See as an example TGI Paris, réf., October 29, 2008, *Nicolas Sarkozy c/ SARL Tear Prod et a.*,: *JurisData* no 2008–001800, with a comment by A. Lepage.

230 The press reported on the injunction issued by a German court for the defamatory content of a humourist's satirical text directed against Turkish President Erdogan's dictatorial policy. The text, in particular, was allegedly considered to be merely insulting, and not justified by any critical – satirical purpose (available online: http://www.reuters.com/article/us-germany-turkey-comedian-idUSKCN0Y82C5 last accessed October 2016).

> tolerate a comedian's eagerness to raise a laugh against people, provided that when he sets about ridiculing our citizens in his comedies, he is not inspired by anger? Or shall we divide comedy into two kinds, according to whether it is good-natured or not? Then we could allow the playful comedian to joke about something, without anger, but forbid, as we've indicated, anyone whatever to do so if he is in deadly earnest and shows animosity. We must certainly insist on this stipulation about anger; but we still have to lay down by law who ought to receive permission for ridicule and who not.[231]

Plato does not seem to doubt that laws should be established about who is or is not allowed to joke; he excludes that "the composer of comedies, or of songs, or iambic verses" should be allowed to "ridicule either by description or by impersonation any citizen whatever, with or without rancour," while the possibility of ridiculing anyone should be limited to those who joke "in a playful spirit and for pure jest."[232] The defense of law against laughter, therefore, should be entrusted to law itself; yet, as mentioned above, this creates an obvious logical short-circuit, since law could only allow, as Plato himself advocates, "harmless" forms of comedy, i. e., devoid of the maieutic (and destructive) capacity of laughter. In short, authority should deprive laughter of its power. The historical examples of dictatorships' vain attempts to prevent comedy or make it the exclusive instrument of their political design show that this is neither possible nor desirable. It would imply a return to the idea of the unity of the cogito and its monopoly on the human, laying the foundations for the monolithic nature of political-institutional and legal systems.

As mentioned above, the aspiration to eternity is a characteristic not only of dictatorships, but also of modern constitutionalism, starting with the Constitution of the United States, which sets safeguarding "the gift of liberty" for "posterity" as a fundamental premise. In fact, it was obviously a certain idea of freedom which paradoxically allowed slavery. This idea of freedom, like every legal construct, has subsequently transformed itself, and will continue to do so.

---

231 Plato, *The Laws*, trans. Trevor J. Saunders (London: Penguin, 1970), 483.

232 In the tenth book of the *Republic*, Plato dwells on the ability of tragedy and humor (forms of poetry that are charachterized by their recourse to *mimesis*, i. e., the pretence of imitation of reality, behind which the author disguises himself) to loosen the dominion of reason over the passions, and thus diminish the capacity for judgment and self-control. Thus, "the only poems we can admit into our community are hymns to the gods and eulogies of virtuous men. If you admit the entertaining Muse of lyric and epic poetry, then instead of law and shared acceptance of reason as the best guide, the kings of your community will be pleasure and pain" (Plato, *Republic*, trans. Robin Watterfield (Oxford: Oxford Univ. Press, 1994), 361). Therefore, rationality should be the only guide. The philosopher subsequently condemns "buffoonish" laughter without appeal.

Lord Shaftesbury wrote in 1709[233]

> Truth, 'tis suppos'd, may bear all Lights: and one of those principal Lights or natural Mediums, by which Things are to view'd, in order to a thorow Recognition, is Ridicule it-self, or that Manner of Proof by which we discern whatever is liable to just Raillery in any subject. So much, at least, is allow'd by All, who at any time appeal to this Criterion. The gravest Gentlemen, even in the gravest Subjects, are suppos'd to acknowledg this: and can have no Right, 'tis thought, to deny other the Freedom of this Appeal; whilst they are free to censure like other Men, and in their gravest Arguments make no scruple to ask, Is it not Ridiculous?

In the context of a clearly avant-garde conception of laughter as a human manifestation of liberation from oppression, the English thinker defines eutrapelia, like Aristotle, as a problem not of law, but of justice, or perhaps, more specifically, of ethics (which helps distinguishing the "just raillery" from the "unjust"). As seen above, neither Leopardi nor Nietzsche succeeded in freeing themselves from the problem of eutrapelia, nor, indeed, did they attempt to do so. Aware of the revelatory and destructive power of laughter, they always saw it as an instrument to lead thought beyond the contingent, and even beyond the human condition itself. More than being a problem of law in the strict sense, the question of eutrapelia concerns the consistency of the ethical foundations of law, and of its communicative capacity, on which its very effectiveness, or transformative capacity, depends.

On the other hand, Nietzsche assigns fundamental importance to communication, as shown by Zarathustra's decision to give himself up to preaching, and break his isolation. Communication and the will to power are not incompatible; on the contrary, the former is the fundamental instrument through which one acquires that "capacity to laugh" (in the right way ...) which is the prerequisite for the new idea of knowledge made possible by the "gay science."

The communication of Nietzsche – Zarathustra, after all, is neither horizontal nor perfectly transparent, but vertical and inspired by precise strategies of persuasion, whose first and most obvious element is style: it is a preaching that emanates from an authoritative source, and is addressed to subjects that tend towards radical transformation. The communication that reveals the value of laughter, therefore, is a transformative communication, based on persuasion. Zarathustra does not possess physical strength or institutional apparatuses at his service, nor does he need them; his ability to communicate and persuade (not indoctrinate) stems from knowledge alone.

233 Anthony Shaftesbury, "Sensus Communis, An Essay on the Freedom of Wit and Humor" [1709], in Anthony Shaftesbury, *Characteristicks of Men, Manners, Opinions, Times* (Indianapolis: Liberty Fund), I, 37–94, 40.

Thus, laughter does not necessarily lead to the aspiration to eliminate the law, but rather suggests a rethinking of it. Since it is difficult, if not impossible, to imagine a society without rules, or "power relations," the problem that laughter constantly denounces, by acting as the spokesman for the phantom of justice, shifts to the foundation and quality of rules.

As Michel Foucault observes

> power relations are not something that is bad in itself, that we have to break free of. I do not think that a society can exist without power relations, if by that one means the strategies by which individuals try to direct and control the conduct of others. The problem, then, is not to try to dissolve them in the utopia of completely transparent communication but to acquire the rules of law, the management techniques, and also the morality, the ethos, the practice of the self, that will allow us to play these games of power with as little domination as possible.[234]

The renunciation of the idea of domination as the foundation of law, the need for an ethical (and moral?) foundation, the recognition of the interaction between the individual and collectivity, and the awareness of the necessarily transient nature of all this are the elements that emerge from the reflection conducted so far on the relationship between law and comedy.

---

234 Michel Foucault, "The Ethics of the Concern of the Self as a Practice of Freedom" [1984], in Michel Foucault, *Ethics Subjectivity and Truth*, ed. Paul Rabinow, trans. P. Aranov and D. McGrawth (New York: New Press, 2003), 281–301, 298.

Chapter 4
In the Vortex of Evil

Comedy and subversion

If, as we have just seen, laughter is the antibody that can heal a sick law incapable of guaranteeing fairness and justice, it is still laughter that becomes a guiding light when the whole of existence falls into the vortex of evil, a vortex that engulfs everything, even law. As Pirandello maintained, the task of humor is to make the reader aware that nothing exists without its opposite. It follows that there would be no sense in a comic representation of the law without acts of subversion regarding those rules that society considers essential to civil coexistence, and that the law aspires to codify and transform into norms.

In point of fact, the struggle between good and evil is innate to laughter. This struggle is never clear-cut, but rather full of nuance and ambiguity. The comic narrative thus upsets the accepted symmetries that define the boundaries between laughter and tears, between the conforming and the dissimilar, in order to suggest a remedy for the incongruity of reality, even if it becomes paradoxical or surreal.[235] In this case, it follows that the comic representation of law cannot help but be full of contradictions, and that the very fairness of the law can be questioned. Laughter challenges both the rationality of the law (see Leopardi's destructive power of laughter) and the dis-values embodied in crime, so as to put the one who laughs in the position of reconsidering both their own personal assessments of the inescapability or arbitrariness of the law and their own potential criminal nature from a 'democritical' perspective.

Sergej Dovlatov: the rebellious laugh

Whereas for Leopardi laughing is an act of rebellion against one's destiny and death, Sergej Dovlatov's literature can be conceived as the anatomy of this condition. The author, the protagonist and narrator of *The Zone* (2002) is surprised at how he was able to smile in the penal colony for common criminals run by the Soviet army, where he had served for three years as a guard:

---

235 See J. Palmer, *Taking humor Seriously* (London: Routledge, 2003), 95 ff.

https://doi.org/10.1515/9783111286778-006

> I saw freedom behind bars, cruelty as senseless as poetry, violence as common as dampness. I saw a man who had been completely reduced to an animal state. I saw what he could be gladdened by. And it seemed to me that my eyes opened. [...] In that world, I saw men with a gruesome past, a repulsive present and a tragic future. [...] The ratio of good and evil, grief and happiness, remained unchanged. [...]
>
> But the content of these concepts was radically changed. The usual hierarchy of values had been demolished. What had once seemed important receded into the background. Trivialities blocked the horizon. A new scale of values for "the good things of life" arose. [...] The world in which I found myself was horrible. Nevertheless, I smiled no less frequently than I do now, and was not sad more often.[236]

One of the underlying themes of Dovlatovian poetics is the lack of a clear distinction between good and evil, that is, a supposed differentiation determined by a cultural order used to classify the world and to associate thoughts. Rather, his poetics is aimed at unmasking the stereotypes of a world that is instead bizarre, paradoxical, multiple, never being normalizable. This revealing process takes place in his works through humor, since humor tends to undermine the ethical structures of society[237] and to become a form of resistance. In the upside-down world of *The Zone*, the guards themselves embody the darkest and most malignant side of humanity, while laughing becomes a strategy to attack life, to prevent destiny from bringing people down. Humor acts as a means of control (or self-control) in a morally and ethically devastating situation. In fact, the novel is not about prisons and prisoners or monsters, but about humankind. Dovlatov suggests, nonetheless, that the exasperated situation in the penal colony can be extended to the entire society outside prison.

One such instance is the character of Kuptsov, a Russian thief by genetic inheritance ("And I come from a long line of Russian thieves.," *TZ*, 58), who refuses to work at the camp like the other inmates, even though this leads him to spend long periods in solitary confinement or even to the self-amputation of his own finger. When one day the narrator fulfills his obligations as a guard and punishes him, we read: "Kuptsov stood up. He was almost polite with me. A grimace of cheerful astonishment had frozen on his face. 'You dish it out, Chief,' he said when I passed the embrasure of his cell." (*TZ*, 59) Kuptsov responds to punishment with a smile. He accepts his fate without showing resignation or a despair that would break his integrity, never mind the integrity of a criminal. By emphasizing how kind he was to his jailer, Dovlatov makes us realize that the prisoner's reac-

---

236 Sergej Dovlatov, *The Zone. A Prison Guard Notes* [1985], trans. Anne Frydman (London: Alma Classics, 2013). Kindle ed., 11–16. Later in the text *TZ*.

237 See the Postface by Laura Salmon to the Italian translation: Dovlatov, *Regime speciale* (Palermo: Sellerio, 2002), 260 ff.

tion was due neither to disenchantment nor arrogance, but rather it was a form of compliance with life, that is, with the law of the colony. The astonishment suggests that he imagined a different degree of understanding with the guard, and in fact the guard perceives this emotion so vividly that he reports it to the reader.

Far from questioning the seriousness of the crimes or the fairness of the punishment, the author aims to call into question our prejudices about criminals. He emphasizes that reality is much more complex than a mere distinction between right and wrong, good and evil, as the two often do not contradict each other. Moreover, a few pages later we surprisingly learn that Kuptsov himself stabs Dovlatov in order to steal his winnings at gambling. After recovering, the latter is happy to see his assailant's smile again and to converse with him. Perhaps in the closed and all-encompassing world of the penal colony, Dovlatov finds a bit of himself in his adherence to Kuptsov's life. Dovlatov says: "Man is capable of anything, of making evil and good. I regret that this is so."[238] When there is no way out of evil, the only way forward seems to be the observation of evil, and the reliance on humor as a form of detachment.[239] Humor reverses the effect that evil has on a person. The diary mainly illustrates the camp guards, who behave as pitilessly as hardened criminals:

> I detected a striking similarity between the camp and the outside, between the prisoners and the guards, between the burglar recidivists and the controllers of the production zones, between the zek foremen and the camp administration officials. One single, soulless world extended on either side of the restricted areas. [...] We were very similar to each other, and even interchangeable. Almost any prisoner would have been suited to the role of a guard. Almost any guard deserved a prison term. (TZ, 48–50)

We have just seen how for Giacomo Leopardi humans do not shy away from the possibility of harming their enemies: although here the guards are not to be under-

238 Salmon, Postface to Dovlatov, *Regime speciale*, 266.

239 It seems appropriate to recall in this context the work of Yue Minjun, the celebrated Chinese painter famous for his fully laughing figures. The observer is confronted with a multiplicity of individuals, all similar to each other, who are characterized by a stereotyped laughter that does not reveal any critical awareness. Where uniformity suggests that there is a shared collective consciousness, it is difficult for the observer to identify a logic, a relation between what is inside and outside the subject, and therefore to identify the meaning that laughter takes on for any individual. Minjun's laughter becomes a mask that marks an absence of communication as well as a profound relationship between individuals. This laughter is more like Andy Warhol's series, where it is shown that mass production cancels out the uniqueness of the individual. Laughter is thus transformed into a powerful and violent instrument of disapproval and denunciation of social dissociation in China. See F. Jullien, "No possible Subject," in *Yue Minjun, L'ombre du fou rire* (Paris: Fondation Cartier pour l'art contemporain, 2012), 31.

stood as the 'enemies' of the prisoners, the violence they demonstrate is mostly gratuitous, vulgar and unjustifiable. The guards become the symbol both of how evil potentially lurks within each one of us, and of how the law, entrusted to the hands of an unjust person, is nullified or can be transformed into a powerful instrument of torture and oppression.[240] In this respect, it is interesting to note the conversation the narrator has, after Kuptsov's aggression, with an officer who offers him a relocation to another penal colony for security reasons. The narrator refuses the opportunity offered, claiming that the situation would not change and that on the contrary he believes "the law should be observed." (*TZ*, 62) To this morally irreproachable reaction, the officer replies: "You planning to stand on your rights?" (*TZ*, 62) as if to say that the world cannot change because it is radically evil and the law is bound to fail. In the maelstrom of evil, the law does not guarantee security, fairness or justice. In actual fact, in Dovlatov's camp, law turns into abuse of power, while the victims seem more inclined to succumb than to react. In this part of the world, the boundaries between good and evil are completely erased. Evil and abuse of power are the norm, and perhaps even the rule.[241] The Russian writer represents very well Nietzsche's claim that 'subjuga-

---

240 I would like to recall the series of paintings entitled *Abu Ghraib Series* created by Fernando Botero to commemorate the torture and humiliation inflicted on Iraqi detainees by American coalition soldiers during the Second Gulf War in 2004.
The famous fat, buttery, exaggeratedly rounded figures (*Boteromorphs*) typical of Botero's poetics are victims of the same tortures portrayed in the photographic reportage. However, despite the brutality of the scenes, the abnormal naked bodies, however humiliated, seem to defy their torturers with humor, so much so that they turn from victims into heroes. Although one cannot laugh at the violence shown, a pervasive sense of the grotesque shields the dignity of the prisoners, while the torturers are ideologically subdued and the strength they display is diminished: the jailers no longer represent the law, nor any principle of Justice. Similarly, symbols of the law, such as handcuffs, chains, the prison, as well as the US Supreme Court's ruling on torture, are also mortified. Where the original bodies, which inspired Botero, are unequivocally and irredeemably tragic, the grotesque depicted by the painter makes us aware of a monstrous human condition and leads us back to an absolute principle of Justice.

241 The harshness and inescapability of the evil of the penal colony makes one look even more tenderly and kindly at Charlie Chaplin's *A Dog's Life*. The society depicted in the film is fundamentally unjust, one sees in this regard the poverty and joblessness, which induce the Tramp to steal in order to eat; the acts of prevarication of the criminals, who not only steal, but also have no qualms about getting the young protagonist fired; but also the insensitivity of the audience, who are moved by a song while not caring about the tramp's fate. Even the fag that sticks under his shoes seems to be a form of injustice. At the same time, although the Tramp steals the flapjack and appropriates a wallet that does not belong to him, we spectators do not feel like accusing him, because we share the motivations of his gesture: to survive and to love his woman. Faced with injustice, we too are willing to accept an illegal act and tend to replace right with feeling.

tion' has pretensions to normativity: everyone wants to impose their own rules and their own profits, even if this goes against common morality and the prisoners' rights (even the Asian cook who insists on preparing a hallucinogenic tea in the presence of the guard, ignores with a stubborn smile the unlawfulness of the gesture). It is in this perverse logic, implemented by the few to the detriment of the many, that laughter becomes a form of liberation of the common human being from a normativity that only respects the values and interests of the strongest.

In this case, the prisoners in the camp are three-fold prisoners: of their own corrupt conscience, of judicial authority and of their jailers. It is also curious to note the importance Dovlatov attaches to the norm "as the most favorable and least painful condition of human existence,"[242] as if to say that staying within the rules (of the atrocious game of life), i. e., sharing common principles or even the law, seems to be the best condition to ensure a worthy existence. In the specific case of the camp, however, the norm seems to be precisely that of the jailers who share with the prisoners a common sense of rebellion against the jurisdiction of the state and the rule. The most worrying thing in this case is that the state does not guarantee protection for the weakest, while laughter emerges as the only possible form of self-defense. Laughing does not annul, but demystifies evil, treating it for what it is without accepting its power; laughing has the power to normalize the brutality of evil by minimizing it and thus making it bearable. In a condition where goodness and justice cannot make their way because they do not exist even in the form of a phantom, laughing challenges evil and makes the one who laughs more cynical, but at the same time responsive and less succumbing. Laughter acts as a conscious act of madness; it is an ethical subversion, as Salmon calls it, that specifically breaks the torturers' abuse of power and, with it, the

---

The policemen, for their part, are not Dovlatov's bad elements, but rather the 'mechanical' agents of an absent justice. These do not prove themselves equal to understanding the situation and merely carry out an arrest procedure: in fact they have no voice, but are the hand of a power that thwarts the value of the citizen.

Between the evil and the good thus schematically divided, only the dog seems to take responsibility for the action and decide where the good lies beyond the law. The dog becomes the *deus ex machina*, the source of justice and fairness. Even if practiced in an unusual and irreverent way of the rules. The law is made far away from the places of the law and its institutional protagonists. One cannot help but smile, however, when one discovers that the dog and the police chief both have the same spot around their eyes. Only justice beyond the law (the one derived from the common sense shown by the dog) makes goodness and love triumph in society. In the film, comedy overturns established knowledge about the relationship between truth and justice, good and evil, right and crime.

242 Dovlatov quoted by Salmon in *I meccanismi dell'umorismo*, 116 [my translation].

cognitive automatisms that make us distinguish the difference between good and evil. Laughter is actively opposed to power, while renouncing violence or direct confrontation: embracing evil so as not to be subjugated and destroyed by it.[243]

This is even more understandable if we consider that for Dovlatov, the world around us is nothing but a mirror of who we are: "According to Solzhenitsyn, camp is hell. Whereas I think that hell is in us ourselves." (*TZ*, 5) The horror of the penal colony is the horror that pervades fundamentally lonely and individualistic human beings, for whom only their own benefit and the imposition of their own rule make sense, rather than the *sharing* of rules with fellow human beings.

This understanding of laughter has nothing to do with the theories of laughter as discussed in the first chapter of this volume; there is no shadow of comedy; it is a form of laughter that does not amuse,[244] that is totally removed from the sphere of the divine, that does not fascinate or cheer. It is a laughter deprived of the hope of redemption, justice and jurisdiction. However, it is a laughter that works as an antidote to despair, because although the protagonist lacks hope, there is still a form of dignity in him that leads him to react and not to conform to the perverse logic/law of the colony. Laughing, therefore, once again acts as a counter-logic.

As a matter of facts, we are not dealing with a satanic laughter, but with a deeply and quintessentially human one. It is human because it is intimately connected with the vital force of survival, but at the same time it is an *escamotage,* which by *deception* tries to make the unbearable reality (and also the law) disappear. If there is no fascination in this kind of laughter, the fascination certainly lies in the act of staging the deception: the person who laughs wants to be seductive to evil, and make people believe that they are participating in the other person's crime or law, while on the contrary they are actually carrying out a form of rebellion. *Escamotage* is a diagonal line, a distortion, and therein lies the creative act of the one who laughs, so much appreciated by Leopardi. Those who manage to laugh in despair realize the immeasurable absurdity of a power that may well be frightening, but cannot or must not be respected. Jurisdiction fails, along with its social role, because it is inadequate in accounting for the complexity of reality. However,

---

243 Finding the will to smile and react to evil is evocative of Roberto Benigni's film *La vita è bella* (1997), in which a Jewish father imprisoned in a Nazi concentration camp makes his little son believe he is taking part in a great game with a wonderful final prize in order to make the horror of that tragedy more bearable for him. Similarly, recent images have gone viral on the web of a Syrian father who teaches his daughter to laugh every time she hears a bomb go off, so as to associate a positive thought with a frightening event.

244 See Salmon, *I meccanismi dell'umorismo*, 137: "Dovlatovian resolution is humorous, not comic, since its main function is not to make the reader laugh, but to violate the postulates of his conscience" [my translation].

law is implicitly saved by laughter, since an ideal of justice is nevertheless recognized as inseparable from the human condition. I like to recall one of Tiziano Terzani's teachings: if someone points a gun in your face, just laugh. Terzani recounts that one evening in Kabul, just before the curfew, he was stopped by an armed man who threatened him to stop. Terzani opened the driver's window and began to laugh, raising his hands. His full Muslim beard and his light laughter broke the cultural automatism that associates a Western man with a danger to be defended with weapons.[245] As Leopardi aspired: "The power of laughter is terrible and awful: anyone who has the courage to laugh is master over the other, in the same way as anyone who has the courage to die."[246]

In point of fact, neither Terzani's nor Dovlatov's laughter constructs a new sense of what is right in human intellects, whereas a new sense of what is right is what the self-confessed culprits of the musical *Chicago* would like to establish in their ideal society.

Rob Marshall's *Chicago:* when what is right is relative

The number entitled *Chess Sun Tango* in the musical *Chicago*, directed by Rob Marshall (2002), is a perfect example of humor addressed against a Law that is apparently incapable of guaranteeing equity and justice, because it is incapable of grasping the sense of reality or of what is right. From the outset, the narrative is highly ambiguous from a semiotic point of view and strongly permeated with the idea of the uncanny.

The Hollywood prison, where the scene is set, certainly lacks the grim despair of Dovlatov's lager and presents itself as the opposite of the panopticon. In fact, we find ourselves in a dreamlike prison, a dark place, not penetrated by sunlight due to the lack of windows, oppressive, hidden from the gaze of both society and the jailers, but paradoxically reminiscent of the suffused atmosphere of the night club. The setting suggests a prison deprived of the ugliness that we usually associate with the punishment dimension of prison sentences, as well as the solidity of the walls, which are both defensive (for the society outside) and offensive (for the prisoner locked inside), like those designed by Giovanni Battista Piranesi.

245 Terzano Terzani, "La vita in breve," from the drama performance *Le parole altre* with Angela Terzani Staude and the Francesco Bruno Ensemble. Available online: https://www.youtube.com/watch?v=YUh7CrxJv78 (last access in February 2020).

246 Leopardi, *Zibaldone*, eds. Michael Caesar and Franco D'Intino (New York: Farrar, Strauss and Giroux, 2015), par. 4391. The word "awful" is in English in the original text.

The musical uses an enveloping space, unlimited, undefined, deeply dark, but penetrated by beams of light that illuminate the protagonists of the scene.

Besides, the most distressing prison ceremonial that feeds the collective imagination, that is, the guards' footsteps thundering through the cells at night along with the deafening opening of the doors, is spectacularized here, to the extent that the guard is transformed into an elegant entertainer in a dinner jacket who seats Roxie Hart at a small table; Hart is the film's female protagonist, recently imprisoned because of the murder of her scoundrel lover. The *mise-en-scène* serves to present Roxie with the confession-show of a group of "six merry murderesses of the Cook County Jail." As with the prison, the women are presented as *subjects* who are in no way mortified by their punishment, but on the contrary, they are extremely vital, sensual, strong, and capable of attracting our attention and will, as if they were modern-day Ulysses sirens. They therefore go far beyond the traditional iconology of the condemned criminal.[247]

It needs to be pointed out that this show is represented in a dreamlike dimension (perhaps it is not by chance that it is set at night), in which all the characters – criminals, guards and lawyers – reveal themselves for what they really are once stripped of their social masks: namely, that of the convict, the guard, the unscrupulous lawyer, the victim, and so on. If in the Soviet penal colony all characters were the embodiment of evil, here all characters are rogues, scoundrels, swindlers, be they criminals, lawyers or people of justice. However, more than anything else, they reveal themselves as artists capable of enchantments, some for their chameleon-like ability like lawyer Billy Flynn and jailer Mama Morton, others for their singing or dancing. In contrast to Dovlatov's humanity, these subjects are completely vital, creative, seductive, absurdly in control of their actions and their unconventionality or transitiveness: in a Nietzschean key, they can be understood as the incarnation of the sensuality and cruelty of the Dionysian. However, deprived of the social mask, i.e., social categories of judgment, they do not suffer moral and spiritual degradation but they are transformed into *beauty* with strong physical connotations. Questionable ethics are combined with aesthetics. The movie director's reading of the criminals predisposes us to accept a different sense of the law, less rigid and more flexible or – at least – as a different one. From a narrative point of view, it is as if Marshall had embraced Thomas De Quincey's lesson, ac-

247 The convicted tempt us as Eve tempted Adam. These women seem to claim "comically," and thus with an inversion of meaning, the disvalue of the repressive legalism introduced by God with the repression of the sexual instinct. Even the protagonist Roxie Hart, at first resigned, sad, faded, will soon be transformed in exactly the same way as the other women, because she shares with them the same vision of law and crime.

cording to which, assuming that murder is morally 'very improper' and unacceptable, it can be treated *aesthetically*, i.e., in relation to *taste:*

> When a murder is in the paulo-post-futurum tense, and a rumour of it comes to our ears, by all means, let us treat it morally. But suppose it over and done, and that you can say it (...) is completed or (in that adamantine molossus of Medea) (...) it is done; (...) then I say, what is the use of any more virtue? Enough has been given to morality; now comes the turn of Taste and the Fine Arts. A sad thing it was, no doubt, very sad; but *we* can't mend it. Therefore let us make the best of a bad matter; and , as it is impossible to hammer anything out of it for moral purposes, let us treat it aesthetically, and see if it will turn to account in that way.[248]

Again, de Quincey reminds us that only the *connoisseur* understands how to examine the aesthetic principles of the criminal act, and the *connoisseur* is a 'judge of a far different calibre than Her Majesty's Assize Judges.' If the English writer and essayist theorizes and illustrates how killing can be an art rather than a trivial, ordinary, and coarse act, in *Chicago* the prisoners are transformed into singers and dancers who stage the performance of their murders and their motivations. At the same time, they question themselves about the appropriateness of the punishment inflicted and the meaning of the sentences. Through very sensual clothing and dance, the merry murderesses, as they are called, tell us how they killed their men for reasons that appear to the spectator to be totally trivial:[249] one because he blew out his chewing gum,[250] one because he was a liar,[251] one because he was too jealous,[252] one because of 'artistic differences,'[253] yet all of them deserved

248 Thomas De Quincey, *On Murder Considered as One of the Fine Arts* (1827–1839) (London: Penguin Classics, 2015), 10–11.

249 For Sergei Dovlatov, "people" – that is, each one of us – "killed for a package of tea." Dovlatov, *The Zone,* 14.

250 Each murder has a title – *Pop, Six, Squish, Uh uh, Cicero, Lipschitz!* – to which as many stories correspond. *Pop* is about an annoying chewing gum: "You know how people have these little habits that get you down, Like Bernie. Bernie, he liked to chew gum. No, not chew, pop. So I came home this one day, And I'm really irritated, And I'm looking for a little bit o' sympathy, And there's Bernie lyin' on the couch, drinkin' a beer and chewin.. No, not chewin', Poppin'. So, I said to him, I said 'You pop that gum one more time', And he did. So I took the shotgun off the wall, And I fired two warning shots, Into his head."

251 *Six:* "I met Ezekiel Young from Salt Lake City about two years ago, And he told me he was single. And we hit it off right away, So, we started living together. He'd go to work, he'd come home, I'd fix him a drink, we'd have dinner, And then I found out: "'Single' he to/ld me. Single, my ass! Not only was he married, Oh no, he had six wives. One of those Mormons, you know. So that night when he came home from work, I fixed him his drink as usual You know, some guys just can't hold their arsenic!"

252 *Squish:* "Now, I'm standing in the kitchen Carvin' up a chicken for dinner, Minding my own business. In storms my husband Wilbur in a jealous rage: 'You been screwin' the milkman,' he

the appropriate punishment they received. The vulgarity and meanness of these men was so unbearable that they deserved death. It goes without saying that also the perverse nature of these women is stigmatized. In fact, they did not shy away from harming those they considered their enemy, but the elegance of their story helps us to empathize with them, making us smile at their abstruse reasons and accept murder as an aesthetic gesture aimed at removing ugliness and evil. The combination of aesthetics and paradoxical logic creates a cultural short-circuit that disorients the spectator.

The stories of these women are reminiscent of Max Aub's *Exemplary Crimes. The Unbearable Encounters of Everyday Life Transformed into Crimes Without Punishment,* in which the surrealist writer recounts crimes that – at least or only intentionally – we all commit every day (or almost every day), but which the protagonists of the stories told *actually* carry out without suffering punishment. However extravagant and banal the reasons for these offenses may be, they are always considered by their perpetrators as mere acts of liberation or in response to a form of injustice suffered. It is as if these characters were stateless rather than anarchists, living in a non-world in which they are the only inhabitants, perhaps not too dissimilar to the uniqueness and solitude of Dovlatov's jailers. They do not seem to feel any sense of responsibility, nor do they seem to recognize, and therefore share, any morals or laws other than their own – so much so that they are surprised when they discover that the law does not conform to their sense of what is right. It is perhaps pertinent to assimilate this attitude to Nietzsche's non-moral, which, as we saw in the previous chapter, places itself at the boundaries of the rule and its enforcement according to an idea of *will* as the source of every moral conception of 'good' and 'evil.' In the other world occupied by the protagonists of *Exemplary Crimes* and *Chicago,* only the individual's will of power defines the limits of what is fair and what is unfair: if greedily chewing gum gave a sense of freedom and domination to the victim, the same act gave rise to an unbearable sense of oppression that deserved a definitive and immediate response. The reader is able to laugh because these tragic tales are treated without a moralistic vein, as Aub himself states in the introduction to his work.

In the Spanish writer's interpretation, contemporary humans want to conform to social models – "We accept, with a deliberate will, everything they impose on

---

says He was crazy, And he kept on screamin': "You been screwin' the milkman." And then he ran into my knife He ran into my knife ten times."

253 *Lipschitz!:* "I loved Al Lipschitz More than I can possibly say. He was a real artistic guy: Sensitive, a painter. But he was always trying to find himself. He'd go out every night looking for himself And on the way, He found Ruth, Gladys, Rosemary and Irving. I guess you could say we broke up Because of artistic differences. He saw himself as alive, And I saw him dead."

us"[254] – but in doing so, they limit their creative impulses and become mediocre, although they may find a spark of originality and vitality in crime. However, if breaking the law proves to be an act of rebellion against social conformity and the conformist intent of the law, even 'humble criminals' become trivialized whenever they seek justification for their deeds. Since not even the wise can find the words to overcome the drift of the contemporary world and, as we know, laughter does not belong to the wise, the artist is left with an absurd tone for the storytelling of the crime: "All that remains is the game that depends on chance."[255] Laughter thus becomes a strategy that reveals human meanness and at the same time its potential.

> 'Better off dead,' she told me. And the only thing I wanted was to give her satisfaction![256]

> He was smarter than me, richer than me, more generous than me, he was taller than me, more handsome, more debonair, he dressed better, spoke better; if you think these are excuses, you are really stupid. I always thought of ways to get rid of him. I was wrong to poison him: he suffered too much. That's what I regret. I would have liked him to die suddenly.[257]

> He was stupid. I explained and re-explained to him three times the way to do it, very clearly. It was very simple, all he had to do was cross the Avenida de la reforma at the fifth crossroads. And each time he got confused in repeating the explanation. I made him a very clear map. He stood there looking at me questioningly:
> And then ... Oh God, I didn't understand.
> And he shrugged his shoulders. He had to be killed. And I did it. Whether I regret it or not is another matter.[258]

Irony, sarcasm, paradox: these are the ingredients both of this book and of Rob Marshall's musical. In the musical, for the spectator the threshold of the unusual is crossed when the chorus starts repeating the refrain "I betcha you would have done the same!" between the women's stories:

> He had it coming!
> He had it coming!
> He only had himself to blame!
> If you'd have been there,

---

254 Max Aub, *Crímenes ejemplares [1957] Crímenes ejemplares/ Exemplary Crimes* (Thule Ediciones, 2007); Italian trans. Lucrezia Panunzio Cipriani, *Delitti esemplari. Gli insopportabili incontri della quotidianità trasformati in delitti senza castigo* (Palermo: Sellerio, 1981), 11 [my translation].
255 Aub, *Delitti esemplari,* 12 [my translation].
256 Aub, *Delitti esemplari,* 13 [my translation].
257 Aub, *Delitti esemplari,* 30 [my translation].
258 Aub, *Delitti esemplari,* 37 [my translation].

> If you'd have seen it,
> I betcha you would have done the same!"

Hypocrite lecteur, – mon semblable, – mon frère! This comment draws the attention directly to the moral and individual responsibility of the spectator, who is drawn into the events not as a *judge*, but as a potential *criminal* or perhaps simply as a *connoisseur.* After all, as Giorgio Manganelli recalls in the *Preface* to De Quincey's volume,

> Now, there is no doubt that murder is extremely interesting and, all things considered, entertaining. The murderer carries a great and dramatic responsibility on his shoulders – he is the proxy for all murderers who do not kill. [...] the murderer is not a peripheral figure, the 'monster,' but is the image of our dreams, of our nightmares.[259]

In short, to quote Dovlatov, the hell is in us. Moreover, among Aub's confessions, we read: "Have you ever felt like eliminating one of those lottery ticket sellers, when they get boring, pushy, supplicating? I have, on behalf of all."[260] Associating De Quincey once again with the confessed Chicagoans, Manganelli writes:

> The unbelievable charm [...] of De Quincey's discourse lies precisely in this indirect speech, by extravagance and hieroglyphics, this fiddling with knives, this disarming with jest, which is in truth serpentine cunning, playful hypnosis that disorients the one who is to be devoured, who is to be turned into an accomplice.[261]

While watching *Chicago*, viewers are torn between the serious and the facetious, between fascination and horror, and their imagination prevails over rationality, as they are involved in acts that they would not dare commit in reality, even though such criminal deeds are already potentially part of their common nature. While they are led to laugh at the claims of these criminals, they experience a maieutic laughter that makes them aware of their innermost nature, or at least induces them to question themselves. The women's comments go beyond common sense, they are able to present reality to us in a different way, to imagine other moralities, other balances and harmonies between what is right and what is not according to the law. The world is thus cognitively deviated to make us all perceive a (different) logic hidden in the illogical, including the fallacy of legal (Apollonian) logic and

---

259 De Quincey, *On Murdered Considered as One of the Fine Arts*, trans. Luigi Brioschi, *L'assassinio come una delle belle arti*, Introduction to the Italian edition by Giorgio Manganelli (Parma: Guanda. 1990), 9 [my translation].

260 Aub, *Delitti esemplari*, 20 [my translation].

261 De Quincey, *L'assassinio come una delle belle arti*,10 [my translation].

human criminal nature. Maieutics is combined with humor in the Pirandellian sense, where humor would be “a rebellion against rhetoric and canons, in other words, it is (…) a sort of ‘sabotage’ of the current conception of the world that inhibits a different understanding of human reality.”[262] Precisely, a non-conformist reality.

The portrayal of day-to-day life in Chicago during prohibition times is marked by (often likeable) crooks and scoundrels, foremost among them lawyer Flynn. Flynn is the irreverent voice of the civil and legal conscience of 1920s Chicago. In his profession, he reveals the failings of the system when he tells his client “There is nothing to fear. It's a three-ring circus, these trials, the whole world is a pure spectacle. But you work with a star!” It can perhaps be said that Flynn exploits the law – and not only the law- for the benefit of his client without any ethical or moral restraints. Justice has nothing sacred about it, but it is a spectacle that needs skilled actors and an audience reminiscent of the Roman Coliseum: an audience that can be manipulated and that, in turn, influences the court's judgment. Here the lawyer proves to be a crime artist as well as the murderesses. Crime and justice once again seem to be on the same level, even if the tone is absolutely ironic, excessive, brazen and not tragically realistic like Dovlatov's.

Similarly, the *night-time* tango act arouses laughter because we perceive a paradox that undermines the norm. In the *Chicago* Cook County Jail, we are immediately caught between a *plausible* dimension, because the women are guilty and we therefore recognize the correctness of the punishment imposed on them according to a realistic logic, and an *implausible* dimension, because the context is revisited in such a way as to unhinge all our certainties regarding the idea of guilt and punishment. According to a non-binary logic of and/and, sense and non-sense are displayed together to offer an anesthetization of prison and punishment. Such aesthetics opens up all possible expectations. The viewer forgets that the show is actually offered to Roxie Hart, the film's protagonist, who is off-screen observing the performance. The viewers tend to believe that the doomed women sing and dance just for them, so much so that they are willing to laugh. The spectators recognize the humor that underlies the work and which emphasizes the idea that logic is the product of ideology, rather than a totally objective system: if objectivity lies in the overcoming of logic, the convicted women's reasoning goes beyond all *clichés* and mediocrity.

As spectators, we laugh especially when the confessed offenders have the audacity to ask us to consider as ‘fair’ criminal deeds that we would consider unacceptable outside that fictitious framework. They ask us to share their reasons in

262 Pirandello, *L'umorismo*, 64 [my translation].

the face of a due process that has not understood them, that has not – *in their opinion* – proved to be fair. The law only assessed the presence of a corpse, not the reasons for the murder, as if to say (cynically) that here are murders, but perhaps there are not crimes:

> They took a flower
> All along In its prime [...]
> And then they used it [...]
> And they abused it
> How could you tell me
> It was a murder
> That I was wrong?
> But not a crime!

The protagonists astonish us by pointing out that theirs are crimes, but not felonies; that is, criminal deeds, but without fault. Absurdly and against every basic principle of coexistence and respect for human life, the women do not understand the reasons for the sentence. Obviously, there is a gap between common logic and morality on the one hand, and criminal logic and non-morality on the other. In fact, a rule – do not kill – is eccentrically compared with a law of nature – the natural instinct for the survival of the species – and in any case the adherence to an instinct that is not culturally or legally conformed. Is this a further reinterpretation of the 'unjust disguised' as legal? The paradox is obvious, and the laughter that the women provoke is not comparable to the sympathy we might feel for criminals like Robin Hood or Arsène Lupin. We are seduced by provocation. I like to recall the definition given by the American writer Ambrose Bierce to the term 'Murder' in his *Devil's Dictionary:*

> "HOMICIDE," *n.* The slaying of one human being by another. There are four kinds of homicide: felonious, excusable, justifiable and praiseworthy, but it makes no great difference to the person slain whether he fell by one kind or another – the classification is for advantage of the lawyers."[263]

The juxtaposition of different logics creates a short-circuit that we perceive as paradoxical, i. e., contrary to common sense, or what most people recognize as the unconditional norm and law in their conscience. The aim of the paradoxist is gener-

---

263 Ambrose Bierce, *The Unabridged Devil's Dictionary: The Cynic's Word Book – Satirical, Ironic and Humorous Definitions* [1911] (Athens: Univ. of Georgia Press, 2001). Also online: http://www.thedevilsdictionary.com (last access in February 2023).

ally to demonstrate an ambivalence or the main dogma that underlines a truth,[264] namely that every truth (including legal and judicial truth, therefore) is the result of a logical, formal, linguistic, cultural construction. Laughter and paradox activate an intuition of *illogicality*, which suddenly and unexpectedly interrupts the narrative flow of reality to make us realize that the initial premises were wrong and therefore also the consequences that followed (however logical the consequences may be in relation to the premises). The convicted women in the musical (but also the protagonists of Aub's confessions) are so convinced of what they are saying that the paradoxical scope of the situations narrated acts instantaneously and instinctively on the spectator, even before reason can intervene to rationally explain the incongruity of the discourse.[265] The short and intense stories of *Chicago* take the same form of paradoxes expressed in aphorisms, parables, artistic sentences and anecdotes that Taoism and Zen Buddhism methodically use as instruments of enlightenment to reveal almost *automatically* how 'truth' is never univocal or normative.[266] In this context, humor reveals what is inaccessible to logic and thus also to any "logic," that is a strict, flat and slavish application of the law. Humor is a 'rebellious' literary communication,[267] and the director of *Chicago* turns the serious upside down, in the name of a violent logic (also that of cause and effect) that deserves to be subverted. He thus subjects the world to a cognitive deviation and allows the logic disguised in the illogical to be suddenly perceived: in this case, that we are all potential criminals.

In the movie, there is no sign of repentance on the part of the confessed offenders, because they are not Don Quixote: they never deny themselves, but rather wish to extend their vision of justice to all of humankind. Unlike Don Quixote, they do not embody any moral or value system such as chivalry. Even though it cannot be said that they have no rules, the rules must rather adhere to their personal aesthetic vision of existence and crime. Like Leopardi's human, they do not endure tyranny and do not consider harm as an evil act in itself.

---

264 See M.V. Ljapon, "O 'grammatike' jumora i strategii ostroumija," in *Logičeskij analiz jazyk. Jazykovy mechanizmy jumora*, ed. Arutjunova (Moscow: Indrik, 2007), 309.

265 Ljapon, "O 'grammatike' jumora i strategii ostroumija," 325.

266 Salmon, *I meccanismi dell'umorismo*, 121–30: "In addition to verbal practice, in Buddhism enlightenment can be achieved through physical work or meditation." It is worth revisiting the *First Epistle to the Corinthians*, where Paul of Tarsus mentions the "fools in Christ," who, contrary to being considered "wise," possess the ability to expose human flaws, attitudes, thoughts, and actions through their examples and irony. These individuals reveal the contradictions within seemingly sensible or pious behavior, unveiling the space for duplicity. Thus, within the madness of these women, truths and the boundaries of logic may be hidden. F. Schlegel spoke of the 'logical chemistry' of the joke.

267 Salmon, *I meccanismi dell'umorismo*, 70.

From a narrative point of view, it is the paratactic narrative structure that standardizes crime, with the result that our perception of murder decreases while the derisive acceptance of law's inadequacy to understand the reasons behind criminal actions increases. This is true at least for those who are endowed with a different sensibility and who question the very concept of the normal and the norm. The spectator is able to see sense and non-sense simultaneously, but as Sigmund Freud also says,[268] it is sense that allows non-sense to pass and make us laugh. Similarly, young Taoist and Buddhist monks are taught to recognize the 'unity of opposites,' the 'non-sense of sense' and the fact that there are questions without answers (*kōan*).[269]

However, these women do not hide their suffering and they reveal a high degree of aggressiveness. It might be interesting to recall Konrad Lorenz's hypothesis about laughter in his theory of aggression.[270] According to the Austrian ethologist, aggression is an innate instinct that guides our behavior and gives us the impetus to do everything we do. Aggression, however, needs to be controlled and one of the possible ways is through laughter, together with knowledge of the consequences of our acts, and moral responsibility for our actions. Greek catharsis and psychoanalysis have taught us that many praiseworthy behaviors are actually the sublimation of aggressive or sexual drifts: one can react by punching the table instead of hitting the opponent, or one can write an enthusiastic pamphlet by curbing one's sense of anger. In the latter case, one can claim that a renewed moral system can be built on the discourse (for Leopardi, the imagination) that replaces the aggressive reaction. The merry murderesses in *Chicago*, as well as the murderers depicted by Aub, relied on instinct and aggression, but the spectacle, and thus the poetic/artistic sublimation of the murderous horror, allows us to laugh and instinctively grasp some of the limits of human behaviors and of the legal system. After all, wasn't irony one of the favorite tools of Socrates' pedagogical method, namely maieutics? The doubt aroused by irony is supposed to awaken the desire for investigation and thus knowledge: while the condemned ask to be understood and justified, the spectator is asked to reverse the message and free himself from aggressive instincts. The irony relies on the fact that the sender, the object and the recipient of the irony recognize this inversion; on the contrary, the women prove to be cold, objective, detached, even prejudiced, in their comments and attitudes. It is the film director

268 Palmer, *Taking Humor Seriously*, 116 ff.

269 Odifreddi, *C'era una volta il paradosso. Storie di illusioni e verità rovesciate* (Turin: Einaudi, 2001), 76. It is perhaps also worth recalling the significance attributed by Leopardi to the imagination as a tool for constructing a moral system freed from the instinct of nature and the constraints of rationality.

270 Lorenz, *On Aggression*, 284 ff.

and the screenwriter who rely on the irony of the spectator to convey their message. In this case, the spectator does not only laugh at what is being told, but above all at himself.

Laughter would thus be a ritualization of a process in which threats are redirected: we laugh at the six female offenders because unconsciously we are as aggressive as they are, and by laughing at them we are able to critically control our instincts. In this sense we know we are superior to the condemned, and this puts us in a free zone from which we can see, laugh and be critical without compromising ourselves, legally or otherwise. Laughter, says Lorenz, always obeys reason and is at the same time a perfect tool for revealing lies and meanness. In fact, the murders are presented as an automatic and inevitable reaction to a provocation suffered, although the dance is characterized by an almost mechanical self-control, as if it were the sublimation of natural human aggression in the aesthetic act.

Aub's and Marshall's stylization of surreal logic allows us to superimpose our world on that of these 'different' minds. By perceiving their illogical nature, we also feel the pleasure of having achieved the unattainable. I wonder if art here does not enable us to reach that moment that Nietzsche associates with the unthinkable. Perhaps the most disturbing aspect is the fact that this realization takes place through a questioning of the role of the law. The law that condemns does not recognize the licitness of a *natural* act, so to speak. Quite rightly, the law exists precisely to stem these human deviations. Can we say that the conflict between nature and culture is being staged? Between vital, creative impetus and a legal system that tends to normalize existence by depriving it of imagination and creativity and therefore of the unthinkable? The women ironically appeal to *humanitas* as a *ratio decidendi*, but obviously they overturn the principles of justice to which we all appeal in our daily lives. Yet even though they are highly disturbing subjects, they do not intimidate us because we know that they are brought to justice: the law has intervened to establish an order without which we could not laugh. If they were outside the disturbing yet reassuring walls of prison, everything would be different. No one questions imprisonment, but it is precisely from our free and safe zone that we can also look at the worst of crimes with hilarity.[271]

The scenes described by the women, as well as the blurring of the victim and criminal roles, are somewhat reminiscent of René Magritte's painting *L'assassin menacé* (1927), inspired by one of Paul Nougé's poems collected under the title *Im-*

271 It would be interesting to compare it with Tim Parks' novel *Cara Massimina*, where the tale of a kidnapping is authentically funny, as are the reasons for a double murder.

ages peintes. The white corpse of a woman is lying on a *dormeuse* and the elegant and beautiful murderer is still listening to some music coming from a gramophone while three men look into the window (perhaps eyewitnesses or policemen) and two others are hidden, perhaps waiting to catch him. In this depiction of crime, there is a strong contrast between the sensuality of the woman (whose posture is reminiscent of a Venerina's[272] body), the horror of the murder and the sense of the perverse suggested by the calmness shown by the murderer. The latter appears to us, however, as the protagonist of the visual narrative, as well as threatened by the presence of strangers. The moment of suspense captured by Magritte in his painting is resolved in the stories of the women, who are as beautiful, elegant, sensual and perverse as the protagonist of the pictorial scene. As in the prisoners' tales, in Magritte's painting the body of the victim is perceived as an estranged element to the meaning of the story: the locutionary act, the pictorial representation and the criminal fact are not the same thing, just as the image of a pipe is not a pipe. Death is such and it only matters to the dead, as Ambrose Bierce would say! In the musical and in the painting, it is the ironic reversal of roles and the complex relationship between good and beautiful, between horror and guilt that draws us into the inversion of the meaning of crime and the Law. The murders become almost an aristocratic fact that have little to do with the obviously degraded environment of the stories and the collective imagination around the prison. In this moment, it is the comic process that allows us to recover an ethical dimension that goes beyond aesthetics, so that we can recognize the difference between good and evil beyond all appearances.

These pages have perhaps shown how laughter makes us aware of ourselves so lightly that we can voluntarily implement strategies of resistance to evil, no matter where it comes from, even from the legal system.

272 Venerina, or little Venus, is a wax anatomical model representing a pregnant young woman. Created in by Clemente Susini (1754–1814) in 1782, it is currently in the historic Science Museum of the University of Bologna. The thoracic and abdominal could be removed to see the various organs. Such models were used by students in medicine.

Chapter 5
The "ridiculous claims" of law

The claim to define subjectivity

Roman law drew a distinction between human beings and *aliquid monstruosum* (something monstrous) born from women, specifying that "non sunt enim liberi, qui contra formam humani generis converso more procreantur."[273] Even if we consider the opposite ("men are those born of women who are not monsters"), the source manifests the claim to define the shape of humankind ("forma humani generis") i. e., at least the outward appearance of humanity: the *monstrum*, as non-human, did not possess any form of legal capacity, and therefore could not be considered a child, or a subject at all.

In his commentary on the *Pandectae*, Pothier restates the quoted passage, pointing out that it could only be considered a "monstrosity" "un corps humain avec une tête d'âne ou de boeuf, l'enfant d'une femme dont la partie supérieure serait celle d'un homme, et la partie inférieure celle d'un poisson, ou d'un veau, et autres du même genre."[274] The *monstrum* is thus relegated to the world of the impossible. Aubry and Rau could only take note of this. While mentioning the passage from the *Digest* quoted above, they add that the rule denying legal subjectivity to monsters "a notre avis, ... est sans application possible, puisque, d'après les lois de la physiologie, le fait qu'elle suppose ne parait pas pouvoir se produire."[275] Modernity has swept away the "monster" from legal treatises, which

---

273 This is a passage from the *Pauli sententiae* (Paul. Sent. 4.9.3 – 4): "mulier si monstruosum aliquid aut prodigiosum enixa sit, nihil proficit: non sunt enim liberi, qui contra formam humani generis converso more procreantur" (if a woman gives birth to something monstrous or wondrous, it shall be of no benefit to her: actually, those who are born against the shape of humankind are not sons), referring to the *ius trium liberorum*, later included, with modifications, in the Digest (Paul. 4 Sent. D. 1.5.14). The *ius trium liberorum* was a piece of legislation granting special benefits to women who gave birth to three or more sons.

274 Robert Joseph Pothier, *Pandectae Justinianeae* [1748] (Paris, 1818), 1.389 (a human body with the head of a donkey, or an ox. A child, born from a woman, with the higher part of man, and the lower of a fish, or a veal, or others of the same kind).

275 Charles Aubry and Charles Rau, *Cours de droit civil français d'après la méthode de Zachariae,* 4. ed. (Paris, 1869), 1.181. Available online: https://gallica.bnf.fr/ark:/12148/bpt6k5858422r/f10.image.-texteImage, last access March 2021) (in our opinion, [...] it has no possible application, since, following the laws of physiology, the facts that it assumes cannot actually take place).

https://doi.org/10.1515/9783111286778-007

have thus renounced the claim to define the human form.[276] Conversely, law has not abdicated the claim to define, or rather to determine, some intangible elements of subjectivity, nor will it ever be likely to do so.

Central to this viewpoint is the concept of citizenship, which on the one hand identifies subsets of human beings, and on the other determines the perimeter of the legal rules applicable to each subject within it, by virtue of its identity-related characteristics that are presumed by law, on the basis of criteria sanctioned by law itself. In classical Greek philosophy there is a very close relationship between citizenship – understood not only as belonging to a territorial community, but above all as eligibility to exercise public functions – and education. As much in Plato's *Republic* and *Laws* as in Aristotle's *Politics*, great emphasis is placed on the need for law to trace a strict educational path, aimed at a well-defined cultural formation of citizens, and of rulers in particular. Modern constitutionalism distinguishes between upbringing, attributing a central role to the family, and instruction, in which the role of the state is pre-eminent. Moreover, it recognizes the universal nature of the right to instruction, which is not merely limited to citizens. Nonetheless, there seems to be no doubt that the constitutional state also reserves areas of cultural conformation for those subject to it, by way of law.

The first and foremost of these is the national character of citizenship: because of law, (almost) every newborn child has a nationality which, in addition to subjection to the state and its rules of law, involves an attachment/belonging to the homeland with all the historical, cultural and value systems that this term entails.

The founding acts of modern constitutionalism, moreover, emanate from representative bodies of (self-defined) national communities, the terms of which are determined by the rules for electing the members of these bodies, and in particular rules granting voting rights.[277] Furthermore, while affirming that it "recognizes" and therefore does not create the subjectivity and personality of individuals (as persons and in the social formations, in the formula of Article 2 of the Italian Constitution), the law claims to identify and regulate almost any institution of social

276 For further references see Carbone and Rossi, "Who is the Monster? Laughing at Friends and Foes."

277 The very recognition of universal human rights contained in such acts emanates from national communities: it is not the humans, who as a vast community do not have a single legal system, nor a single institutional structure, who recognize universal human rights, but the French, the Americans, the Italians, or, in the case of international conventions, groups of nation-states. In fact, with an apparent paradox, universal rights come into existence only when they are recognized by national communities, and institutional apparatuses undertake to protect them. See also Hannah Arendt, *The Origins of Totalitarianism* [1946–1948] (New York: Harcourt Brace, 2004), 290.

control (and personality formation): family, school, associations of all kinds, religion. Thus, it can be said that personality is formed and acts sometimes according to the manners prescribed by law (including rules on the content and modalities of teaching, albeit free), and sometimes within the margins of autonomy that are in any case identified by law.

The same subjectivity under private law, on the other hand, shows an aspiration of the law to determine some cultural characteristics of the subject. Think about the notion of *capacité juridique* or *capacità giuridica*, understood as the capacity to be the holder of rights and obligations. This notion implies that all subjects, even those who are not completely self-conscious (such as, once again, the newborn child) immediately become part of a series of legal relations with other individuals and things, which qualify them as sons/daughters (legitimate, natural, etc.), relatives, heirs, owners, creditors, debtors. Law, in other words, aspires to define, or at least to help define, the personality and culture of the subjects whose actions it intends to regulate. Given that law regulates, first and foremost, the very modalities of its own mutation or its own permanence, it aims in some way to ensure that its recipients continue to culturally consider these modalities as acceptable, i. e., that they shall not question the legitimacy of the law's right to command.

At a lower level, the law aims to guarantee the permanence of the cultural conditions needed so that its own fundamental values and logic are not undermined. Replacing, for example, the Western concept of property with the Aboriginal Australians' conception of the relationship between humans and territory (i. e., doing exactly the opposite of what the colonizers did in Australia)[278] would entail radical modifications of the legal sources, starting with the constitutional ones, but above all a complete change in the mental attitude of members of society, which would be difficult to achieve "with the legislation in force," and which would most probably require recourse to oppression (as was the case in Australia).

Law is certainly part of the culture of those who produce it and to whom it applies; it is determined by the broader cultural conditions within which it is situated, but at the same time it contributes to determining them. At the very least, it aspires to contribute to determining them, with varying modalities and degrees of success. For this reason, law can be traced back to the area of communicative phenomena,[279] and its positivistic separation from all the other spheres of expression

---

278 For further references see Paola Carbone and Giuseppe Rossi, "Celsus and Chatwin Go Walkabout," *Pólemos* 9 (2015): 175–197.

279 For further references see Giuseppe Terranova, *Elogio dell'approssimazione. Il diritto come esperienza comunicativa* (Pisa: Pacini, 2005).

and communication that characterize historical and social experiences[280] seems increasingly arbitrary. Every individual is born into a legally determined environment, which helps to define his or her subjectivity.

Nationality is a real comic cliché, starting with the simplest forms of comedy, such as jokes. At first glance, comedy based on nationality often appears to be an expression of chauvinism; by emphasizing the faults of the foreigner, it seems to offer confirmation of laughter as an expression of superiority. Law and comedy would thus seem to agree in affirming that nationality is a defining element of the subject, if not even a necessary element to this end, given that the protagonists of comedy based on nationality are often characterized solely through it. Slightly deeper reflection, however, shows that what generates laughter is not so much the ascertainment of the superiority of one's own nation over others, and thus the quality of the rule of law that allows (or rather obliges) one to call oneself "Italian," "French," and so on, but the paradox. Let us take a joke like "What does a Belgian do if the water in which he is washing his son is hot? He puts gloves on."

Laughter begins as we think about the stupidity of the individual, then of the paradoxical idea that there is a whole population of individuals capable of equally stupid conduct, and thus that all Belgians fall into this population (but, as it is well known, we are all someone else's Belgians ...), with the result that Belgium would have a one hundred percent stupidity rate.[281] What is laughable, in fact, is precisely the idea that nationality can define the individual, and that therefore all Belgians, Italians, etc. have the same characteristics; in reality, comedy attributes universal traits to national types which are traditionally represented by masks (cunning, credulity, stupidity, avarice, etc.), and mocks the claim of law to reduce the universal to a limited sphere, in this case by the legal criteria that attribute nationality.

---

280 Paolo Heritier, "Nessi multiformi tra diritto e narrazione," *Tigor: rivista di scienze della comunicazione* 2 (2010): 4–13, 6: "once the breach in the dam of the impossibility of distinguishing law from morality within the pure theory of law has been opened, then why should we stop at the analysis of the links between law and science, economics, religion, without extending the field to the analysis of the links between law and art?" [my translation]; see also Paolo Heritier, *Estetica giuridica* (Turin: Giappichelli, 2012).

281 This assumption is contradicted by the Second Fundamental Law of Human Stupidity: "'The probability that a certain person be stupid is independent of any other characteristic of that person": Carlo M. Cipolla, *The Basic Laws of Human Stupidity* [1976] (Bologna: Il Mulino, 2011), 48. An example of French humor on the alleged characteristics of the Flemish mentality is offered by J. Verne's short story *A Fantasy of Dr. Ox* [1872], trans. Andrew Brown (London: Hesperus Press, 2003, 4), set in the imaginary town of Quiquendone: "[...] there's nothing to be said or thought against the Flemish inhabitants of western Flanders. They're decent people, sensible, a bit tight-fisted, sociable, even-tempered, hospitable, perhaps a bit slow in speech and not very quick on the uptake ..."

Compared to most examples of humor, or comedy in general, about nationalities, ethnicities, religions, and so forth, Jewish humor has a peculiarity which Freud already pointed out in his 1905 essay: the jokes about Jews "[...] are invented by Jews and aimed at Jewish characteristics. The jokes made about Jews by outsiders [*Fremdem*] are mostly brutal comic anecdotes, in which [the effort of making] a proper joke is saved by the fact that to the outsider the Jew counts as a comical figure."[282] And again, according to Freud many examples of Jewish witticism can be explained by pointing out that

> the prevention of an insult or an abusive reply by external circumstances happens so often that the tendentious joke is a particular favorite for use in enabling criticism or aggression towards persons in high places who claim authority [to be voiced]. The joke then represents a rebellion against such authority, a liberation from the oppression it imposes.[283]

Despite appearing self-deprecating, at least part of Jewish humor has as its true target anti-Semitism, and its premise that every Jew is the bearer of an original and unfixable guilt, no matter what.

Irony, in this highly hostile context that has accompanied almost the entire history of the Jewish people, is a weapon,[284] or at least an instrument of defense. Understood in this way, Jewish humor about Jews confirms the ludicrousness of the homologizing claim that is inherent in the legal concept of nationality and is exasperated by nationalist ideologies, and/or hinged on hostility towards ethnic, religious, racial, ethnic groups, and by the rules of law that have embraced them historically, and in contemporary times.

The oral tradition in the transmission of the revealed word, that is to say of "interpreting orality," opens up a radically dialectical culture due to the inevitable heterogeneity of accounts and interpretations. Many have related the connection

---

282 Freud, *The Joke and Its Relation to the Unconscious*, 108–109.

283 Freud, *The Joke and Its Relation to the Unconscious*, 102. The origin of the Jews' "participation" in the mottos created about themselves is identified in the same mechanism underlying the joke of a character of Heinrich Heine who, when narrating that he sat next to a very rich banker, reports that the latter "treated me just like his equal, quite familionairelly." The joke is, in turn, traced back to Heine's suffering at being marginalized by his own rich relatives.

284 In the words of the Chief Rabbi of England, Hermann Adler, in an 1893 essay, Jewish humor is "a weapon with which a beneficent Maker has provided His feeble creatures, whereby they have been enabled to survive in the fierce struggle for existence ... the iron hand of bigotry ... the soul-chilling venom of contempt": Hermann Adler, "Jewish Wit and Humor," *The Eclectic Magazine* 57 (1893): 530–538. Piero Stefani, "Riso ed ebraismo," *Servitium* 23 (1999): 247, while acknowledging a foundation to the thesis that Jewish humor represents "an irony directed at first against oneself, but, in reality, directed above all against others," considers it inadequate to account for the breadth and heterogeneity of the phenomenon.

between the Jewish *witz* and the tradition of orality.[285] "[B]oth the oral Torah and Jewish humor live insofar as they are recounted, interpreted, expanded and actualized, while both lose consistency as soon as they are simply codified."[286] Moreover, the link between Jewish humor and "the existential precariousness of the Diaspora" which generates a (genuine) "melancholic self-mockery now proverbial"[287] has been highlighted.

As a particular form of comedy, humor – but we could more generically say laughter – thus again shows its connection with becoming, if not with actual wandering, of which the Jewish diaspora is perhaps the most powerful symbol.

Comedy emphasizes the dialectic between the individual and the community,[288] but also the tension between the aspiration to the permanence of law and the ineliminable becoming of historical facts, perhaps affirming, in a general and non-evaluative way, the recessiveness of law with respect to individual culture and feeling. In such comic representations, what is "just" is what individuals consider good for themselves, the rule that best reflects their personalities.

The story narrated in the 1958 film *La loi c'est la loi!*, centered on the travails of a French gendarme who discovers he is, despite himself, Italian (the work will be analyzed in detail in the next chapter), shows that law can impose or grant *status*, citizenship and nationality, just as it can annihilate a man as an individual and member of society, but it cannot change his inner feelings: the Frenchman remains French, even when he becomes, by rule of law, Italian. The artificiality of political and institutional borders in the film symbolizes the artificiality – and the potential danger – of the legal construction of the person, first and foremost as a subject belonging to a given positive legal system, and subordinate to it. This is a crucial theme, which not only traversed the history of post-unification Italy, but also marked the events of colonization and decolonization,[289] and manifested itself dramatically in the period of crisis experienced by the European Union in the first two

285 Within the Jewish community, as well as outside: see Stefani, "Riso ed ebraismo".
286 Stefani, "Riso ed ebraismo" [my translation].
287 Gad Lerner, "Il Don Chisciotte sconsolato che generò l'umorismo ebraico," introduction to Shalom Alechem, in *La storia di Tewje il lattivendolo* (Milan: Feltrinelli, 2000), 7–8 [my translation].
288 See Giovanni Bombelli, "'Comunità tra identità e diritto," in *Luoghi della filosofia del diritto. Idee, strutture, mutamenti*, ed. Bruno Montanari (Turin: Giappichelli, 2nd edition 2012), 272: "the 'community' always oscillates, ambiguously, between utopia (emancipating) and ideology (all-encompassing)" [my translation].
289 The influence of the former colonizer's legal system on the legal experiences of the former colonies is a theme that has been widely developed in comparative law. See, for example, with reference to Africa, Gianmaria Ajani, Barbara Pasa and Domenico Francavilla, *Diritto comparato. Lezioni e materiali* (Turin: Giappichelli, 2018), 383.

decades of this century (at the moment subdued, though not definitively resolved, by the health emergency).

The claim to shape society

Obviously, the transformative aspiration of law does not merely focus on the subject, but it also extends to the relationships between subjects, or at least to a numerous series of these: the legally relevant relationships, from which, *de facto*, very few forms of human interaction seem to escape. The law dictates rules of behavior, whose foundation may be traced back to a pure relationship of force. Constitutional democracies, which refuse the idea of law as the outcome of mere force (but even autocracies still need some legitimation), assume a link between the law and the feeling that legal rules are just rules, or at least rules that are justly produced, and will be justly applied, even by dissenters – or against them.

Even in a democratic context, it is hard to imagine that all rules of law are universally agreed upon, i. e., that each of them constitutes the result of an authentic general will, in the sense envisaged by Rousseau, according to whom dissent represents a necessary but transitory phase. Thus, the rules of law that require unanimous agreement, or with respect to which unanimous agreement can be presumed (pretended?), must be reduced to an essential core that characterizes the system as such. The core of these characterizing rules is represented by constitutional charters. Part of this essential core are, for example, the rules which attribute sovereignty, those defining the form of a state, those enshrining the fundamental modes of production of the other rules of law, starting with political representation and the majority principle in a democratic context. The dissenters will therefore be legitimately bound by the rule of law they do not agree with, since it has been produced in accordance with shared modalities, including, first and foremost, the majority principle. It goes without saying that the latter is quite different from Rousseau's idea of a general will, since it admits the existence of a minority not as a transitory fact, but as a structural element of the system.

At the level of the essential core, legal systems tend to manifest the aspiration to permanence, if not perpetuity, in the strongest manner. The citizenry manifests its will not to change, not to desist from certain principles that provide the legal order with its core values. Therefore, some key constitutional rules protect the community from the temptation to depart from the fundamental values enshrined in the constitution itself. The Italian Constitution's prohibition to revise the republican system is an example of this, but also the US Constitution displays an aspiration to perpetuity (at least) of its own essential core. This is revealed in the preamble, in the reference to the preservation "to ourselves and our Posterity" of the

"Blessings of liberty," as well as in the irreversibility of the partial transfer of sovereignty from the states to the federation. The 1688 English Bill of Rights, with its reference to the indubitable character of the rights and liberties claimed by the Lords and Commons, shows both the aspiration to perpetuity and the intention to erect a legal barrier to renunciation, precluding the possibility of it at any time.

For the sake of simplicity, through what I have designated as the "essential core," the law shows the claim to make at least some aspects of society unmodifiable (the republican afflatus of the Italians, the attachment to freedom of the Americans), i.e., to sterilize them with respect to historical becoming or, as Nietzsche would say, to rescue them from eternal return. The legal experiences that were inspired by Marxian doctrine as interpreted by Lenin,[290] which saw law exclusively as an instrument to pursue a political end, represented by the transformation of society towards communism, seem to be at the opposite extreme. However, the desired transformation should have had the character of irreversibility. The peculiar manifestation of the finalism of socialist law, in fact, seems to be nothing more than a different form of law's aspiration to immortality, even as the capacity to generate (or rather, to help generate) a perfect and perpetual society.[291] Conversely, in the original texts of modern constitutionalism the essential core has a fundamentally negative content. On the one hand, it enshrines the finalistic character of state organization and the law it produces, serving to guarantee the "happiness" and "natural" rights of every human. On the other hand, it sets the

---

290 Vladimir Ilič Ulianov (Lenin), *State and Revolution* [1917] (New York: International Publishers, 1932), 78: "and so, in the first phase of Communist society (generally called Socialism) 'bourgeois' right is not abolished in its entirety, but only in part, only in proportion to the economic transformation so far attained, i. e., only in respect of the means of production. 'Bourgeois right' recognizes them as the private property of separate individuals. Socialism converts them into common property. To that extent, and to that extent alone, does 'bourgeois right' disappear ... The state is withering away in so far as there are no longer any capitalists, any classes, and, consequently, no class can be suppressed. But the state has not yet altogether withered away, since there still remains the protection of 'bourgeois right' which sanctifies actual inequality. For the complete extinction of the state, complete Communism is necessary."

291 See the political programme set out in the preamble to the 1977 Brezhnev Soviet Constitution: "Developed socialist society is a natural, logical stage on the road to communism. The supreme goal of the Soviet state is the building of a classless communist society in which there will be public, communist self-government. The main aims of the people's socialist state are: to lay the material and technical foundation of communism, to perfect socialist social relations and transform them into communist relations, to mould the citizen of communist society, to raise the people's living and cultural standards, to safeguard the country's security, and to further the consolidation of peace and development of international co-operation" (https://www.departments.bucknell.edu/russian/const/1977toc.html, last access September 2022). For an analysis see Paolo Biscaretti di Ruffia, Gabriele Crespi Reghizzi, *La Costituzione sovietica del 1977* (Milan: Giuffrè, 1990).

limits that the rules of law must not overstep, lest they betray this purpose, degenerating into misrule and tyranny. Rather than aspiring to create a new order, the aim of law seems to be to not disturb, and if possible, to strengthen, a pre-existing and "natural" order. Both the Declaration of Independence of 1776 and the Declaration of Rights of 1789 were based on "a certain idea" (liberal) of humans and humanity, or at least of a certain part of humanity, belonging to nations and even before that to races, that could be considered "civilized."[292]

"We hold these truths to be self-evident, that all men are created equal, that they are endowed by their Creator with certain unalienable Rights, that among these are Life, Liberty and the pursuit of Happiness. – That to secure these rights, Governments are instituted among Men, deriving their just powers from the consent of the governed" states the Declaration of Independence. The preamble and Articles 2 and 4 of the French 1789 Declaration have entirely similar content. In this perspective, the function of the law (and of the government) is to ensure the fulfillment of the "natural" rights that have as their object "liberty, property, safety and resistance to oppression" (Art. 2 of the 1789 Declaration), the only limitation being that other members of society are guaranteed the enjoyment of these same rights (Art. 4).

In the infamous *Dred Scott* ruling of 1856, the Federal Supreme Court wrote that

> the legislation and histories of the times, and the language used in the Declaration of Independence, show that neither the class of persons who had been imported as slaves nor their descendants, whether they had become free or not, were then acknowledged as a part of the people, nor intended to be included in the general words used in that memorable instrument.[293]

---

292 This brings us back to Roscoe Pound's considerations on civilization as the foundation of all legal experience, on which we refer again to Rossi, "The Search for the Workable Legal Precept."

293 *Dred Scott v. Sandford*, 60 US 393 (1856), 407. Dred Scott, a slave who claimed to have gained his freedom after being taken to a state where the Missouri Compromise (a federal law passed in 1820) did not allow slavery, was denied legal standing by the Supreme Court on the grounds that he could not qualify as a citizen due to his status as a slave. The Court also found the Missouri Compromise contrary to the Constitution, insofar as it prevented the owner from taking his slaves back with him to a slave state, after having taken them to a state where slavery was not permitted by federal law itself. The bibliography on the case is vast. See: David T. Konig, Paul Finkelman, and Christopher A. Bracey (eds.), *The Dred Scott Case: Historical and Conteporary Perspectives on Race and Law* (Athens: Ohio Univ. Press, 2010); Alison Morretta, *Slavery and Citizenship: the Dred Scott Case* (New York: Cavendish Square, 2018); Tim McNeese, *Dred Scott v. Sandford. The Pursuit of Freedom* (New York: Chelsea House, 2007).

This interpretation, which contradicts the Declaration of Independence's assumption that "all men are created equal" is motivated by considerations based, first and foremost, on "public opinion" and history:

> It is difficult at this day to realize the state of public opinion in relation to that unfortunate race which prevailed in the civilized and enlightened portions of the world at the time of the Declaration of Independence and when the Constitution of the United States was framed and adopted. But the public history of every European nation displays it in a manner too plain to be mistaken. They had for more than a century before been regarded as beings of an inferior order, and altogether unfit to associate with the white race either in social or political relations, and so far inferior that they had no rights which the white man was bound to respect, and that the negro might justly and lawfully be reduced to slavery for his benefit. He was bought and sold, and treated as an ordinary article of merchandise and traffic whenever a profit could be made by it. This opinion was at that time fixed and universal in the civilized portion of the white race. It was regarded as an axiom in morals as well as in politics which no one thought of disputing or supposed to be open to dispute, and men in every grade and position in society daily and habitually acted upon it in their private pursuits, as well as in matters of public concern, without doubting for a moment the correctness of this opinion.

The opinion of the Court continues by denying that slavery, and the conception of humanity on which it was based, were indigenous products of the American colonies:

> And in no nation was this opinion more firmly fixed or more uniformly acted upon than by the English Government and English people. They not only seized them on the coast of Africa and sold them or held them in slavery for their own use, but they took them as ordinary articles of merchandise to every country where they could make a profit on them, and were far more extensively engaged in this commerce than any other nation in the world.

The opinion of the Court makes it clear that:

> It is not the province of the court to decide upon the justice or injustice, the policy or impolicy, of these laws. The decision of that question belonged to the political or lawmaking power, to those who formed the sovereignty and framed the Constitution. The duty of the court is to interpret the instrument they have framed with the best lights we can obtain on the subject, and to administer it as we find it, according to its true intent and meaning when it was adopted.[294]

At the same time, however, the Court sees the interpretative key to circumscribing the scope of the Declaration of Independence and the Constitution precisely in the (alleged) historical *communis opinio* on the justice of slavery. In his dissenting

294 *Dred Scott v. Sandford*, 405.

opinion, Justice McLean observed that: "In the argument, it was said that a colored citizen would not be an agreeable member of society. This is more a matter of taste than of law."[295] The judgment shows a logical short-circuit, in which an alleged feeling of justice is used to interpret the rule, which in turn is supposed to legitimize a result that is actually the result of "taste." In France, neither the Declaration of 1789 nor revolutionary legislation put a definitive end to slavery and the lucrative trade it ensured.[296]

There is a paradoxical and sinisterly comical tension between the naturalistic and liberal assumptions of the founding texts of modern constitutionalism and the historical context that generated them. This is revealed by the weakness of their first tests of application: *Dred Scott*, but also the French revolutionary legislation itself, among the most illiberal in history, up to the paroxysmal slaughter during the Reign of Terror. After the two world wars, contemporary democratic constitutionalism attempted to resolve this tension. There was an extensive critical reflection on the formal nature of the liberal (or "bourgeois," according to the Marxian critique),[297] principle of equality. This led to an acquired awareness that neither equality itself, nor fundamental (perhaps "natural") rights are self-enforcing.[298]

Alongside the usual negative limits, the law has thus been assigned a positive role of guaranteeing and promoting the effectiveness of the social – and sometimes, but more subtly, cultural – prerequisites on which the entire construction of the legal system is based. At the same time, "programmatic" norms have appeared in constitutions and legislation. The function of these norms is, with different degrees of cogency, to enunciate just objectives, towards which the law should help push society. Labour law is one of the areas where this tendency is clearer.

Law should thus shape society and the individuals living within it, by not only preserving it from unwanted changes, but predefining the modes of desired changes, i. e., preventing the "eternal return." Certain dilemmas should be resolved forever, in order to finally ensure perpetual peace to the phantom of justice, like the ghost of Canterville. For example, having established once and for all that all people are equal, the law should not only treat equal situations accordingly,

295 *Dred Scott v. Sandford*, 533.

296 See also Clara Palmiste, "La Francia e la schiavitù: storia, memoria e politica," *Passato e presente* 69 (2006): 129–136; Costanza Margiotta, "La schiavitù tra diritto, memoria e ricerca storica: il caso francese," in *Il senso della Repubblica. Schiavitù*, eds. Thomas Casadei and Sauro Mattarelli (Milan: F. Angeli, 2009), 23.

297 On which Horkheimer and Adorno dwell in order to highlight, following Marx, its inherently oppressive nature.

298 As observed, in particular, by Hannah Arendt.

but also make every effort to ensure that existing inequalities are removed[299]. This way, nobody shall be deprived (at least) of the effective enjoyment of fundamental rights. As mentioned above, comedy is particularly sensitive to the provocations of the phantom of justice: it accepts wandering as an inherent condition of existence, scoffs at fixity and knows from experience that the most solemn utterances are often also the most vacuous. In the works dedicated to the character of Fantozzi the accountant, Paolo Villaggio has masterfully shown how no rule of labour law (or constitutional law ...) can ever free the protagonist – or possibly any other employee – from his condition of "inferior" (the appellative used by Countess Serbelloni Mazzanti Vien Dal Mare during a famous gala dinner) condition, not to say of a real metaphysical loser. Fantozzi's condition of servitude is inevitable because it is, above all, mental and cultural. Every attempt at redemption is in vain.[300] Whether it is the ephemeral adhesion to Marxism, or the rebellion triggered after decades of abuses and humiliations by the umpteenth viewing of *Battleship Potemkin*, in conjunction with the Italy-England football match, when Fantozzi finally decides to exercise his freedom of thought with a blunt and very well-known critical judgment.

The (tripolar) dialectic between the legal rule, social sensibility and individual feeling is the constant feature of all battles for civil rights – which of course Fantozzi also enjoys, at least in theory. As a matter of fact, the legal rule sometimes precedes and sometimes follows the transformations of social feeling – and especially majority feeling – depending on the composition and assessments regarding political expediency of the group of institutional decision-makers – especially when what is at stake is the right of minorities to be "taken seriously."

The U.S. Federal Supreme Court's case law on racial segregation offers important data. In *Plessy v. Ferguson* (1896),[301] which deals with segregation in railway carriages, the dialectic is clear. On the one hand there is the Court's opinion, in

299 Article 3(2) of the Italian Constitution, which assigns the Republic the task to "remove those obstacles of an economic or social nature which constrain the freedom and equality of citizens, thereby impeding the full development of the human person" is emblematic (https://www.senato.it/documenti/repository/istituzione/costituzione_inglese.pdf, last access September 2022).

300 The redemption is in vain not only for the accountant Fantozzi, but for society as a whole. At the first appearance of Fantozzi "[...] one could think that what Fantozzi's mask represented was the previous stupidity, the residual ignorance, the late-feudal servility, the crude and impotent machismo that advanced modernity would sooner or later annihilate, with the ecumenical capacity to enlighten and elevate. We thought we were laughing at the danger we had escaped [...] We were having fun laughing at Fantozzi: but instead the Fantozzian was beginning, in that very moment, to laugh at us": Stefano Bartezzaghi, "Così Fantozzi," in Paolo Villaggio, *Fantozzi rag. Ugo* (Milan: Rizzoli, 2013), 4 [my translation].

301 *Plessy v. Ferguson*, 163 US 536 (1896).

the sense of compatibility with the constitutional rule of equal protection of the segregationist doctrine, which was summarized in the "separate but equal" formula. On the other hand, there is Justice Harlan's dissenting opinion. A comparison of the two opinions shows a clear dichotomy. The majority follows a formalist conception of law inclined to the interpretation of constitutional principles aimed at making them conform to widespread prejudices in the social body on the basis of political expediency.[302] Justice Harlan's approach is based on a progressist view, which instead attributes to these principles a propulsive function of socio-cultural transformations still in the making, if not at an embryonic stage, in the name of the full effectiveness (of the "seriousness") of these principles.[303]

The Supreme Court's 2015 ruling on the unconstitutionality of state regulations that impeded same-sex marriage[304] shows a similar dichotomy. The majority emphasizes the importance of interpreting the Constitution, and in particular the due process clause of the Fourteenth Amendment, to remove barriers to the full realization of human personality and equality: "The right to marry is fundamental as a matter of history and tradition, but rights come not from ancient sources alone. They rise, too, from a better informed understanding of how constitutional imperatives define a liberty that remains urgent in our own era."[305] The minority opinions, on the other hand, argue that it is not the task of the court to introduce changes of great social significance, which would require parliamentary intervention at the very least (thus guaranteeing political representation): "Those who founded our country would not recognize the majority's conception of the judicial role. They after all risked their lives and fortunes for the precious right to govern themselves. They would never have imagined yielding that right on a question of social policy to unaccountable and unelected judges" (according to the dissenting

---

302 As expressed in the opinion of the Court by Justice Brown: "Legislation is powerless to eradicate racial instincts, or to abolish distinctions based upon physical differences, and the attempt to do so can only result in accentuating the difficulties of the present situation. If the civil and political rights of both races be equal, one cannot be inferior to the other civilly or politically. If one race be inferior to the other socially, the constitution of the United States cannot put them upon the same plane."

303 According to Justice Harlan's dissenting opinion: "We boast of the freedom enjoyed by our people above all other peoples. But it is difficult to reconcile that boast with a state of the law which, practically, puts the brand of servitude and degradation upon a large class of our fellow citizens, – our equals before the law. The thin disguise of 'equal' accommodations for passengers in railroad coaches will not mislead anyone, nor atone for the wrong this day done."

304 *Obergefell v. Hodges*, 576 U.S. 644 (2015).

305 *Obergefell v. Hodges*, 19. The language of Justice Kennedy's *opinion of the Court* echoes that of rulings on racial segregation, starting with Justice Harlan's above-mentioned *dissenting opinion* in *Plessy*.

opinion of Chief Justice Roberts[306]). Justice Thomas' minority opinion expressly excludes that the legal system may have a propulsive function with respect to social sentiment: "Our Constitution – like the Declaration of Independence before it – was predicated on a simple truth: One's liberty, not to mention one's dignity, was something to be shielded from – not provided by – the State."

The alternating prevalence of one or the other tendency explains why, within the same Western constitutional tradition, we find contrasting rules on subjects such as same-sex marriage,[307] capital punishment, euthanasia and other major "ethical" questions, to be resolved by interpreting open principles. Not even law, therefore, escapes the "eternal return" and wandering: every solution is by definition provisional and ephemeral, subject as it is to the continual need for sharing as well as a true and proper ethical endorsement, on the part of the citizens, or the majority of citizens.

The claim to define ethics / morality

It would be misleading to assume that humor, when it uses the juridical to provoke laughter, always implies an unambiguous and unanimous concept of *bonum et aequum*, to be contrasted with the disappointing one embraced by the law, or with the

306 *Obergefell v. Hodges*, 25. In similar terms the 'great conservative' Antonin Scalia: "With each decision of ours that takes from the People a question properly left to them – with each decision that is unabashedly based not on law, but on the 'reasoned judgment' of a bare majority of this Court – we move one step closer to being reminded of our impotence. According to Judge Thomas: "By straying from the text of the Constitution, substantive due process exalts judges at the expense of the People from whom they derive their authority."

307 Italian Constitutional Court, 14 April 2010, No. 138, held that the requirement of sex diversity between spouses was compatible with the principles of equality and social solidarity, as well as with the constitutional protection of the family, on the basis of a historicist reading of the Charter, founded on the preparatory works and expressly rejecting the evolutionary interpretation, which was considered to be beyond its powers (notwithstanding in Article 3, paragraph 2 of the Constitution) "[…] it is true to say that the concepts of family and marriage cannot be considered to have been 'crystallised' with reference to the time when the Constitution entered into force, because they are endowed with the flexibility that is inherent within constitutional principles, and are therefore be interpreted taking account not only of the transformations within the legal system, but also the evolution of society and customs. However, such an interpretation cannot go so far as to impinge upon the core of the provision, modifying it in such a manner as to embrace situations and problems that were not considered at all when it was enacted" (https://www.cortecostituzionale.it/documenti/download/doc/recent_judgments/S2010138_en.pdf, last access in September 2022).

law's own lack of effectiveness. Justice, as already mentioned, is a phantom: it has no definite consistency or form, but is constantly changing.

Especially in the systems that assign a pre-eminent role to normative sources to the detriment of judge-made rules, law tends to assume that the legal rule always pre-exists the behavior it is supposed to regulate. In this way, law should direct human action towards results that can be considered *just* (or rather, lawful). In some cases, comedy shows that unlawful conducts are not socially felt as unjust. This may be the outcome of a gap between the "official" statement of underlying values and the way such values are actually felt by people. In those cases, rather than reaffirming the value of the just as opposed to the legal, humor generates or reinforces *doubts* in the audience as to what *bonum et aequum* actually is. In this way, the comedian snatches the phantom of justice from the perpetual peace that the law would have wanted to assure it, bringing it back to its own perpetual torment.

In a very famous scene in the film *Totòtruffa '62*, Totò and Nino Taranto, petty swindlers, sell the Trevi fountain to a foreign tourist. In the film there is no blame for this and other frauds, nor is any sanction by law shown. On the contrary, the two swindlers systematically evade the law, thanks to the benevolence of a commissioner, a former schoolmate of Totò's, whose surname is Malvasia. The damage caused by the scams perpetrated by the two accomplices (who end up unwillingly harming the commissioner's son, who is in love with Totò's daughter) will not be neutralized in the end by the law, but by a providential intervention: Totò unexpectedly receives a billion-dollar inheritance from America, thanks to which he will be able to compensate the victims and ensure that he and his relatives can live an honest life.

It can be said that the repression of fraud is one of the common elements of all legal experiences and that it has very ancient origins: one might assume that there is unanimous consensus that defrauding is unjust conduct, that the defrauder must be punished, and the victim protected. The film's comic effect, on the other hand, stems from the viewer's implicit solidarity with the fraudster,[308]

---

308 Note what Umberto Bosco, following Croce, observes in his commentary on Canto XXI of Inferno, where Dante resorts to grotesque terms in describing the albeit atrocious torment of the barterers (petty swindlers, but also corrupt officials): "[...] there are sinners, such as barterers, thieves, counterfeiters, against whom high-level religious and political resentment would be disproportionate to the mediocrity of the faults, and also useless for teaching purposes because they are faults under the eyes of all and condemned by all (but without bitterness: especially that of swindlers: it is an experience one has every day)": Umberto Bosco, "Introduzione al Canto XXI," in Dante Alighieri, *La Divina Commedia. Inferno* (Florence: Le Monnier, 1979), 313 [my translation].

who "has to make a living," and also a lack of empathy with the victims, who after all pay a price for their own stupidity – but not even a high one, given their utter cluelessness and the small amount of the ill-gotten gains. Anyway, in the end providence will sort it all out ...

The prosecution of Pinocchio in the village of Trap for Blockheads offers us a similar situation: Pinocchio is condemned by the judge-gorilla for having been cheated by the Cat and the Fox, who persuaded him to sow his money in the Field of Miracles. His guilt, in essence, consists in having been clueless. Although the episode expresses a clear distrust of jurisdiction, the moral lesson to be drawn from it is not one of reproach towards the judge, but a plea to not trust too much in the protection offered by the law. The latter cannot help those who are so credulous as to be inexcusable: law, Collodi teaches, does not protect fools. That is why the judge, although softened by Pinocchio's tale, nevertheless sentences him to prison.[309] Current consumer protection regulations have long since downgraded civil law categories and rules such as the *dolus bonus*, or the *caveat emptor* principle (buyers beware, since any seller is a potential liar: *omnis mercator mendax*).[310] The problem of setting a threshold remains open, however. One may wonder whether the law should incentivize absolute credulity, since the credulous shall always rely on its protection, and thus will never see the need to become more careful.

Dworkin himself is well aware of the difficulty of identifying what is exactly just, i. e., to be "taken seriously," especially when principles need interpretation, and values lead to conflicting results. In his extensive reflections on the subject, he does not however forgo finding a unifying element of morality (understood as a set of rules that govern relations between subjects), ethics (understood in the sense of a set of rules by which the individual determines his or her actions),

---

309 Collodi, *Pinocchio*, 67–68: "Pinocchio related in the presence of the judge all the particulars of the infamous fraud of which he had been the victim. He gave the names, the surnames, and other details of the two rascals and ended by demanding justice. The judge listened with great benignity, took a lively interest in the story, was much touched and moved, and when the puppet had nothing further to say, he stretched his hand and rang a bell. At this summons, two mastiffs immediately appeared dressed as gendarmes. The judge then, pointing at Pinocchio, said to them: 'That poor devil has been robbed of four gold pieces; take him up, and put him to prison immediately'. The puppet was petrified on hearing this unexpected sentence and tried to protest; but the gendarmes, to avoid losing time, stopped his mouth, and carried him off to the lockup."

310 See also Giuseppe Rossi, *La pubblicità dannosa. Concorrenza sleale, "diritto a non essere ingannati," diritti della personalità* (Milan: Giuffrè, 2000), for an in-depth analysis of the origins of the ban on misleading advertising.

and politics.[311] In doing so, he opposes empirical and/or economistic perspectives that deny the objectivity of moral rules, or at any rate of rules that are not codified by positive law. This unifying element is seen in human dignity,[312] which should justify, if not impose, choices that do not maximise individual utility or even individual well-being, such as giving up a high-paying job in the tobacco industry.

However, although comedy is not devoid of a moral sense and actually tends to exalt it by contrasting it to the immorality of others (e.g., that of legislation, jurisdiction, the police, etc.), it does not see an insurmountable limit in human dignity and is prepared to laugh at it and make others laugh at it, as long as it seems just to do so – just like anything else. A fundamental element of anti-Semitic comedy, for instance, is represented by the "denunciation" of the covert power of Israel, understood as a state and as a religious community which is allegedly based, among other things, on the exploitation of the Shoah, which is therefore made the object of denial and derision. The comedian Dieudonné M'Bala M'Bala, for example, who is evidently inspired by his own personal interpretation of "human dignity,"[313] has had (or had) considerable success in France. His audience could be made up of anti-Semites, anti-Islamists, the frustrated, the curious, those intolerant of the dominance of political correctness, or simply individuals willing to laugh at crude jokes steeped in cruel stereotypes: perhaps all these categories of people, variously mixed.[314] In any case, ignoring the existence of this audience, or considering it as a pure expression of a pathology or deviance to be repressed,[315] could prove to be a dangerous choice.

---

311 Ronald Dworkin, *Justice for Hedgehogs* (Cambridge, MA: Harvard Univ. Press, 2011), 191 ff., 255 ff., 417 ff.; Ronald Dworkin, "What is a Good Life?," *New York Rev. of Books*, February 10, 2011, online: http://www.nybooks.com/articles/2011/02/10/what-good-life/ (last access March 2021).

312 In the sense of awareness of the value of one's own life, and the assumption of a "special responsibility" with respect to the identification of what constitutes success, and conduct consistent with that identification (Dworkin, *Justice for Hedgehogs*). For a critical analysis see Kenneth W. Simons, "Dworkin's Two Principles of Dignity: An Unsatisfactory Nonconsequentialist Account of Interpersonal Moral Duties," *Boston Univ. Law Review* 90 (2010): 715–735.

313 The special responsibility that Dworkin speaks of should consist in exposing to public opinion inconvenient truths that others have withheld, with the hardly definable moral result of gaining by spreading religious hatred.

314 Benoît Hopquin, "Dieudonné: la posture du paria, un ascenseur pour son succès," in *Le Monde*, December 28, 2013 (online: http://www.lemonde.fr/societe/article/2013/12/28/dieudonne-la-posture-de-paria-un-ascenseur-pour-son-succes_4340971_3224.html, last access October 2016) reports a large audience in attendance "pour éprouver le frisson de l'interdit, par conviction, par esprit frondeur ou par simple curiosité."

315 Dieudonné himself, with obvious cleverness, observes "Ce n'est pas moi qui suis malade, c'est la société" (as referred in Hopquin's newspaper article).

This kind of phenomena show that the values on which *bonum et aequum* is based, and thus by extension the legal system that constitutes its political and technical expression, are constantly changing and must be widely shared among members of society, institutional decision-makers and influencers. In a democratic system, members of society, institutional decision-makers and influencers operate in continuous interrelation with one another. In this case, it is not so much a matter of taking the rights of minorities seriously (Dieudonné M'Bala M'Bala's fans represent one of them), as of reaffirming and showing with facts that the majority is convinced of its principles of freedom, equality and democracy, and that these do not represent mere enunciations of the Charters, but real rules of conduct for institutions, before being for individuals (a subject on which the recent Covid emergency regulations would require very extensive reflections).

Institutions and laughter: the emperor's new clothes

Contrary to his reputation as an author of sad fairy tales, Hans Christian Andersen[316] wrote a comic tale in 1837 that amuses the reader, although no one laughs in it: *The Emperor's New Clothes.* In reality, it is a tale full of paradoxes and logical traps, which begins with the possibility to predict the ending (the punishment of the vain and renegade emperor in his duties of government), but actually ends in a quite unexpected way. Indeed, the ending could be said to be mis-educational, the ultimate extravagance for a fairy tale: the swindlers profit from their embezzlement, and are even honored, while the frivolous and inept ruler, far from being dethroned, remains firmly in place. As is often the case with fables, the apparent simplicity hides a plurality of messages that are not always reassuring, and at times provocative.

The beginning of the story offers, on the surface, the portrait of a bad ruler who is vain, a spendthrift and inattentive to government: the emperor "was so fond of new clothes that he spent all his money on being well dressed." He "had a coat for every hour of the day, and, instead of saying, as one might, about any other ruler, 'The King's in council', here they always said 'The Emperor's in his dressing room'."

"In the great city where he lived," adds Andersen, "life was always gay" and "every day many strangers came to town." A superfluous description for the pur-

---

316 All quotations are from Hans Christian Andersen, "The Emperor's New Clothes," in Hans Christian Andersen, *Andersen's Fairy Tales*, trans. Jean Hersholt (New York: Heritage Press, 1942), 79–87.

poses of the story (it would have sufficed to say "one day two strangers arrived at court …"), but above all disconcerting. A wasteful, narcissistic ruler, far removed from the affairs of state, is the source of misrule, and under misrule life is anything but "very gay." Andersen, therefore, with a logical reversal typical of the comedy, seems to suggest that the "good" ruler might be precisely the one who does not take too much interest in the affairs of state.

Among the many travellers were "two swindlers" who "let it be known they were weavers, and they said they could weave the most magnificent fabrics imaginable." They added that "this cloth had a wonderful way of becoming invisible to anyone who was unfit for his office, or who was unusually stupid." The rascals put the emperor in front of two equally negative alternatives: if indeed accepting the offer would have entailed the risk of deception, refusing it would have led the onlookers to think that, in reality, the emperor feared he was inept at the role, or excessively stupid if he failed to see the wondrous fabric.

"'Those would be just the clothes for me', thought the Emperor: 'If I wore them I would be able to discover which men in my empire are unfit for their posts. And I could tell the wise men from the fools'." The emperor's thinking reveals that the rascals were not only mocking him through vanity, but also through another, no less powerful lever: the pursuit of immunity from doubt and irresponsibility in choice (the doubt and choice that he had, until then, avoided by disinteresting himself in government). To exercise power without assuming the burden of uncertainty and the responsibility of decision is the ambition of every ruler, yet this ambition is unattainable, to the good fortune of those who are ruled.

On the other hand, the assertion of the swindlers about the miraculous properties of the cloth conceals a kind of coded message: the cloth will remain invisible to those who are "unusually stupid." The message is hidden not only from the emperor, but also from the reader: it is for good reason that Andersen entrusts it to the words of the swindlers, i. e., those whom, in fairy tales (but not in reality), the reader knows not to trust. The message is this: there is a usual degree of common stupidity that is part of the human condition, and from which no one is immune, whatever his or her education, social position, or institutional position, if any.[317] This is an observation that comedy would probably approve of. A first consequence follows: the rule defining the degree beyond which stupidity becomes "illegitimate" will inevitably be formulated by stupid people. So, it will be a stupid rule. There is another corollary: the aptitude for the role will depend on the degree of stupidity that the role requires. If we assume that immunity from doubt is an

317 Andersen goes further, claiming that every human being carries within him or her a certain amount of stupidity.

index of stupidity (and the fable, as we shall see, suggests so), it follows that the more a role will require those who occupy it to be immune from doubt, the more it will be suited to persons with a high degree of stupidity.

The emperor, who is anxious to check the progress of the weavers' work (to whom he had already supplied very valuable materials, which they had appropriated) and worried about not being able to see the cloth – even though he knew quite well that "it couldn't have been that he doubted himself" – nevertheless thought it preferable to "send someone else to see how things were going." After all, the villagers in the town "were impatient to find out how stupid their neighbors were."

Stupidity is a characteristic of neighbors, and the emperor refrains from putting himself to the test not out of doubt about his own stupidity, but out of fear of appearing stupid. The "honest old minister" and "the trustworthy official," whom the emperor sends at different times to verify the work of the weavers (who in the meantime have continued to collect the precious materials supplied to them), both decide to report to the emperor that the work is proceeding magnificently and that the garment will be of unequaled beauty, even though they see nothing on the loom. There is a nuance of difference in the thoughts of the two dignitaries standing in front of the empty loom, that deserves highlighting. "'Heaven have mercy!,' thought the 'old minister,' 'Can it be that I'm a fool? I'd have never guessed it, and not a soul must know. Am I unfit to be the minister? It would never do to let on that I can't see the cloth'." The "trustworthy officer" thinks, instead: "I know I'm not stupid ... So it must be that I'm unworthy of my good office. That's strange. I mustn't let anyone find out, though." The thought of the "old minister" unveils the moral of the tale, already "encrypted" in the swindlers' words: it is difficult to admit doubt (to oneself, and all the more so in public) about one's own stupidity, and in general to admit the innate narrowness of human judgment. The "trustworthy officer" is not even touched by this doubt.

When the minister and the official accompany the emperor – who has been reassured and has finally made up his mind – to visit the weavers, their situation is a prisoner's dilemma. Either of them could reveal the truth and (perhaps) earn the emperor's favor, to the detriment of the other, for foiling the scam. Or, they could both be dismissed if the sovereign is still afraid to appear stupid and decides not to trust them. With this uncertainty, and with perfect Nash balance, both of them choose to lie: "'Magnificent' said the two officials already duped: 'Just look, Your Majesty, what colors! What a design!' They pointed to the empty looms, each supposing that the others could see the stuff'." Not only the emperor, but the entire populace is thus led to believe that the two rascals were, in fact, weaving a beautiful dress.

Finally, the moment of the solemn parade arrives. "'If Your Imperial Majesty will condescend to take your clothes off,' said the swindlers, 'we will help you on with your new ones here in front of the long mirror'." By laying down the clothes he wears, the emperor is invited, metaphorically, to disrobe his institutional figure; looking at himself in the mirror, wearing his new clothes, he will be forced to measure himself against himself, and thus to decide whether or not to finally face the challenge of doubt. If certainty is demanded of the institution, and thus frees men, at least temporarily, from their condition of doubt, the man in the mirror is forced to look at himself, and thus judge himself, for what he actually is. The man-institution in the mirror is led back to his own humanity, to his own innate condition of doubt, to the inevitable realization in himself of a common stupidity which, Andersen would say, no-one escapes. However, in the tale the emperor is not alone, and therefore he cannot and does not want to step out of his role as a being who embodies the institution. The rascals deceive him with their gestures and lies, which are immediately taken up by all the courtiers, who in unison praise the quality of the fabric and clothing. When the master of ceremonies announces that "Your Majesty's canopy is waiting outside" the emperor replies "'Well, I'm supposed to be ready' and turned again for one last look in the mirror, for he wanted to make as if he were minutely examining his own clothing."

Unlike people, institutions are necessarily part of an order constructed by law which unfolds in a grand and disciplined gala procession. The task of the emperor is to be at the head of this order, and therefore he looks at the mirror not to question it (and thus question himself), but simply to find in it a confirmation of what he already knows: the sovereign institution wears splendid ornaments, because it is the origin and foundation of the order, without which everything would collapse.

At the very least, and here we come closer to the deeper meaning of the story, it is necessary that the appearance of this order be maintained, in order to avoid the surfacing of unavoidable (lawful) individual and collective stupidity, and the re-emergence of omnipresent and unavoidable doubts. These would lead to the realization that not only the emperor, but all of us are naked. We are all wearing fictitious clothes made of knowledge and convictions that will sooner or later prove to be illusory, whether in whole or in part. The scam engineered by the rascals progressively unveils this conclusion, and that is why Andersen lets them off the hook, wealthier and unpunished, thus running the risk of conveying the miseducational message that crime pays. Nor is it surprising (and not only because every bystander is afraid of appearing too silly or unsuitable for their jobs by not seeing the clothes), that the appearance of the naked emperor solemnly leading the parade, though evidently ridiculous, elicits no reaction from the crowd other than praise.

When the child shouts that the emperor is naked, the truth gradually spreads through the crowd. Everyone shouts that the emperor has nothing on, but no one laughs. The laughter of the people would have meant the end of the procession, of the emperor and the courtiers, a prelude to the establishment of a new order, through a new emperor, perhaps more dedicated than the first to the affairs of state (and this would not necessarily have been a good thing): laughter is transformative, not decisive. It does not break the eternal return, Nietzsche would say, but opens up new forms of knowledge. "'This procession has to go on'. So he walked more proudly than ever, and his noblemen held high the train that wasn't there at all."

The emperor, who confirms himself as a "good" emperor, understands that the most important thing is the "decorum of the procession;" not the order itself, but the appearance of order, or the dignity of the institutions, which must be safeguarded no matter how ridiculous the situation in which those who embody them put themselves. Law is not overwhelmed by laughter because the idea of the institution, the idea of law (the idea that humans can sometimes give themselves just rules, despite their inherent stupidity, or perhaps even because of it, due to its ability to counterbalance the excesses of logic), survives by transforming itself through laughter.

Justice is not of this world (jurisdiction is …)

Jurisdiction and the trial with its actors (judge, lawyers, parties) are obviously among comedy's favorite topics when it comes to law.

If law aspires to transform the world, or some part of the world, the trial is the instrument par excellence for this to be accomplished. Through the trial, the violation of the rule of law should be punished, and the *unicuique suum* should be realized. Through the trial and its ritual, the "ridiculous claim" of law is nothing less than to do justice, or at least, after ascertaining the truth of the facts, to give way to what the rule of substantive law deems to be right in that case, in that place and at that historical moment.

Inevitably, here humor mocks the inanity of the trial, shown as a tiring and self-referential activity, unable to reach the truth, and thus to ensure justice. The case is to be traced back to the ritual/formal nature of the trial at court and/or to the unreliability (fallacy, dishonesty) of its protagonists, starting, of course, with lawyers and judges. The ritualism and formalism of the trial are perceived by comedy as a source of protractedness, which benefits the players in the trial itself, and first and foremost the lawyers (the longer a litigation lasts, the greater the commitment and remuneration of the lawyers: *dum pendet, rendet* …). This triggers a conflict of interest between the lawyer, who is interested in the duration and increased costs of the trial, and the client, who is interested in speed and affordability. The figure of the lawyer who fleeces clients, persuading them to cultivate fruitless litigation, is commonplace in satire (an example for all are the cartoons of Daumier), as well as in representations that oscillate between the tragic and the grotesque, such as Charles Dickens' *Bleak House.*

The link between duration and the need to hear the position of both parties, and thus to grant a fair balance between trial efficiency and guarantees, tends to slip into the background. Humor simplifies, or perhaps perceives that the balance between efficiency and procedural guarantees is fluid (errant): an impulse that the phantom of justice continues to transmit to law, which offers solutions that are always provisional and changeable (especially in a system like the Italian one, prone to a certain frequency of procedural reforms).

In the *Story of the Grail* of 1180–1181, Chrétien de Troyes narrates the assault suffered by the valiant knight Gawain, barricaded in a tower in the company of a maiden, at the hands of a host of "commoners." The attack is described in grotesque terms, almost giving the episode the character of a humorous interlude in the arc of the chivalric novel:

> you would have seen a host of furious commoners taking up axes and halberds; one took a shield without any straps, another took a door, another a great winnowing-basket. The town crier raised the cry and all the townfolk gathered, and the bells of the commune rang so that no-one should stay behind; even the most base-hearted souls snatched up a pitchfork or a flail or a pick or a cub. Not even a pack of Lombards off to kill a slug ever made so much commotion.[318]

The very defense of the besieged has humorous overtones. Gawain uses a chessboard as a shield, and the maiden "took the chessmen that were lying on the flagged floor and hurled them at the mob in fury. She tore wildly at her clothes, swearing in her rage that, before she died, she would have all the rabble destroyed if she could."[319] When the local ruler arrives, an entangled situation is revealed. The latter considers Gawain guilty of misdeeds against him, and has therefore sent him a challenge through his champion, which the knight has taken up. The people, having recognized the author of the alleged misdeed, feel they can do justice to the sovereign by attacking the knight. Moreover, when Gawain entertains the maiden, he violates his commitment to not enter the castle or any other city of the sovereign until the challenge has been faced. Moreover, the girl is none other than the king's sister, whom the king himself had entrusted to Gawain, having met him

---

318 Chrétien de Troyes, *Perceval. The Story of the Grail*, trans. Nigel Bryant (Cambridge: D.S. Brewer, 1986), 64.

319 de Troyes, *Perceval. The Story of the Grail*, 64.

shortly before, without recognizing him... A contrast therefore arises: the "commoners" attack Gawain while he is protected by the king's hospitality, but the knight, by accepting the latter, has violated a previous commitment. The matter is resolved with the intervention of a "vassal ... a native of the town, who gave advice to the whole country because he was a man of great wisdom." In the wise vassal's words: "God help me, sir, all this can be sorted out. To whom should one appeal, if the mob have assaulted him? The debate would go on and on and on until the great Day of judgment! No, it shall be settled according on the will of my lord the king here."[320] The solution sought by the king (that is actually suggested by the wise vassal himself) involves Gawain taking on a chivalrous commitment: he will deliver to the king "the lance whose head sheds tears of the clearest blood" (the lance that struck the side of Christ, forerunner of the Grail – chalice?) or, if he fails, he will have to surrender himself to the king. Gawain accepts this proposal, which safeguards his knightly honor.

All this, of course, would have pleased Don Quixote, who in all likelihood had Chrétien's "Story" on his bookshelf: chivalrous rule is far preferable to trial, which by its very nature is useless and certainly not worthy of a noble knight, whose word is more than sufficient to ensure justice. It is no coincidence that the "wise vassal" compares the trial with the "great Day of Judgment," the only truly reliable occasion for judgment. Although in the Middle Ages the subject of procedural warranties was certainly not of great importance (to put it mildly), Chrétien considers the trial itself synonymous with unnecessary length, with the certainty of being well understood by his readers. The writer does not even need to give any details on the specific characteristics of that trial, and thus explain why it would be of interminable length. The equivalence of trial-unnecessary length is an axiom.

In Chrétien's episode the judge does not even appear, nor is there any mention of what rules would govern the trial. The trial is an inane activity whoever the judge is, unless he is the Almighty, and whatever the rules that govern its course. One might instead think that the usefulness of the trial depends on the quality of the rules that give it structure, and on the judge who applies them; hence, that the effectiveness of the trial in ensuring the just application of substantive law depends precisely on these qualities. Comedy always questions what good law is, including procedural law, and who the "good" judge is (just as it questions who the "good lawyer" is, as we have seen).

---

320 de Troyes, *Perceval. The Story of the Grail*, 66.

Rabelais recounts the episode of Judge Bridlegoose[321] who, for a long time and obviously unbeknownst to the parties, decided cases by rolling the dice until a single decision, thus made, turned out to be incorrect. The story reports the judge's extensive and refined defense when accused of violating the rules of the trial and failing in his function. The judge's self-defense is a perfect example of a sixteenth-century harangue, dense with quotations from Roman and canonical sources and the works of glossators and commentators. Bridlegooses's central thesis is that he perfectly respected the rules of the trial, and followed all its formal articulations. He gave the parties ample opportunity to present their pleas in lengthy documents, which he scrupulously read. He thus allowed the lawyers to earn a proper profit from their profession, the contentiousness of the parties was able to find an outlet, and time was given adequate opportunities to perform its peace-making function, thanks perhaps to the death of the parties, or the exhaustion of their assets. As a wise judge, he always knew how to identify the moment when each trial had reached its maturity, and thus the time to make a decision, obviously with a roll of the dice. The defense is entirely approved by the wise Pantagruel, who knows the law no less than any other discipline. Bridlegoose proves himself the wisest of judges, entrusting the decision to divine intelligence, which moves the dice. It is indeed remarkable that in one case the decision of the dice was not correct. It would be easy to object that the decision of the dice is arbitrary, unfounded, and therefore antithetical to the modern and contemporary conception of judicial decision-making. This is an equally easy objection to overcome: it is (almost) always possible for the judge to provide the decision of the dice with a posthumous motivation, which gives legal sustainability to the response of the dice. It is no coincidence that the parties offer opposing legal reconstructions of the same issue, so the trial offers at least two alternative legal solutions, in addition to the many others that the judge's imagination can offer him/her. Between the decision and the reasoning, it cannot be taken for granted which precedes the other. In the Bridlegoose episode, the trial is reduced to mere representation even though its rules are fully respected, starting with the principle of hearing the pleas of both parties. This does not mean that it is devoid of any social function. As mentioned, its function simply does not lie in settling the dispute according to law. There is in fact no connection between the outcome of the trial and the law, although the law is at the heart of the trial itself, through the ritual and the references contained in the parties' acts. This does not imply, however, that there is no connection between trial and justice: the just outcome of the trial, in fact, is ensur-

---

321 Rabelais, *Gargantua & Pantagruel*, 438–458. For more extensive considerations see Rossi, "Contradditorio processuale e formazione della regola di diritto," 324 ff.

ed neither by its rituality nor, in a broader sense, by its juridical nature, but by its unfolding (and here Rabelais's irony is transparent) in a world in which divine will has imprinted a providential orientation towards goodness. Thus, even if justice were of this world, it would certainly not be so due to law, let alone trials.

It follows from the episode of Bridlegoose and the above-mentioned case (in chapter 1) between Lord Kissbreech and Lord Suckfist that, according to Rabelais, just law does not necessarily belong to the sphere of the non-human (the other-worldly). Rather, it requires a knowledge of humanity through history, and a solid moral foundation.[322] Just law, in other words, does not generate just human-kind, but it assumes it.

In its usual wandering spirit, humor thus sets out in search of the "good judge," who applies the right law in a fair trial, but it keeps discovering that humans on trial continue to manifest only the merits, and above all the flaws, of their humanity, while the phantom of justice continues to be a phantom. To what extent the human can be just when called upon to use a delicate technical instrument with circumscribed possibilities such as law, through a highly ritualized activity such as the trial, is a matter of opinion.

During a period of imprisonment following his participation in an anti-absolutist conspiracy, in 1831 Angelo Brofferio, Piedmontese lawyer, poet-dramatist and politician wrote several songs in the vernacular that were published in Lugano in 1839, including one entitled *La pratica legal* (legal practice).[323]

The first stanza reminds us that from the first day when people decided "to live together as good friends," on the one hand they shared the land (taking "each a piece" of it), and on the other hand they all agreed unanimously on the need for justice. A gallery of grotesque figures follows, with obvious humorous effect: the President who "took everything that was good and beautiful for himself" in order to honor his job, without any malevolence but out of a mere spirit of justice; the Count who "does himself the honour of making his creditors come down with asthma" (and here one can't help but think of the famous scene of the funeral of justice in the *Marquis Del Grillo* movie, mentioned in chapter one above); the "very serious magistrate," who falls asleep while sitting in the Senate wearing a hat and a wig that "know the code better than he does,"[324] and who makes decisions according to the quality of his sleep the night before; the "amiable senator," who loves the gallows and "would even hang justice." Of all these, the only pathetic figure is the defenseless "poor man father of ten children," whom a scoundrel has

---

322 See Rossi, "Contraddittorio processuale," 322 ff.

323 The original text is available online: http://www.piemunteis.it/wp-content/uploads/La-pratica-legal.pdf (last accessed October 2020); the quotations above are my translations.

324 A character that would not be out of place in William Hogarth's painting *The Bench*.

"flayed alive with two lines of transaction"; after being led by lawyers to Herod and Pilate, "jaundice came upon him, and death did justice." Brofferio's conclusion is unequivocal, in the sense that there is only one law, that of the strongest: "always the cunning is right, behind the back of the fool / always the weak will be wrong, if he takes on the strong." The final exhortation is, at last, quite blunt:

> if a relative wants to take your bed
> give it to him now, and be quiet
> if a friend breaks your arm
> thank him and go for a walk
> Woe to him who lets the lawyers put him in the sack
> Woe to him who takes a fancy to obtain just justice

People laugh at the judge, sung by Edgar Lee Masters and Fabrizio De Andrè, for being a dwarf. In De Andrè's text (1971)[325] he even goes so far as to presume an arbitrary moral condemnation without remission in dwarfism, which clearly imagines mockery as a punishment: "a dwarf is a carrion for sure." Such brutality arouses a resentment in the dwarf that leads him to study and move from the "cathedral pews'" to the "sacristy," thus counteracting the equally brutal use of law, degraded to an instrument of revenge. The social brutality in mocking the dwarf is thus contrasted with the institutional brutality exercised through the abuse of jurisdiction, to the point where the judge, "arbiter on earth of good and evil," "at the hour of farewell," must "genuflect." The judge thus lowers his own stature yet again before the "stature of God," whom he admits to "not knowing at all," despite having passed his law exams and thus having adequate and certified knowledge of the legal system. These verses, which emphasize at once the distance between justice and the law, and that between the "sacristy" and divinity, do not deny the possibility of justice itself, but place it (with Rabelais), if not necessarily in the sphere of the otherworldly, certainly outside the places where law is made and applied.

Compared to the reconstruction sketched above of the tripolar relationship between laughter, law and justice, in the case of De Andrè's judge, laughter does not denounce the inconsistency between law and justice: laughter and judicial vengeance are both inconsistent with justice (which belongs to God). Masters' poem[326] comes to an even more radical conclusion. Judge Selah Lively is forced to see that brutal mockery, associated with dwarfism and poverty, is indifferent to any

---

325 Fabrizio De Andrè, *Un giudice*, a song included in the album *Non al denaro, non all'amore né al cielo*, of 1971, inspired to some poems of the *Spoon River Anthology.*

326 Edgar Lee Masters, "Judge Selah Lively," in *Spoon River Anthology*, 67.

attempt at redemption through effort and merit. He has worked as a grocery store clerk, studied by candlelight (i.e., at night, in the hours off work, and not "by the light of rancour," as in De Andrè's text), employed "diligence" and "regular church attendance" – not necessarily in a negative sense – to become an "attorney at law," "representing all the widows in the Probate Court," but nevertheless,

> They jeered at your size, and laughed at your clothes
> And your polished boots.

Therefore, once he became a judge, and called upon to judge

> all the giants
> Who had sneered at you,
> Well, don't you think it was natural
> That I made it hard for them?

Masters' poem does not leave the reader with the idea that we find in the rather consolatory ending of De Andrè's text, where the judge is humbled by the ascertainment of the existence of divine justice, but rather with a question whose rhetorical nature is by no means obvious. In fact, the readers are forced to question their own moral sense, and thus how they would have acted if they had been in the judge's place, as well as what is, or is not, "natural." The problem, then, is to overcome the risk of the logical fallacy in which two injustices create justice. This idea can be found in retributive justice, which attributes to the judge the power to inflict suffering in order to counterbalance other suffering. For this, law is not enough, as Bohumil Hrabal's stunned monologue warns us, when he recalls the noblewoman whose daughter

> married the handsome judge Just, the one known for throwing the book at all the rowdies and the drunk, Tónek Opletalů once boxed his hears because he gave him thirteen months for slitting Říha's throat during an academic debate, but Christ, healer of the nations and mainstay of the poor, knew way back then that man, predisposed as he is to villainy, soon sheds tears, which is why he had the strength to load that girder on his back for us all and lug it the two kilometers to Golgotha, all bloody and bruised, to these days priests go wild at the thought of it, though they prefer telling children about the Holy Trinity [...].[327]

The judge is completely part of the vicious circle of injustice that is supposed to do justice, with the same regular alternation of "villainy" and "tears," destined to not

327 Bohumil Hrabal, *Dancing Lessons for the Advanced in Age* [1964], trans. Michael Henry Heim (New York: Harcourt, Brace & Co., 1995), 6–7.

be broken until Christ arrives, and capable of bearing the unjust sufferings inflicted on him until death, without asking for reparation. This kind of choice is "difficult to get one's head round," not only for parish priests but also for jurists – not excluding, if I may say so, judges.

Auto da fé: a law without a world / a world without a law

In a 1973 essay, Elias Canetti recounts the genesis of his (only) novel, *Auto da fè.*[328] On 15 July 1927, Canetti reads a newspaper headline while sitting at a café in Vienna:

> I can still feel the indignation that overwhelmed me when I took hold of the Reichpost; it had a gigantic headline: 'A Just Verdict'. There had been shooting in Burgenland, workers had been killed. The court had acquitted the murderers. The judgment was designated, no, trumpeted, as 'a just verdict' in the organ of the government party.[329]

Canetti adds that

> It was that mockery of any sense of justice rather than the acquittal itself that triggered an enormous excitement in the workers of Vienna. From all parts of the city, the workers marched in closed processions to the Palace of Justice, which with its sheer name embodied injustice for them.[330]

The origin of the feeling of injustice does not lie in the outcome of the trial, which was held in a courthouse whose name is, in itself, evocative of injustice, but in the propagandist attempt to subvert the feeling of justice. The injustice of formal law and therefore of the trial does not outrage the workers because it is connatural to the law itself, which is not made by them nor for them:[331] it represents a natural

328 Elias Canetti, "The First Book: Auto da Fè" [1973], trans. Joachim Neugroschel, in Elias Canetti, *The Conscience of Words. Essays* (New York: Seabury Press, 1979), 203–213.

329 Canetti, "The First Book," 205. The episode referred to by Canetti concerns the riots in Schattendorf on 30 January 1927 between militants of the Social Democratic Party and the nationalist paramilitary grouping Frontkämpfervereinigung Deutsch-Österreichs. Three members of the latter were charged with double murder, and later acquitted in self-defense.

330 Canetti, "The First Book," 205.

331 Jurisdiction is an alien authority, like the Police Headquarters before which, a few years earlier (and with the interval of the war) Švejk, not yet a "good soldier", had appeared: "The spirit of an alien authority pervaded the building of the police headquarters – an authority which was ascertaining how enthusiastic the population were for war. With the exception of a few people who were ready to admit that they were sons of a nation which had to bleed for interests completely

outcome. Indignation is triggered because the government and the media outlet subservient to it disawoved the feeling of justice. Justice, therefore, does not lie in law. It cannot be in the law, or in the buildings that herald its name, but in the world, or rather in the feeling of the world of those who invoke it because they feel the need for it (a feeling that cannot be eliminated, whether or not they are aware of the ectoplasmic nature of justice).

The crowd sets fire to the Palace of Justice, an uprising breaks out and ends with ninety killings. Canetti recounts being dragged along by the crowd (to which he dedicates his best-known essay), transforming himself into a part of the throng, which absorbed him into itself completely. Nevertheless, he retains a singular ability to "grasp all the concrete details occurring before my eyes."

One of these scenes is narrated in detail:

> in a side street, not far from the burning Palace of Justice, but still off to the side, a man, very sharply distinguished from the crowd, stood with high flung arms, wailing and moaning over and over again: 'The files are burning! All the files!.' 'Better than people!,' I told him, but that didn't interest him, all he could think of was the files. It occurred to me that he might have some connection to the files, an archivist, he was inconsolable. He struck me as funny, even in this situation. But he also annoyed me. 'They have been shooting down people!' I said angrily, 'and you carry on about files!'. He looked at me as if I weren't there and repeated with a moan: 'The files are burning! All the files!.' He was stationed to the side, but it was not undangerous for him, his lament was not to be missed, I too had heard it.[332]

The distinction between "the files," where the law is, and "the people," where the aspiration for justice is – as well as the capacity to destroy and kill (the tendency to alternate wicked behavior with tears, of which Hrabal speaks) – could not be clearer. Moreover, the "man of the files" is both a humorous figure, insofar as he despairs about paper rather than about humans and is capable of arousing indignation due to his insensitivity to tragedy and injustice, but he is also worthy of some respect when he exposes himself to danger (albeit "to the side") to defend something which, for him at least, has value, and which may indeed not be entirely without value.

The episode is clearly reflected in the structure of *Auto da fé,* with its division into three chapters. "A Head without a World" recounts the existence of the "man of books," the erudite sinologist Peter Kien, who lives exclusively in the company of

alien to it, police headquarters presented the finest collection of bureaucratical beasts of prey, to whom gaols and gallows were the only means of defending the existence of the twisted clauses of the law": Jaroslaw Hašek, *The Good Soldier Šveik and His Fortunes in the World War* [1921–1923], trans. Cecil Parrott (London: Penguin, 1973), 44.

332 Canetti, "The First Book," 206.

books, in a studied attempt to do without the world and those who inhabit it. Kien marries his wife Therese for the sake of utility, and in the fallacious belief that he could lead her to somehow loving the books. In "Headless World," Kien is thrown out of the house by Therese. He is forced to face the world, which is symbolized by a pawnshop (the Theresianum ...), a place of venality. Kien tries to save the books from those who would offer them as pawns, and from the "pig," hidden on the sixth floor of the building, who will devour them. In the world, Kien falls victim to sordid and unscrupulous thugs and dealers, violent policemen, profiteers and brutes of all sorts. Finally back in his flat, Kien now has "The World in the Head": but the coexistence of "books" and life experience will prove to be impossible. In the last chapter Kien's self-deception is heralded by the burning of the Theresianum, which had actually been anticipated by one of the rumors that had arisen from the brawl in which Kien had been involved in during one of his visits to the mount, animated by an attempt to save the books[333]:

> On the sixth floor of the Theresianum the beasts are bidding each other good night; there they keep thousands of books unjustly in durance, tens of thousands, against their free will, guiltless, what can they do against the hog, cut off from terra firma, close under the BROILING attic roof, starving, condemned, condemned to the devouring FLAMES.[334]

Kien hears the cries of the books, of his own books; he realizes that he is powerless, that he cannot hope for help, not even from his brother and illustrious psychiatrist, thanks to whom he had managed to regain possession of his house and books. All that remains for him at this point is to acknowledge the inevitability of the fire, the *need* for the books to burn, and he with them. The world "cannot stay" in the head, it cannot be faced with the head alone: with its destructive force, it will prevail anyway. The parallel between the books imprisoned in the Theresianum and the files in the courthouse is crystal clear. Kien's grief is similar to that of the "man of the files," and his desperate plea for the innocence of the books suggests that the man who despaired outside the courthouse might have uttered a similar plea for his files. It is not the fault of books that "hogs" and fire exist. It is not the fault of law that human beings are unjust, and files burn to atone for this injustice. Perhaps, books and files, and the law they both contain, have a value and a beauty of their own. That is why both Kien and the "man of the files" are not just humorous figures. However, books and files cannot contain the world, exhaust it,

333 Elias Canetti, *Auto da fé* [1935], trans. C.V. Wedgwood (New York: Stein and Day), 291: "The unemployed are starving. What's he want with a pearl necklace. String 'em up I say! Mean it too. The whole lot of them. And the Theresianum too. Burn it! Make a nice blaze!"

334 Canetti, *Auto da fé*, 460.

or claim to shape it. The law without a world succumbs to the world without law, and the world is too big and ever-changing (Kien would say "bad") to be in the law.

The antinomy between "world" and "'head," between humans and books – files (between "world" and "law") burns at the stake, and in the final laugh of Kien, who "climbs up to the sixth step, looks down on the fire and waits. When the flames reached him at last, he laughed out loud, louder that he had ever laughed in all his life."[335] Kien's laughter, a far cry from Zarathustra's, is pure surrender to the (tragic) comedy of existence.

335 Canetti, *Auto da fé*, 464. In the chapter, the number six symbolically recurs.

Chapter 6
Who am I and where do I live? Persona, law and laughter

Italian by law: Totò and Fernandel

As we have seen so far, for Conan Doyle and Aristophanes the law is not able to guarantee justice because of a structural weakness in the system; for Stan Laurel and Oliver Hardy it is a judge's lack of professionalism and ethics which undermine the *principium* of justice; while with some obvious differences, for Dovlatov and Marshall it is not always easy to distinguish criminals from innocents, and law-abiding citizens from a law that does not respect citizens. Now, there is another aspect worth investigating from a narrative point of view that was already explained in the previous chapter, namely when the law legitimizes itself to tell us who we are or what we are not.

When authors start writing a story, they first give an identity to their protagonists, such as a gender and a nationality: in facts, a social frame of reference is established in which the readers can project or recognize themselves. In particular, since a name is the keeper of memories, it allows the character to become a *unique* representative, to be mentionable and recognizable.[336] In life, through one's name an individual becomes a "person," i. e., the mask that will make that person intelligible to the world throughout his or her existence. In this regard, it is worth remembering that being given a name is a right recognized by the United Nations Convention on the Rights of the Child, Article 7 § 1: "The child shall be registered immediately after birth and shall have the right from birth to a name, the right to acquire a nationality and, as far as possible, the right to know and be cared for by his or her parents." And also in Article 8 § 1: "States Parties undertake to respect the right of the child to preserve his or her identity, including nationality, name and family relations as recognized by law without unlawful interference."

Analogous principles are also enshrined in other international conventions and national codes.[337] Name and nationality thus imply a principle of belonging

336 Roland Barthes, "Proust et les Noms," in *Le degré zéro de l'écriture* suivi de *Nouveaux essais critiques* (Paris: Seuil, 1972), 89 ff.

337 See also The United Nations High Commissioner for Human Rights, http://www2.ohchr.org/english/law/ccpr.htm (last accessed in December 2009): "Article 24:2 – Every child shall be registered immediately after birth and shall be given a name."

https://doi.org/10.1515/9783111286778-008

that places the child not only within a community, but also within a cultural system that makes them a subject of rights and duties. It is thus through this procedure that a child becomes part of the *polis,* that is to say, part of a system of beliefs, symbols and rules that pre-exist the birth, and which will define the ethnicity, religion, sex, language, traditions, historical and cultural heritage which, in turn, will negotiate the child's social net of relationships from the moment of birth onward.[338]

On first sight, therefore, it would seem that the acquired right to a name and nationality are guaranteed from birth as a legal, cultural and *natural* act. However, literature, cinema and life show us that things are different and can take on more disturbing aspects unless a sense of humor intervenes to make us accept the unacceptable. One example is the film *The law is the law* (*La loi c'est la loi*), directed by Christian -Jaque in 1958. The film stars Totò as the Italian smuggler Giuseppe La Paglia, and Fernandel, alias Ferdinand Pastorelli, a French border guard by profession.

Right from the start, the two protagonists are portrayed as both friends and enemies, as they are involved in a role-play between guards and thieves which always ends in a light-hearted verbal diatribe where, in any case, the rules are always respected. Indeed, at the very beginning of the narrated events, we see the gendarme leading Totò to prison at the end of a French veteran's parade, amidst merry children, fanfares, the applause of the crowd and the head of the gendarmes scolding the dutiful Pastorelli because he could have postponed the arrest until later. The festive context immediately places us in a comedy.

The story takes place in a small mountain village on the French-Italian border, where the two communities live peacefully, albeit with some light-hearted rivalry. The criminals are never too bad and the righteous never good enough, as can be seen both in the figure of the smuggler, who is a nice good family man who has married Pastorelli's first wife, and in the figure of the gendarme, who behaves fairly and rigorously with La Paglia, but is never considered competent enough by his superiors. The former, moreover, describes himself to his children as a "poor man who works all day honestly to defraud the law," as if to say that a professional criminal can also be a good man, a worker with his own particular deontology. La Paglia is an honest fraudster, an oxymoron in short. Although his behavior is neither morally nor legally justifiable, we do sympathize with Totò, but this is very different from the perverse sharing of

---

338 See Benedetto Vecchi, *Zigmunt Bauman, Intervista sull'identità,* trans. F. Galimberti (Rome and Bari: Laterza, 2009), 80. See also Zygmunt Bauman, *Identity: Conversations with Benedetto Vecchi* (London: Polity Press, 2004).

human nature we have just experienced with the women in *Chicago.* Despite the fact that La Paglia buys and sells alcohol illegally, his trade does not have real victims but rather co-conspirators, who know exactly what they are doing when they buy his goods – so much so that not even the head of the *gendarmerie* considers the Italian smuggler dangerous. He knows that La Paglia will not run away and needs that 'job' to support his family. Maybe the captain himself is one of his clients! Up to this point, the principle of reality prevails over a law which seems to be taken seriously only by Pastorelli, for whom the violation of the principle of legality comes first and is therefore more important than any charge or crime. From the very first scenes of the film, the impression given is that the law is not necessary to regulate common living in the village. It goes without saying that the film director winks at the spectator and lures him into embracing this dimension of peaceful conviviality, even if it is not exactly in accordance with the rules of law. The world depicted is based more on shared values than on the compliance with or fear of a sanctioning and punitive law.

The narrative turning point comes when Pastorelli discovers that he was born in the kitchen rather than in the bedroom of the hotel across which the state line passes. Suddenly, at the age of 45, the upstanding French gendarme learns that he is Italian and therefore has no right to work as a border guard, and even less to stop the scoundrel Giuseppe, who straight away escapes arrest. The legal status acquired as a child at birth through registration at the registry office and which determined his place in the community is suddenly denied to Pastorelli. He officially ceases to be what he has always been, and what he feels he is. From being a subject of law, he becomes an object of law. It is at this point that comedy[339] intervenes to create a strong distortion between the exceptional nature of this discovery, the immediate repercussions on the arrest (Totò unexpectedly gets the better of justice, because the very representative of the law is actually more of an outlaw than the smuggler himself!), and the overwhelming rigor of the principle of causality expressed by the Italian scoundrel during a surreal conversation that makes Pastorelli aware of his national 'non-identity.' The drama of the gendarme is treated so light-heartedly that it clashes with the latter's strict respect for the institutions:

> LA PAGLIA: You're not even French ... so ...
> PASTORELLI: I'm not French?
> (brawl)
> [...]

339 See Emilio Banfi, "Il linguaggio comico: tra pragmatica e strategie linguistiche," in *Sei lezioni sul linguaggio comico,* ed. Emilio Banfi (Trento: Univ. of Trento, 1995), 17–70, 21.

LA PAGLIA: One moment, let's think about it. So, you were born in Italy, of Italian mother and unknown father. What are you?
PASTORELLI: French
LA PAGLIA: Come on, give me a break: I-T-A-L-I-A-N. Eh eh.
PASTORELLI: Are you crazy, Italian?
LA PAGLIA: Because maybe it's a disgrace to be Italian?
PASTORELLI: No, it's not a disgrace to be Italian. I respect and greet the Italians (he says addressing directly two soldiers and not the other patrons of the bar).
PASTORELLI, turning to La Paglia: So because I was born in a kitchen I would be Italian, so if I had been born in a stable I would be a horse!
LA PAGLIA: No, you would be a donkey!
PASTORELLI: A donkey?
(brawl)
[...]
PASTORELLI: Be thankful I'm in uniform otherwise ... poor Giuseppe.
THE STRAW: Who, moi?

It is clear that poor Pastorelli does not identify with Italian citizens, whom he only respects when they wear a uniform. The linguistic paradoxes, to which the conversation is entrusted, have the advantage of preventing the situation from degenerating into an attitude of aggression against a people on the basis of commonplaces and *clichés*. This inherently contradictory situation places the two enemies on the same level for the first time: the guardian of the law and guarantor of the French state's power finds himself likened to an oxymoron-man. Once again we find ourselves facing a degradation of power, as happened with Brassens' judge and the one in *Do Detectives Think?*, but in this case it is the law that delegitimizes its representative, a condition that would be unbearable if the comic dimension did not step in.

Contrary to the linguistic technicalities of the law, which make it an abstruse subject that is difficult for a citizen to understand, the film opens up a clash on a linguistic level between legal rigor and comic paradox. As we will see, the dialogues are all marked by an overturning of the relations between form and meaning. Elements of novelty and surprise, which arise from the dystonia between the exceptionalism of an utterance and the ordinariness of an answer or vice versa, aim at breaking behavioral patterns and predictable models, thus provoking laughter in the spectator.[340] In the dialogue we have just seen, where Pastorelli suggests – absurdly and provocatively – that if he had been born in a stable he would have been a horse, La Paglia takes his words literally and uses them to his own advantage to discredit his interlocutor. For Pastorelli, obviously, there is no coincidence between the truth statement and the fact, but

340 See Banfi, "Il linguaggio comico: tra pragmatica e strategie linguistiche," 21.

Totò's comic performance exploits this incongruity, so much so that Fernandel reacts by getting angry: as Bergson maintains, the subject who mocks wishes to humiliate the object of derision. In Pastorelli's world a paradox contains a truth (the truth of law), whereas La Paglia consciously plays with the possibilities offered by language to mock the authorities (rather than the man). A paradox within a paradox is created. Here it is interesting to see how comedy never loses sight of the truth, even though the final aim may be either to bring out the incongruity of reality with respect to common sense and what is right (how can a man divest himself of his cultural identity from one moment to the next?); or a perlocutionary act aimed at creating an effect that may be provocative and potentially unjust, such as the feeling of anger. Ferdinand wants to make his enemy Giuseppe understand his position, but the other mocks precisely this communicative intention: Giuseppe exploits the paradoxical situation to demote the powers of authority even below his own criminal status, since Pastorelli does not legally exist and therefore has no 'value' (so much so that he can be considered nothing less than an Italian!). The insensitivity shown by Giuseppe is purely comic, since it would not be possible to laugh at the victim if one did not first anesthetize the heart.[341]

Since Fernandel is thoroughly law-abiding and aware of the institutional responsibility of authority – to the point of being an emblem of the righteous man – he does not find anything funny in what is happening to him. For him, authority and law coincide, and do not correspond to the privileges of power as they did for Philocleon. He feels fully part of a social body when he wears the uniform and acts in the name of the law: he wears his truth (identity and existence) along with the uniform. When Pastorelli is forced to accept that being born in Italy from an Italian mother and an unknown father means being Italian, even if one has been registered at the French registry office, his ordeal begins. From one day to the next, poor Ferdinand loses his national and cultural identity along with his job, but he is also seen as a bigamist and a draft-dodger, and for this reason is mocked by his fellow citizens.

Suddenly, he becomes the unlikely victim of an unstoppable series of harmful consequences, and this only because the statutory law, which tells him who he is and, above all, who he is not, is strictly and unquestionably enforced. During a conversation between him and the two chiefs of the French gendarmerie and the Italian carabinieri – both of whom do not want Pastorelli on their territory – he asks whether, in their opinion, he exists or not. The unanimous answer is "Not before the law": how is it possible that the law denies such evidence?

---

341 Bergson, *Laughter*, 5.

> PASTORELLI: So, if I've understood correctly, for you the existence of a man doesn't count at all. Only the identity card counts.
> FRENCH: The law must not be discussed, especially by its guardians!
> ITALIAN: Exactly, that's how it is in Italy, in France and everywhere else!
> PASTORELLI: I get it, the world goes on with law, papers and regulations. Soon you will need a permit to live, duly stamped in order to breathe.
> CUSTOMERS TOGETHER: Ehhh....
> PASTORELLI: All right, I admit I'm guilty. Guilty of being born in a kitchen where some imbeciles have made a frontier pass. La *frontiére*, nice invention.
> ITALIAN: Oh no! Now you are exaggerating
> FRENCH: You are insulting the frontier, you are a customs officer!
> PASTORELLI: I'm not a customs officer anymore. I'm nothing anymore, you see, I'm nothing anymore.

This scene recalls another one described in Flann O'Brien's extravagant novel *The Third Policeman*,[342] in which, during a conversation with Sergeant Pluck, it emerges that the protagonist is "invisible to the law" because he has no name: he cannot denounce anyone or avail himself of any rights, and yet he can be sentenced to death:[343]

> "Do you recall that you told me that I was not here at all because I had no name and that my personality was invisible to the law? [...] Then how can I be hanged for a murder, even if I did commit it and there is no trial or preliminary proceedings, no caution administered and no hearing before a Commissioner of the Public Peace?"[344]

After careful consideration, Sergeant Pluck replies that since he has no name, he is not *de facto* a person and can therefore be hanged without fear of any retaliation: "The particular death you die is not even a death (which is an inferior phenomenon at best) only an insanitary abstraction in the backyard [...]."[345] In both stories, the lack of a legally recognized identity transforms the territory into a no-man's land, where legal principles fail along with common sense and the principle of reality, which reduces even the death of a man to a minor fact, to an unhealthy abstraction in the backyard.

The code seems to be an evil authority that not only cannot be questioned ("The law must not be discussed"), but that leaves no room for common sense and even less for the network of identity and existential relationships woven by

342 Flann O'Brien, *The Third Policeman* [1939–1940] (London: Harper Collins, 2007).
343 Patrizia Nerozzi and Mara Logaldo, "Intertextuality and Parody of Law in *The Third Policeman* by Flann O'Brien: a Literary and a Linguistic Reading," in *Pólemos* 10.2 (2016): 431–452, 103.
344 O'Brien, *The Third Policeman*, 103.
345 O'Brien, *The Third Policeman*, 105.

a person over the years as citizen and, for Pastorelli, even more as an enforcer of order. He is ideally expelled from the *polis.* He loses his political power, and his life enters into chaos: he no longer has any recognized cultural reference points, but a nationality that he does not feel as his own, so much so that he calls himself "a fake."

In this case, the law has not only proved unable to uphold respect for human dignity (and perhaps fundamental rights) as well as the rights protected by the United Nations, but it has even denied the citizen the possibility of narrating himself by establishing congruous and plausible relations with the rest of the community. Following a disjunctive logic, the law has thrown him into an apparently unquestionable indeterminacy; it has made him a barbarian in spite of himself, that is, it has officially declared him Other than himself. Heedless of evidence, the law assumes the right to 'validate' a (juridical) subject and a human being at the same time, decreeing what is authentic and what is not. In this case, the film confronts us with the fact that if, on the one hand, the Western legal tradition recognizes the quality of legal subjects holding inviolable rights, on the other, we have no choice but to accept the identity decided for us by the legal system into which we are born. For a man like Pastorelli, officialdom has no appeal, it leaves him no way out. The film demonstrates in all its drama just how artificial and traumatic the rule of law is, if comedy were not to intervene to question it and bring it back into the realm of the *bonum et aequum.*

The inefficient law enforcement of the beginning is countered by a rigorous and uncompromising practice of law, which manifests itself on the linguistic and dialogic scale. First of all, it should be noted that the film undermines the meaning of the words "nation" and "nationality," which are used in a parodic fashion as a meeting/clashing point for two different fields of law. Smuggling, as the import/export of illegal goods between different countries, initially regulates the interpersonal dynamics between customs officer and smuggler, between justice and lawlessness, for the protection of the national economic heritage. Subsequently, the idea of the 'nation' turns into a question of personal rights which, among its first effects, delegitimizes the uniform worn by the protagonist, as the ultimate sign of belonging to a legal and value system. Whereas comic favors the polydiscursive character of reality, the law severely limits it by relegating its members to inexorable logic and terminological rigor, as happens to Pastorelli when, in accordance with the law, he is unreasonably asked to prove his nationality by means of his birth certificate: "The administration is not obliged to lend faith to the words of individuals, but only to their certificates, duly stamped and endorsed."[346] In the film, the dialogues are designed so that what happens to Pastorelli does not satisfy the conditions of truth expressed by the articles of law. However, the rigidity of the principle of causality demonstrated by Totò earlier does not correspond to an equally rigorous manifestation of logical on the part of the law. The contrast between the logic of reason and administration and the logic of imagination makes the spectator laugh; the latter recognizes that the paradigm of the '*just* law' has been subverted, and thus the practice of interpreting the new meaning begins.

The *weakness* of Pastorelli from a legal and social point of view emerges in his difficulty to express discomfort verbally. The *injustice*, on the contrary, is expressed precisely by continuous and bothersome linguistic acts which will be resolved, as we shall see, in the tautology 'the law is the law' used to underline how there is no way out for the victim. It is as if Pastorelli's absurd condition did not have a linguistic statute capable of describing his tragic experience and thus attaining justice. Apparently, this case brings to mind another film – *The Terminal* – directed by Steven Spielberg in 2004 and starring Tom Hanks. The plot was inspired by the true story of Mehran Karimi Nasseri, who was forced to live in Terminal 1 of Paris' Charles De Gaulle airport for 18 years due to an anomalous bureaucratic issue related to his status as a political refugee. There is nothing funny about this latter case, but it can perhaps be said that in both situations, the legislator had not foreseen the exception to the rule and was not prepared to rectify the anomaly, at least by using common sense. In both cases, the system proves to be rigidly codified and closed, mainly because the protagonists are not willing to deviate from the written law. Perhaps this is also why we find La Paglia and his good-natured attempts to defraud the state endearing. This point reminds us in some ways of what happens also in *The Hound of the Baskervilles* and the destructive strictness of the judicial system, as discussed above.

The fact that there is no legal loophole in the film is a source of laughter for us viewers. The more we recognize the integrity, correctness and respect for the law by the good gendarme, the more incongruous (or even Kafkaesque) the injustice inflicted on him appears to us. The spectators are able to laugh at Pastorelli's misadventures only because they can laugh at the juridical system to which

346 Even acquiring a certificate in accordance with the law is not always easy due to the public administration, as Asterix and Obelix show us when they try to get the A38 Pass. The task constitutes one of 12 challenges that the two Gauls must complete in the classical period of ancient Rome. Available online: https://www.youtube.com/watch?v=RatpMrD5aeM&t=5s (last access in January 2020).

they themselves may be victims. They laugh at a system of judgment, of stereotypes, of false syllogisms.[347]

The comedy revolves around a lawsuit filed *ex officio* at the bar or in the street with a defendant who is innocent, but guilty by the people for something he could not have done originally, i. e., registering *himself* at the wrong registry office at the time of his birth, or which *he* did in complete good faith afterwards. All this happens in a whirlwind of the continuous overturning of the truth, of climaxes and anti-climaxes, of illusions and disillusions,[348] which come about because everyone believes they know how to read and interpret the Code, or because they pretend to know how to do so in *bad faith* or out of *opportunism*, against a man who is deprived of the word because he is deprived *a priori* of legitimacy. As Seneca teaches us, Pastorelli needed a good lawyer who could speak for him, code in hand!

The film also features the arrogant figure of the legislator, who shows that he knows the law very well:

> MEMBER OF PARLIAMENT: Until there was a court ruling he was French (... now) he risks being arrested for usurpation of identity: forgery and use of forgery.
> PASTORELLI: But are you really sure?
> MP: Do you want me not to know the law? It was me who did it!
> PASTORELLI: You could do it better. A law that makes an idiot out of a man who only follows his conscience ...

The writing of a new law is an act of abstraction that aims to address abstract cases of crimes, or even to regulate actions and behavior that only potentially exist yet. But a poorly written or poorly conceived law – as for example when it has to adhere to a political compromise – annihilates the sense of justice and law. The law should be an act of political and civil responsibility generated by reason, but it is reason itself that should come to our aid when law and order fail. On the contrary, against all reason, in the film the law proves to be a point of reference for everyone; everyone relies on the law to assert *their own* will and authority, although this is done without discernment or good faith.[349] The script suggests

347 Salmon, *I meccanismi dell'umorismo*, 67.

348 Cicero excludes over-loved objects from laughter and speaks of the disappointed expectation by referring to the misunderstanding as a source of comedy, into which we fall when we expect something while finding something else. Specifically, these disillusions make Pastorelli's character weaker and weaker in our eyes and therefore more and more easily attacked by his enemies.

349 The foolishness of the law can also be seen in the episode of the gold watch in *The Third Policeman* where we read:

> "I came here to inform you officially about the theft of my American gold watch." [...]
> "Why should anybody steal a watch when they can steal a bicycle?" [...]

that even the law, like any other text, constitutionally contains its weakness within itself since the *interpretation* of the law can make the original text and the intention of its authors a mere hypostasis.

In point of fact, the tragi-comic adventures of the protagonist underline how law, when not enforced according to principles of humanity and fairness, becomes a very powerful weapon against the citizen and the community. We expect a law to guarantee *humanitas,* that is the dignity of the individual, their personality, education and freedom in observance of shared values, just as, in observance of the law's value (a civic principle more than a mere rule), Pastorelli had always tried to fight crime in the name of French law. It was precisely his professional and personal integrity that damaged him because, as soon as the opportunity arose, those who had the power to decide, i. e. the mayor and a number of officials, applied the rules by following a *literal* interpretation of the code, in the name of a social interest that appears to be more *humorous* to us the more it is *convenient* for those in power.

It can be noted that the original title of the film in French, *La Loi c'est la loi,* emphasizes the duty to respect the law, even against one's will. Obviously it is a tautology, and it is worth remembering how for Wittgenstein a tautology is unconditionally true and describes the scaffolding of the world, or rather presents it. Specifically, the law manifests itself as the symbol of the structure on which reality is founded, a symbol captured at the point of its dissolution.[350] The impossibility of defining the Law is also taken up by W. H. Auden in the poem "Law like Love":

> "Law, says the judge as he looks down his nose,
> Speaking clearly and most severely,
> Law is as I've told you before,
> Law is as you know I suppose,

"Who ever heard of a man riding a watch down the road or bringing a sack of turf up to his house on the crossbar of a watch?"

"I did not say the thief wanted my watch to ride it," I expostulated." "Very likely he had a bicycle of his own and that is how he got away quietly in the middle of the night" (TP, 63).

"I know what you mean," he said. "But the law is an extremely intricate phenomenon. If you have no name you cannot own a watch and the watch that has been stolen does not exist and when it is found it will have to be restored to its rightful owner. If you have no name you possess nothing and you do not exist and even your trousers are not on you although they look as if they were from where I am sitting. On the other separate hand you can do what you like and the law cannot touch you" (TP, 64). See Nerozzi and Logaldo, "Intertextuality and Parody of Law in *The Third Policeman,*" 435.

350 Nerozzi and Logaldo, "Intertextuality and Parody of Law in *The Third Policeman,*" 450.

> Law is but let me explain it once more,
> Law is The Law."[351]

The poem tells us how different people – the priest, the old man, the young man … – see the law. In this stanza in particular, the man of law cannot explain what the law is except, indeed, with a tautology, leaving the supreme ideals of justice hanging in a metaphysical *vacuum*. While it should only be the law that knows the difference between good and evil (what is just), in practice it proves to be ineffable, yet it is accepted the same way as Love is accepted:[352]

> Like love we don't know where or why,
> Like love we can't compel or fly,
> Like love we often weep,
> Like love we seldom keep.[353]

According to Celsus, the law should always strive to find normative, hermeneutic and implementing solutions capable of satisfying those needs of balancing opposing interests, whereas on the contrary, the poor French border guard has everyone against him: the authority who lays down the law – Code in hand – does not accept a (fair) cross-examination:

> OFFICER: Reading: "Art 145 of the Penal Code 'The civil registrar who knowingly makes a false declaration will be liable under the law etc. etc. etc. etc."
> PASTORELLI: Why "etcetera etcetera"?
> OFFICIAL: Please listen: "you will be liable to 5 to 10 years of hard labour."
> PASTORELLI: No.
> OFFICER: You know better than me: the law…
> PASTORELLI: …is the law.

The fact that articles of law are read or recited means that the written discourse enters the oral language without being re-encoded. In this way, formal correctness depersonalizes events, which once again become the abstraction of a crime: a question of justice and law becomes bureaucracy. Pastorelli stops being a man to become a case, a case in point, an abstraction. From subject, he becomes object;

351 W. H. Auden, "Law Like Love" [1939], in *Collected Shorter Poems 1927–1957* (London: Faber & Faber, 1969), 155.

352 See Daniela Carpi, "'Law and…': A Proposal for Further Interdisciplinary Approaches," in *Recht und Literature im Zwischenraum/Law and Literature in-Between*, eds. Christian Hiebaum, Susanne Knaller and Doris Pichler (Berlin: transcript, 2015), 105–117.

353 W. H. Auden, "Law, say the gardeners is the Sun" (1939).

the citizen with a name and nationality, rights and duties becomes a *mere* legal entity. This act is also manifested verbally in the rhythm of the sentence, which changes as the legal statement is recited. The content becomes mere form but, as mentioned in the first chapter of this volume, law needs seriousness to be believed and respected. However, in doing so, the script deprives legal language of its solemn aura and turns it into an object of parody in an alternating high and low register.

The previous lines emphasize how mockery acts on the recipients to confirm stereotyped patterns, which in this particular case is also highly disconcerting. The confrontation between the citizen and the law becomes a conflict between the citizen and the authority, which does not show respect for the fate of a fellow citizen. But just as the desire to enforce the principle of fairness proves to be a very tortuous path for Pastorelli, the bad faith and lies of the city authorities are hidden in the folds of the language that humor emphasizes. One must, however, distinguish the comic attitude of La Paglia, who is aware of being an outlaw but esteems his rival, from that of the gendarme's real enemies, namely the mayor and his councilors, who use the book of law as if it were a weapon. The latter also enjoy making fun of Pastorelli, but above all they want to hurt him, humiliate him, corner him, demonstrating not a carnivalesque wickedness, but an unquestionable prejudice that can be understood as a form of torture. While carnival usually ends after a few days, on the contrary, the city authorities want to eliminate Pastorelli forever. The sneer of authority is demonstrated in its immense monstrosity, emblematic of the moral degradation of the guardians of the law.[354] Perhaps only a lawyer would have been able to guarantee justice, testifying to the fact that jurisprudence is not for everyone, but only for professionals who know the rules and know how to demand respect for them.

Although specular, these two examples show how the law proves incapable of fulfilling its task of satisfying the needs of humans, condemning a person to a condition of disorder, discomfort and repression of individual will: *humanitas* vs *aequitas*. Only the lightness introduced by comedy allows the spectator to endure a condition of strong ethical and moral ambiguity, before the legal one. The rules of civil coexistence are annihilated by an abuse of power cloaked in strictness

354 See Charles Baudelaire, "De l'essence du rire et généralement Du comique dans les arts plastiques" (1855), in *Flowers of Evil and Other Works: A Dual-Language Book* (New York: Dover Publication Inc., 1992), 170–183, 176: "J'ai dit qu'il y avait symptôme de faiblesse dans le rire; et, en effet, quel signe plus marquant de débilité qu'une convulsion nerveuse, un spasme involontaire comparable à l'éternuement, et causé par la vue du malheur d'autrui?"

and obtuse legalism. In reality, what has been called the '*vacuous* disguised as legal' is represented here.

Although nothing about the law and its practice is changed, order and the truth about Pastorelli's identity are restored by Giuseppe who manages to discover that the innkeeper, responsible for having registered Ferdinand at the French registry office at the time of his birth, had in fact lied about the border line passing a few meters further away, just to make his hotel more attractive to tourists. Giuseppe thus proves that Pastorelli was really born in France and that it is the border line that is misplaced, contrary to common opinion and the groundless beliefs of the border authorities. It is thus La Paglia who shouts to everyone "Ferdinand is French!"

The film shows that there seems to be no way out of the system's distortion or human malice, and questions the very nonsense of a legal rationality that, in technical language, claims to shape the world and define it in a definitive and unappealable way. Just as Leopardi wondered what the real necessity of law was, the law of which Ferdinand is victim is absolutely arbitrary and unjust, especially since it is going after someone who is totally respectful of the law. It is also curious to note that while the law and the authorities are picking on poor Ferdinand, no one really seems to be interested in Giuseppe La Paglia's dealings. Once again, we could define such an attitude as non-moral and totally incongruous for a rule of law. However, it is precisely this drift of justice that makes us laugh, even though the injustice suffered by Pastorelli is clear.

Persepolis by Marjane Satrapi, or an innocent gaze on the law

When the *bonum et aequum* is imposed by law because the law is guided first and foremost by a religious belief, the sharing of common values in the community gives way to the *law of good*, a good that is imposed as a universal and immutable principle in time. This is the main theme of *Persepolis*, an autobiographical graphic novel in four volumes published by Marjane Satrapi in 2000. The comic book[355] tells the story of the protagonist's life from 1979, the year of the Islamic revolution in Iran, until some twenty years later when she finally leaves her homeland,

355 Satrapi prefers the word 'comic book' to 'graphic novel' because she believes the former has equal dignity to the latter: "I don't really like the term 'graphic novel'. I think they created this term so that decent people are not afraid of comics. As in, 'Here, this is the kind of comic book that suits us'." Mara Famularo, "Marjane Satrapi e la rivoluzione di *Persepolis*," *Fumettologica* (November 22, 2019). Available online: https://www.fumettologica.it/2019/11/marjane-satrapi-persepolis/ (last access in February 2023).

choosing voluntary exile in Paris. The comic book was an unexpected success when it was first published: it sold about a million copies, was translated into 24 languages, and was made into a film in 2007, written and directed by Vincent Paronnaud in collaboration with Satrapi herself. *Persepolis* is still considered one of the most important contemporary comics and *The Guardian* ranks it 47th among the 100 most representative books of the twenty-first century.[356]

Unlike Christian-Jaque's film, in which we are immediately immersed in a clearly fictitious and at times farcical comedy, in *Persepolis* the principle of reality is applied: all the narrated facts are true, and the personal and family dramas are intertwined with Iranian politics and the historical moment in which the story is set. In many interviews, the author has said that she wrote this book so that she would no longer have to answer all those in the West who asked her how she had lived through the war and the impositions of a theocratic government. However, in the introduction she also writes how, after September 11th:

> [...] the image of this ancient and grandiose civilisation has been inextricably linked to fundamentalism, fanaticism and terrorism. But, as an Iranian who has spent more than half of her life in Iran, I know that this image is far from the truth. That is why writing *Persepolis* was so important to me. I believe that you cannot judge an entire nation by the mistakes of a few extremists. And I don't want to forget all those Iranians who lost their lives in prison to defend their freedom, who died in the war against Iraq, who suffered repression from different regimes, who were forced to leave their families and flee their country. One can forgive but one must not forget.[357]

Far from being a dissident's indictment of her homeland, *Persepolis* is more an act of love for a country that is misunderstood by the West and therefore degraded to an object of prejudice. Since she is neither a historian nor a politician, the author immediately realized that she could only speak of her personal experience in the first person. Perhaps this text constitutes a *manifesto* of the freedom to be what one is: the author refuses to always justify the history and culture of her country to the world and, implicitly, to justify herself and her choices. Yet not even the autobiographical dimension was enough to trigger the writing process:

> When I started drawing the book I was too full of hatred and anger – I would have killed them all! Everyone had to be punished. I wrote a couple of pages in this state and: hell, I was just like them. I was exactly like them and they had won, because they had made me equal to them. So I decided to take my time, to calm down and understand what was happen-

356 "The 100 best books of the 21st century," *The Guardian*, 21 September 2019, https://www.theguardian.com/books/2019/sep/21/best-books-of-the-21st-century (last access in June 2020).
357 Mara Famularo, "Marjane Satrapi e la rivoluzione di *Persepolis*" [my translation].

> ing to me. And that's the moment when you really understand: you don't justify what happened, but you can analyse it better.[358]

If she had drawn ten years earlier, the comic would have described a world sharply divided between good and evil, between the just and the unjust, between the brave and the cowardly, between religious fundamentalists and liberals, whereas reality is complex for Satrapi. *Understanding* and *remembering* are therefore two keys to interpreting her work, which takes the theme of the law far beyond the framework of the narration. Only a detached and distant point of observation allowed her to identify the unique and winning feature of the narrative: namely, that subtle humor which, since childhood, had allowed her both to become accustomed to the conditions of war and to keep her inner critical thinking alive. As we have seen before, the author emphasizes that when all seems lost, the only way to make the unbearable bearable is to laugh about it.[359] Indeed, there are many laughable moments in the book, such as when on the same page Satrapi juxtaposes a vignette in which numerous young Iranians die in the war with their golden key to paradise hanging from their necks, and one in which the protagonist attends her first party with the caption: "Meanwhile I went to my first party, not only did my mother let me go, but she also made me a jumper full of holes and a necklace with chains and nails. Punk rock had arrived."[360]

This juxtaposition not only makes the story of so many poor young men's deaths bearable for the reader ("The key to paradise was for poor people"), but it also gives a sense of how, in the despair of war, one must still find a semblance of 'normality' that gives the impression of being able to overcome pain. Laughter and pleasure are thus once again presented as a form of power and control. After all, the very idea of the golden key, which would open the door to the pleasures of paradise, relies on a similar concept.[361] Besides, in the comic strip the grandmoth-

358 Famularo, "Marjane Satrapi e la rivoluzione di *Persepolis*" [my translation].

359 Marjane Satrapi, *Persepolis I and II: The Story of a Childhood and The Story of a Return* (London: Random House, 2008), 262.

360 Satrapi, *Persepolis I and II*, 102.

361 In the comic strip one manages to smile even at this event. The maid of Marje's family cries one day at work because at school her son received the golden key with which, if he was lucky enough to die in the war, he would open the door to paradise. The desperate mother says that if this is religion, she, as a religious woman, stops believing. Marje's mother makes herself available to talk to the boy about what was actually happening. During the meeting, the woman asks him if he doesn't want to go to college, but his astonishing answer is, pointing his finger at Marje, "I'll marry her!" The scene ends with a slap in the face for the young boy completely lost in himself, and Marje organizing the party. Besides emphasizing how even war is a thing for the poor (martyrdom is more for the rich), the humor conveys a reality in which the meaning

er, who is a key figure in the narrative as we shall see, tells her teenage granddaughter before she leaves for Vienna: "There is nothing worse in this world than rancor and revenge. Try always to keep yourself honest and worthy of yourself." A sense of humor is Satrapi's way of staying true to herself without falling into the snare of those who would want her resentful or vindictive. Humor would therefore have a thaumaturgic power both for the protagonist and for the readers.

There is no doubt that the mastery of passion and vital impulses belongs in an evolutionary stage to maturity, but the book *Persepolis* is the story of a childhood: it tells the story of Marje's life from primary school until she leaves for Vienna in her teens. In this first part of the comic, we see Marje grappling with what she cannot understand, because she is involved in sudden and radical changes in her hitherto happy existence, and because she does not have the cognitive tools to discern it all. Her life of privilege and comforts, as well as intellectual stimuli, is disrupted first of all by the obligation to wear a veil ('Wear it!'[362]).

The cartoon opens with this imposition. The discomfort of complying with the new rule is portrayed in the first vignette by a series of girls placed next to each other and homologated in their headgear. Although the context is not described since the background is completely white, we have to assume they are at school during class hours. However, soon afterwards we see them on the playground using their new veils as if they were toys. The veil, as a symbol of the female role in relationship to the male sex, is objectified by the girls and considered only for what it is: a bulky and warm piece of fabric. It thus happens that within a framework of inflexible behavioral rules, the girls immediately have a physical and creative reaction aimed at satisfying a *pleasure principle.* Through a playful activity they give form and meaning to their new reality, they investigate it without being subjected to it. The girls respond through imagination ('I am the monster of darkness'), by miming punishment ('execution in the name of freedom'), or simply by shouting out their discomfort ('It's too hot!'). The reader can only participate in the game and observe the many ways that object can be interpreted. The sometimes-fierce criticism of a Western observer is replaced by a positive sense of defiance and resistance of imposition and law: a law that appears senseless and that is not agreed upon, but respected in the name of what is *good* and *just*

of life for young people is tied to immediate satisfaction without ample expectation for the future. This lack of temporal perspective also allows illiberal governments to take root and make their way more easily into the most inexperienced minds, compared to what happens with adults who can, on the contrary, establish relationships and recognize more or less positive differences.

362 Satrapi, *Persepolis I and II*, 3.

As a counterpoint, the adults march in the square, opposing the pro-veil faction to the pro-freedom one: freedom becomes the object of desire and contention in the Iranian society of the revolution, and the veil becomes the first symbol of oppression. Far from the playful dimension, women who are against the veil, like Marje's mother, seriously risk incrimination or retaliation. It is a well-known fact that saints and revolutionaries do not laugh! I like to remember Jean Paul Sartre's words about play and freedom:

> Seriousness involves taking the world as one's starting point and attributing more reality to the world than to oneself; or reality to oneself only to the extent one belongs to the world .... It is obvious that the serious man at bottom is hiding from himself the consciousness of his freedom ...Man is serious when he takes himself for an object. ... What indeed is play if not an activity of which man is the first origin, for which man himself sets the rules, and which has no consequences except according to the rules he has set? ... the act is not his own goal for itself, neither does its explicit end represent its goal and its profound meaning; but the function of the act is to make manifest and to present itself the absolute freedom which is the very being of the person.[363]

Therefore, freedom is the primary characteristic of a human being. It is only when the individuals place themselves at the center of their own world, rather than the world in which they are merely an object, that they dictate the rules and are therefore free beings. Not man, woman, child, Iranian, French or American, but the human being (in an existentialist perspective for Sartre) sets its own rules for interaction in society. This principle also envisages a world in which the *bonum et aequum* is uniformly shared and present, but we know that this is not always the case (or even never!), and that is why the law exists to compensate for this absence. The game, conceived as a means for formulating rules of behavior, would thus replace the law in the role of regulator. This act requires the subject to become aware of and responsible for its actions and choices. The French philosopher thus correlates seriousness, freedom and rule, while Satrapi's entire work establishes a bond between seriousness, the constraints imposed by the theocratic government and the principle of freedom and self-determination that are methodically restricted in the name of Islamic morality. Moreover, Sartre's generalization makes us realize that perhaps little girls and their mothers in any country in the world would behave in the same way as the protagonists: although strongly characterized culturally, this comic involves principles that are transnational and transcultural, so much so that any reader can identify with the protagonists in the narrated events.

---

363 Jean Paul Sartre, "Play," in *The Philosophy of Jean Paul Sarte*, ed. R. D. Cumming (New York: Routledge, 1965), 310.

Marje's bewilderment at the events that she was unwillingly involved in, eventually, becomes enriched by her perplexities and doubts. What she does not understand is how to make her idea of God coincide with the veil. In fact, she has a direct relationship with *an* eternal father who is represented with a large white beard. She is also convinced to be a prophetess: the only female prophet in a group of male prophets (of course, any doubts about the suitability of a female prophet come from the men, not the girl).[364] Marje recognizes the validity of all religions and takes what she considers to be the best from each prophet to draw up her own programmatic plan that includes a series of rules based on social equity and goodness, such as: everyone should have a car (her father has a Cadillac, but he is a privileged), servants should eat at the table with their masters (her family's servants do not), no one should suffer physically (her grandmother has bad knees). Once again, two situations that are not comparable – the bloody revolution and the naive goodness of a little girl – represent the key that triggers the comic process: little Satrapi's perception of what is right and how life should be clashes with the adults' ruthlessness. If on the one hand we smile, on the other we cannot help but appreciate her willingness to participate in the collective good. Marje's God is certainly not that of the Ayatollahs' imposing rules. This paradox allows the author to launch a fierce criticism of the Iranian government, so much so that Satrapi has been accused of being Islamophobic by Iranian authorities. To these accusations, Satrapi replies that she is neither a religious commentator nor a political creature, but only an artist. We might add that she is also an artist who wishes to understand and remember. Once again, it is the same principle of reality that is transformed into humor as well as into political and social criticism. Can one really believe that the naive reflections of a young girl can question a power that rules in the name of God?

Nevertheless, in the child's imagination God is soon supplanted by the great revolutionaries: Fidel, Che Guevara, Trotsky and Marx. The desire to fight by taking part in the protest of dissent became clear from the outset, and was to accompany her throughout her life. However, her limited education and experience lead her to make atrocious mistakes, such as when she emulates the bad practices of the guardians of the revolution – who are also influenced by propaganda – by instigating her two friends to punish a classmate because his father is guilty of war crimes; or when she believes the regime's propaganda because she does not have the knowledge needed to understand the complexity of what is being proposed (this underlies, however, how law is also a question of the communication

364 Satrapi, *Persepolis I and II*, 6.

of shared values or truth among citizens). As a matter of fact, the girl is guided by her parents, rather than by the state, the school or the law.

On the one hand the state, consistently embodied in intransigent, threatening, sullen representatives, imposes its own truth and tells young female students what they are and how they should or should not behave: namely, that they are female, Muslim, rebellious, wrong. On the other hand, there are state laws that shape behaviors to ensure the protection of public morals against symbols of decadence such as jewellery, sneakers, American music, parties and so forth. However, the young protagonist establishes a moment of justice when she tells us about the male equivalent of the veil:

> "But, let's be fair. If women faced prison when they refused to wear the veil, it was also forbidden to men to wear neckties (that dreaded symbol of the West). And if women's hair got men excited, the same thing could be said about men's bare arms. And so wearing short-sleeved shirts was also forbidden" [...] "There was kind of justice after all."[365]

Shortly before this, Satrapi gives us two vignettes with the women's and men's dress codes of the revolution: the fundamentalist woman wears a *chador*, the modern woman lets a lock of hair show through the *hijab*. The fundamentalist man wears a beard and a shirt outside his trousers, the progressive man the mustache and a shirt tucked into his trousers. The narrator's two comments are: about the women: "You show your opposition to the regime by letting a few strands of hair show," and for the men: "Islam is more or less against shaving." In the same vein, the mother advises Marje to always reply that she prays during the day, in case someone asks her. The little girl's serious comment is:

> At first it was a little hard, but I learned to lie quickly.
> "I pray five times a day," says a boy
> "Me? Ten or eleven times ... sometimes twelve." says Marji.[366]

The naive simplification of Islam makes us smile, but while the rules of law should encourage a constant renewal of adherence (or wandering) to constitutional values, in Iran the rights that had been won up to 1980 are revoked in the name of an order recognized by many as outdated. The Islamic law represented by Satrapi does not seem to take into account the natural evolution of culture and its core values. Music, fashion and technology are all considered forms of decadence rather than cultural products of a continuously evolving contemporaneity.

---

365 Satrapi, *Persepolis I and II*, 75.
366 Satrapi, *Persepolis I and II*, 75.

Although here it is not possible to go into the merits of Islamic jurisprudence, of which the author does not speak explicitly, it is only possible to record the practical effects of how the Koranic law is enforced in the lives of citizens. In this regard, we must not forget the unbearable practices denounced in the comic strip, such as condemning a young virgin woman to death and forcing her to marry a revolutionary guard before her execution because the law forbids killing a virgin, which is what happens to little Nara in the comic strip. Or the executions of dissidents and their families in the name of divine justice: "We are the deliverers of divine justice."[367] Propaganda conveys these practices by leveraging religion and terror in order to also create social types that are recognizable or classifiable, and therefore easy to execute if necessary.

The guardians of the revolution's aim is to enforce the rule. It is their belief that they are not flawed or wrong, but this is precisely their worst flaw. Their ontology is also their meaning: they are what they mean to themselves and what they have transferred into law. In Iranian society, there is no contradiction, let alone confrontation, but we now know that it is precisely contradiction that gives voice to humor, which in turn makes existence and law tolerable.[368]

A major difference between the film *The Law is the Law* and *Persepolis* lies in the fact that Ferdinand finds himself, for a short time, alone and with an identity in which he does not recognize himself, while the young Satrapi is forced to adapt to values that she does not recognize as her own, but which are treated as Truth by the guardians of the law. In the representation offered, the Islamic state wants to form/create the believer by means of the rule, so that the law becomes a prohibition, a censorship of one's individual freedom not so much in the name of God as of *duty*. Not only that, the Iranian people are also told not to question the legitimacy of the right to command.

Often Marje consciously applies a strategy against her teachers or those who want to impose rules on her, i. e., shouting louder than them, attacking in order to defend herself, in an attempt to break a mechanism of social control and thus cre-

---

367 Satrapi, *Persepolis I and II*, 66.

368 Being a graphic novel, the visual aspect also plays a role in the narrative. Regarding the guardians of the revolution, we must say that they are always portrayed in the act of imposing their authority. Marje's narrative point of view turns these fearful figures into caricatures because of their posture, tone of voice, attitude towards the citizen. The reader does not laugh at these figures, except through the child's reading of them, but at the imposing culture of a totalitarian power. In the presence of these subjects, we do not laugh at human weakness, as with Honoré Daumier's *Men of Justice*, but at the possibility of resisting evil; laughter is a reaction to the desire for autonomy from a power that wants to impose an identity on people. This is how the reader feels superior to the power of these revolutionaries, even though he is aware of the danger of opposing them.

ate a creative chaos that usually sees her winning. Whenever she implements this communication strategy, she warns the readers so that they can share her strategy of concealing power, and she does not run the risk of being assimilated into her tormentors. On the contrary, Marje's sense of rebellion makes her react, and she takes on dangerous attitudes in Iran, such as wearing American clothes, listening to Camel's prog rock or Kim Wilde's bubblegum pop, and sporting pins with Michael Jackson's face, passing him off as Malcolm X. Since all this puts her in serious danger, she is sent away by her parents to study in Vienna.

Once in Europe, she comes up against a revolution made of young people who call themselves anarchists, but who know nothing of what it really means to fight for one's existence and freedom as Uncle Anoosh, and so many other true martyrs of freedom, had done. Weapons and prisons give way to slogans, guitars around bonfires and a few drugs. For Marje, the only way to avoid dictatorial states and laws that, in her opinion, are openly liberticidal, is to get involved in person, to actively express dissent in the streets, to come down from the ivory tower. The reality principle always governs her existence. The protagonist finds herself learning what it means to be an adult without any real guidance, relying on those she meets, but above all clashing with other cultural and racial prejudices that undermine her freedom to express her own identity once again. She herself recounts how, in order to feel part of a community, she had to deprive herself of her original culture and end up as a foreigner everywhere, at home and abroad. It goes without saying that this condition has nothing to do with official and legal declarations of identity, but belongs to the private sphere, a bit like how Ferdinand Pastorelli continued to feel French even though he was Italian, or *almost* Italian, according to his stamped papers.[369]

Marje's time in Vienna was a succession of attempts to be an autonomous person who respected her ideals, but the failures were such that she finally decided to return home. Returning puts her to the test, so much so that she is unable to say anything about herself when she sees what her city has become after four years of war and destruction. While always a rebel, as a young woman Satrapi begins to conform more to Iranian lifestyles, to the point of deciding to marry at a young age in order to have her own love story. But above all, one

---

369 In the comic strip, there is an interesting episode in which the Superior Nun in Vienna of the boarding house where she was staying insults her by telling her that Iranians are all rude, just because she went to the common room to watch an episode of Inspector Derrick while bringing her dinner. The cultural prejudice is evident and the young woman's reaction is not long in coming. Marje insults the nuns and for this she is expelled without even trying to understand the reasons for that aggressive reaction. Satrapi's comment is that all religions have their fundamentalists and their vain truths about the world and people. Satrapi, *Persepolis I and II*, 178 ff.

day she decides to go so far as to denounce an innocent person, in order to not be arrested by the police herself. She explains how describing that careless, irresponsible and wrong behavior allowed her to highlight how fear can lead to seriously wrong conduct. The grandmother will never forgive her for this act, because with this gesture she failed in her dignity, which is what she had advised Marje never to give up. According to Satrapi, her grandmother, who had always been her supporter and fellow rebel, was not a moralist but had a great sense of justice:

> "Do this, it is good, Don't do this, it is bad," but she always told me "Marjane, if you go to a party and you don't talk to anyone, they will say "Who does she think she is," but if you go to a party and start laughing with everyone they will say "Oh, look at this bitch." So, no matter what you do, if people want to talk about you they will talk about you, so do what you think is right. If you don't feel like talking, don't. If you feel like laughing, laugh. Because she had a great sense of justice. And she was not an educated woman. She hardly knew how to read and write, but at the same time, what was the most important to her was justice."[370]

Of course, rather than law, what we are talking about here is a personal sense of what is right, which finds its justification in a type of ethics that is never fundamentalist but rather respectful of other people's will and freedom. Freedom is obviously not understood as the autonomy to do what one wants, but to behave respectfully in regard to one's own aspirations, talents and dignity and those of others. By having an innocent man arrested in her place, Marje had assimilated herself into the overbearing forces of the Iranian revolution and law. She had allowed her ethics to bow to power and its instruments of repression. When Satrapi recounts what happened, she does so while laughing or rather ridiculing a very serious situation, which offends her grandmother even more:

> "And you find that funny?"
> "Don't you?"
> "No, I think that you are a selfish bitch! That's what I think!!! Have you forgotten who your grandfather was? He spent a third of his life in prison for having defended some innocents! And your uncle Anoosh? Have you forgotten him too???! He gave his life for his ideas! What have I taught you? Humhm? "Integrity"! Does that mean anything to you?"[371]

Eutrapelia. Ridicule always mixes pleasure and pain, making the laughing subject bear part of the characteristics of the person who is being ridiculed. One can

---

370 Annie Tully, "An interview with Marjane Satrapi," in *Bookslut* (October 2004). Available online: http://www.bookslut.com/features/2004_10_003261.php (last access in June 2020).
371 Satrapi, *Persepolis I and II*, 293.

laugh at the evil and ignorance of others, but such a feeling is only right when referring to enemies and not to friends, because then a sense of injustice intervenes. We can laugh if someone slips on a banana peel, but how can we laugh at having an innocent person arrested, when we know that we are putting a life in danger? This is one of those situations where you can only be serious. Needless to say, the girl immediately understands her mistake and the reader is reassured that the she will continue to be a positive character and guardian of her own values. The image of Satrapi, as a manipulator of power and justice against an innocent person, had aroused a sense of disappointment in the reader. It must be emphasized that the guardians of the revolution are never really ridiculed or laughed at because they are so nasty and dangerous that one cannot laugh at them. One can only take on a defiant attitude and make a revolution against the revolutionaries: we smile at Marje's rebellious behavior because she intentionally chooses to devalue her enemies by distorting reality. The distortion is not inherent in the ridiculous subject, but is the result of intentional interventions, of choices of depreciation and devaluation. It follows that we do not laugh at Iran's totalitarian government, but rather at, and for, Marje. Comedy becomes an alternative model to totalitarianism insofar as it becomes an instrument of ideological legitimization in favor of the claims of the marginal, the low and the peripheral.

With respect to Charles Baudelaire's categorization, which distinguishes *significant* comic from *absolute* comic, I think it can be said that Satrapi's belongs to the first category. Contrary to the Iranian government's belief that it has to teach the proper way of living, the meaningful comedy of *Persepolis* aims to strike at the vices and bad customs of power, and stems from the (paradoxical) superiority of the small and defenseless girl in relation to the political and judicial power of her homeland. Needless to say, as Baudelaire himself pointed out, *significant* comedy also reveals an absoluteness and a metaphysical emanation that, in this context, takes on the name of *freedom.*[372]

After a divorce, a voluntary exile in Paris and the success of her comic book *Persepolis*, Satrapi states even more firmly that individual freedom and the essence of the individual does not lie in its classification by gender, nationality, or religious faith. In an interview she states:

> I was brought up with the idea that "you are a human being." They never told me "you are a girl" or "you are a boy." They told me "anything that a human being can do, that is humanly possible, you can do." [...] The only person who stops you from being free is ourselves. Nobody can take your freedom. I mean, I have lived in a dictatorship. I know what I am talking about.

372 See Banfi, *Sei lezioni sul linguaggio comico*, 103.

> [...] I have lived in a dictatorship. There was a ban on everything! Was I less free in my mind? No, I wasn't. Did I become a stupid person? No, I didn't. Because no matter how much they looked at me, they could not get into my mind. That belongs to me. And that is under my control if I decide it is. And I can only decide that if I train it. If you don't use it, it shrinks, and if you use it, it grows. So it is up to us.[373]

As Sartre intended, Satrapi has placed herself at the center of her world, given herself rules and won her game. The lesson given to her by her grandmother also makes her say now that everyone has the right to freedom. Rather than a law to be obeyed, Satrapi seems to adhere to an idea of a rule that responds to shared desires, and not as the imposition of models that should correspond to a logic of good and fair in moral terms. More than morality, she seems to desire an ethical and conscious adherence to what is right and good.

Regarding the French law[374] that would have prevented Muslim girls from wearing the veil, the author states:

> When they banned the veil in schools, I was against that. It became complete nonsense, because instead of understanding why the girls were putting the veil on their heads, they just made a law. And if by just making a law you could stop things, it would be so easy. Forbid persecution, and it doesn't exist any more? Of course it will exist, it will just become hidden. Just get rid of the veil and it will come out in another way. So the law is not a good idea for me. Then they cannot go to school to get an education, and the one way they have to become emancipated is then lost.[375]

Satrapi is opposed not to religions, but to fundamentalism, including Catholicism, which she experienced in Austria when she was very young:

> I am against fundamentalism. I am not against any religion, Islam, Judaism, Christianity etc. It is the use of an ideology to kill people that I am against. ... "I really believe in a society where

---

373 Emma Watson, "Emma Watson Interviews Persepolis' Author Marjane Satrapi," in *Vogue* (August 1, 2016). Available online: https://www.vogue.com/article/emma-watson-interviews-marjane-satrapi (last access in February 2023).

374 In 2010, the Sarkozy government passed a law banning girls from wearing the niqab at school. In 2018, the United Nations declared that law an infringement of human rights because it disproportionately interferes with the right to freely manifest one's religion. As a reaction, remember, many girls had shaved their hair completely before going to school, and many others had felt they had to wear the veil as a form of protest against a law that did not respect their culture of origin.

375 Tully, "An Interview with Marjane Satrapi."

> if someone wants to walk in the street completely naked they will be able to, and if someone wants to wear a veil they will also be able to.[376]

In short, a law cannot tell us who we are. No law can tell us that we are human beings.[377]

---

376 Simon Hattenstone, "Interview Confessions of Miss Mischief," in *The Guardian* (March 29, 2008). Available online: https://www.theguardian.com/film/2008/mar/29/biography (last accessed in February 2023).

377 *Persepolis* was followed up with *Persepolis 2.0,* a short comic book story written by two young Iranians living in California – Sina and Payman. In 2009, in the wake of the elections that saw the victory of President Ahmadinejad, popular uprisings broke out all over Iran that were brutally suppressed by militias loyal to the government. On this occasion, a young woman – Nada – was killed and became the symbol of the protest and the fight for freedom. Aware that communication via social media alone would not have had sufficient resonance, Sina and Payman asked Satrapi's permission to make a remix of the same images from *Persepolis,* but adapting them to the story of the uprisings contemporary to them. Within a week, the text was made public online with a request for disclosure, but the narrative, while respecting the Satrapi family's point of view and the voices of dissent, does not enjoy the same objective detachment and levity as its source. Perhaps the very fact that Satrapi had let a lot of time pass before writing *Persepolis* justifies the penchant for laughter it demonstrates. Sina and Payman, *Persepolis 2.0. Iran Postelection Uprising: Hopes and Fears Revealed,* 2009. Available online https://www.flickr.com/photos/30950471@N03/sets/72157620466531333/ (last access in June 2020).

A final paragraph in the guise of a conclusion

Perhaps Ulpianus suspected he might be making an overstatement when he wrote that "Iuris prudentia est divinarum atque humanarum rerum notitia, iusti atque iniusti scientia" ["Jurisprudence is the knowledge of divine and human affairs, the science of what is just and unjust."]. Perhaps he did not even really write those words; their authors could be the compilers of the *Corpus Iuris Civilis* (who introduced various changes in the sources they were restating: the *legum permutatio* ...), or some later modifier.

They certainly make a fine impression in the incipit of the *Institutiones*, alongside an equally sculptured definition of justice: "Iustitia est constans et perpetua voluntas ius suum cuique tribuens" [Justice is the constant and perpetual will to give each person their due]. Of course, it is not clear how one understands what one's *suum* is, but the definition certainly tells us that a *suum* exists, thanks to law, and that it will always exist, thanks to the perpetual *voluntas* of jurists, which will never know extinction. Undoubtedly, the students of the *Institutiones*, and all the more so the trained and experienced jurists, had a lot to get excited about, and still do.

Still on the first page of the *Institutiones*, the reader is reassured that the knowledge of just and unjust (*scientia iusti atque iniusti*) rests on three unshakable pillars – whose very existence the reader need only accept – on which the whole edifice can be built: "Iuris praecepta sunt haec: honeste vivere, alterum non laedere, suum cuique tribuere" ["These are the foundations of law: to live honorably, not to injure another, to pay to each his own"]. Again, there are many questions: does honesty always coincide with lawfulness? Isn't there something lawful but dishonest, and vice versa? When does one harm someone else? Is every injury unlawful? So, has law eliminated from human beings the idea of competition (with or without weapons), and therefore of lawful defeat? What is mine or yours? Is there something that is not and cannot be anyone's, or is it necessarily everyone's?

What matters, however, is not so much that some questions are clearly answered in the *Institutiones* or in the rest of the *Corpus Iuris*, while others are not. The important thing is that from the very first page of the "manual," the aspiring jurist is taught that the law contains the right answers, or that these right answers, through the law, can be found by means of a method called *scientia*.

From then on, Western law has never renounced the idea of its own scientific nature (its nature of positive knowledge), borrowing different ideas of science, and even of "true science" from philosophy, theology and nowadays epistemology (the true philosophy "veram philosophiam," which, in the passage that opens the

https://doi.org/10.1515/9783111286778-009

Digest, Ulpian indicates as the sole topic of research for jurists – high priests of law, as opposed to fake philosophy – "simulatam").

Law and the jurist, who is its "priest," thus take on all the seriousness of the human being who possesses the true science-knowledge, who can tell others what is just and unjust: the knowledge of good and evil (which caused the progenitors to be expelled from the Earthly Paradise, in which, as Grant Gilmore[378] recalled, there is no law ...). It is no coincidence that the Ulpian definition of *iuris prudentia* includes the knowledge of the divine – *divinarum rerum notitia,* alongside that of the human – *humanarum.* The comedy, by laughing and making people laugh at law, those who form it and those who enforce it in various ways, deprives law not only of seriousness, but also of its pretensions to truth and true, definitive justice. Law belongs to the world, and more specifically to that portion of the world represented by the human. Comedy reminds us that law shares all the characteristics of the human being: the aspiration for justice, a phantom that humans cannot stop pursuing, along with the capacity to wish for and achieve the ruin of others, the continuous succession of provisional truths and falsehoods, in the constant repetition of questions that will never find a just (definitive) answer.

Comedians and the fun they provoke do not replace the certainties of the law with other certainties; on the contrary, they return the law to the dimension of doubt, reminding it that it too participates in the changing nature of existence, shaking its susceptibility to error in its face.

Moreover, humor and laughter remind the law that the claim of immunity from error is harmful. In a world dominated by error, where error is the precondition and the road to any (transitory) discovery, law cannot help but be necessarily errant, and therefore transitory and provisional.

Finally, law, like any outcome of trial and error which comedy never fails to emphasize, is above all about experience. This experience does not concern the use of coercion (otherwise the best legal system would be one that is most capable of punishing, and the best judge one who is generous with exemplary punishments, and so on), but the ability to arouse trust through a message (an argument) that is heartfelt and capable of gaining consensus among the recipients, rather

---

378 Grant Gilmore, *The Ages of American Law* (1977) (New Haven/London, Yale Univ. Press, 2014), 110–111: "Law reflects but in no sense determines the moral worth of a society. The values of a reasonably just society will reflect themselves in a reasonably just law. The better the society, the less law there will be. In heaven there will be no law, and the lion shall lie down with the lamb. The values of an unjust society will reflect themselves in an unjust law. The worse the society, the more law there will be. In hell there will be nothing but law, and due process will be meticulously observed."

than arousing their laughter through the flair of some comedian. What is trustworthy is not ridiculous.

There is a reason why, at the beginning of the *Digest* (but not in the *Institutiones*, as the great Roman law scholar Filippo Gallo did not fail to observe), the Ulpian definition of *iuris prudentia* coexists (in a somewhat tense way) with the definition by Celsus: "ut eleganter celsus definitus, ius est ars boni et aequi" ["law, as elegantly defined by Celsus, is the art of what is good and fair"]. The Italian judge and legal scholar Mariano D'Amelio[379] considered Ulpian's definition "richer in emphasis than in exactness," and Celsus' words "beautiful in simplicity and truth."

The learned, self-important certainty-bearer, who claims to impose good and evil on others, offers countless inputs to the comedian. On the contrary, no temptation to laugh arises when one thinks of the craftsman practising the "art of what is good and fair." The latter is well aware of his own limitations, and in an effort to learn from his mistakes tries to perfect a job, even though he knows that this goal will never be achieved and that the result of his toil will be destroyed or transformed by time and by the work of new craftsmen.

This does not mean that the *ars boni et aequi* should shun comedy, but, on the contrary, that it shares its fundamental nature; like the comedy, it lives as a wanderer, it is aware of the inevitable risk of failure and paradox, it pursues a goal – justice – which will always be elusive within an eternal return that will continue, mockingly, to propose the same unresolved issues.

Without having to turn its back on the scientist, whatever the paradigm of science accepted at the time, the law can and perhaps must dialogue with the humorist, and perhaps stand next to the poet, continually divided, as if uniting Heraclitus and Democritus, between tears and laughter, to be reminded that

> every day in this grand little café of life I sit waiting to see how our little civilization develops, not to mention how our little consciousness might develop (oh what ecstasies, what despair!), and there's a sign outside the café that says HAPPY HOUR EVERY DAY 4–7. It's only 10 a.m. And no one is happy yet.[380]

379 See the term "Giurisprudenza" [Jurisprudence] in the *Enciclopedia Treccani* (1933).
380 Lawrence Ferlinghetti, *Little Boy* (London: Faber &Faber, 2019), 163–164.

Appendixes by Giuseppe Rossi

Appendix 1
The Good Lawyer and *Bardell v. Pickwick*

Suppose you were a middle-aged Victorian widow…

Suppose you were a middle-aged Victorian widow named Mrs. Martha Bardell, the mother of a single son still in his childhood, running a household in Goswell Street, London. Your widowhood has been quite long-lasting, and you do not exclude any possibility of a new union. In your household there lives a single gentleman with some fortune, named Mr. Pickwick. He is always very polite and pleasant with you and your child; he definitively seems to be a very enjoyable person. One day, he suddenly addresses you in this way: "Do you think it a much greater expense to keep two people, than to keep one?"[381] For sure, this is not a Romeo-style love declaration, but it clearly hints at family life and household management. Imagine that, after you have reddened and tried to escape the question, your interlocutor insists in order to learn more. It is not surprising that you answer something like: "That depends a good deal upon the person, you know, Mr. Pickwick; and whether it's a saving and careful person, sir." The answer is "That's very true, … but the person I have in my eye (here he looked very hard at Mrs. Bardell) I think possesses these qualities; and has, moreover, a considerable knowledge of the world, and a great deal of sharpness, Mrs. Bardell, which may be of material use to me." At this point, Mr. Pickwick's talking runs wild, as if he has finally found the courage to fully disclose his heart: "I do … I do, indeed; and to tell you the truth, Mrs. Bardell, I have made up my mind," "You'll think it very strange now … that I never consulted you about this matter, and never even mentioned it, till I sent your little boy out this morning—eh?," "When I am in town, you'll always have somebody to sit with you. To be sure, so you will," "And your little boy … He, too, will have a companion, a lively one, who'll teach him, I'll be bound, more tricks in a week than he would ever learn in a year."

No wonder that, hearing such a crescendo, you fling your arms around his neck, "with a cataract of tears and a chorus of sobs." Suddenly, Mr. Pickwick seems embarrassed. He fears that someone may come. You hear the steps of many people running up the stairs. You are scared and confused. You faint in his arms, just like any other respectable Victorian widow would do. Many people appear, you slowly return to your senses. A man, that you recognize as one of Pick-

381 Charles Dickens, *The Pickwick Papers* (Oxford: Oxford Univ. Press, 1986), 183: further references in the text, abbreviated as TPP.

https://doi.org/10.1515/9783111286778-010

wick's friends who used to visit him, helps you down the stairs. Then, Mr. Pickwick and his company leave, and you hear no more from him. What would you do if you were Mrs. Bardell? Would you follow the advice of a friend of yours? She told you that there is a pair of skilled solicitors in town, Dodson & Fogg, who could help you to settle the matter, by having the rascal ordered by a court to pay you a good amount of money. What would you do, if you were Mrs. Bardell?

The law and matters of the heart

That promises to marry are to be complied with is surely a moral rule, and it is of paramount importance for Mr. Pickwick. Although he himself sometimes acts with some excessive though delicate lightness towards women,[382] he thinks that marriage is to be taken very seriously, to the point of despising and even trying to physically attack one of his acquaintances, Mr. Jingle, precisely because the latter had tried to use such a noble institution improperly (by seducing the spinster sister of another friend of Pickwick, Mr. Wardle, in order to put his hands on her fortune).[383]

According to the rules applicable at the time the *Papers* were set, the breach of a promise to marry entitled the other party to an award for damages, under a kind of mixed application of the law of contracts and the law of torts.[384] Promises to

---

382 "It may be reasonably supposed that Mr. Pickwick had not been very discreet, or sufficiently cautious in his general behaviour to his landlady. As we know, he was rather too effusive in his relations with the fair sex. One of his weaknesses was kissing. He would kiss everybody who was young or good-looking. [...] It should be borne in mind also that Mr. Pickwick was almost invariably drawn into his more serious scrapes and embarrassments by this devotion to the sex": Percy Fitzgerald, *Bardell v. Pickwick. The Trial for Breach of Promise of Marriage held at the Guildhall Sittings, on April 1, 1828, before Mr. Justice Stareleigh and a Special Jury of the City of London* (London: Elliot Stock, 1902), 8.

383 The episode is narrated in chapters VIII–X of TPP.

384 In 1879, the House of Lords moved for abolition of the action for breach of promise to marry, except in cases where actual pecuniary loss was incurred by reason of the promise, the damages being limited to such pecuniary loss (e.g., in cases when the plaintiff had faced costs to organize the wedding ceremony). The parliamentary report is available online: https://hansard.parliament.uk/Commons/1879-05-06/debates/4a6b87e6-e590-495a-8c0d-f5ce2de3b3d1/BreachOfPromise (last access in November 2022). In England, the tort was formally abolished by sec. 1 of the Law Reform (Miscellaneous Provisions) Act, 1970, following and ad hoc report by the Law Commission (available online: https://s3-eu-west-2.amazonaws.com/lawcom-prod-storage-11jsxou24uy7q/uploads/2016/08/LC.-026-BREACH-OF-PROMISE-OF-MARRIAGE.pdf – last access November 2022). The issue was highly debated also in the United States. For a critical review, see Harter F. Wright, "The Action

marry are a matter of the heart, but once they are broken the law steps in. Alongside law comes money, and with money temporality steps to the foreground. We cannot say that moral rules lie outside of temporality, since they are the outcome of specific facts happening in specific places (today's morals, of course, are very different from those of *Pickwick* times). But the law brings the moral rule into a different dimension of temporality. Such a shift involves at least three different aspects: the political and economic aspects, which influence the definition of the rule, and the judicial aspect. Once the rule is turned from moral into legal, the trial shall be used for enforcement. At this point, different things can happen:

a. a moral rule can be modified/corrupted once charged by the law with political and/or economic implications: e.g., the rule that awards damages for the breach of a promise to marry can incentivize opportunistic behaviours on the side of the plaintiff and/or her solicitors (this is how Mr. Pickwick considers Mrs. Bardell's claim);

b. the judicial enforcement of moral precepts encoded into legal rules may strengthen the moral rule, or, on the contrary, it may lead to immoral outcomes (this is what Mr. Pickwick thinks after losing his case; if he won, he would think that, point a. notwithstanding, the noble and learned judicial system of England discovered the fraud, and prevented the swindlers from reaching their goal).

The law is particularly ill-equipped to deal with matters of the heart, or of the soul (the preferential playground of morals), because of at least four different reasons:

i. The remedies used by the law are making liable people pay money to the victims/their heirs (like in the law of torts or in the law of contracts), and/or making liable persons suffer (like in criminal law). Although getting some money, and/or seeing other people suffer for their faults may be of some help, it is hard to believe that injuries of the heart or of the soul shall completely heal this way. Comedy has plenty of chances to emphasize the greed, superficiality, dishonesty, or revengefulness of the victim, or alleged victim, who seeks awards for damages and/or punishment of the liable person. In Dickens' story of *Bardell*, this is a central aspect.

ii. The law speaks a technical, objectifying language, completely different from any language of feelings. Legal language is never the language lovers, relatives, or friends speak. When the law meets the language of feelings, a comical effect arises. This happens in *Bardell*, when Serjeant Buzfuz, pleading for Bardell,

for Breach of the Marriage Promise," *Virginia Law Review*, 10 (1924): 361–383. In some states of the US the so called "heartbalm actions" are still allowed, but damages are strictly limited.

quotes Mr. Pickwicks' messages to her, trying to convince the jury that they were love letters under disguise, or when the judge questions a witness about the nicknames that her husband uses to address her. The interpretation of texts allegedly containing love messages under disguise between alleged lovers in hiding was a central theme in *Norton v. Melbourne*, the real case that inspired Dickens.[385] In order to enable the law to properly talk about feelings, we should imagine, alongside the "gay science," a "poetic law" that speaks a non-objectifying language. Personally, I am not astonished nor disappointed about this idea, but it would surely raise deep troubles with reference to two fundamental aspects of the law – at least according to Western legal thought – like certainty and predictability. The operation of a certain and predictable law in an uncertain and unpredictable world offers great opportunities to comedy, as we have seen above.

iii. Rules of evidence demonstrate all their roughness and limits when it comes to giving/evaluating proof of facts involving a sentimental side. The counsel for the defendant in *Norton* stressed this issue, and this was a victorious strategy. It discredited all the clues against the alleged illicit lovers Mrs. Norton and Lord Melbourne – such as messages, frequent visits, confidential attitudes towards each other – holding that those were normal aspects of an innocent relationship between acquaintances. Buzfuz uses an opposite strategy in *Bardell*. He charges normal behaviours in a landlady-and-tenant relationship with implied meanings which would be transparent only to those engaged in a love affair. The counsels for Pickwick are unable to counteract. The outcome of a trial is often determined by the evaluation of evidence, which depends on the way it is presented to the jury. This is one more aspect of the comical mechanism in Dickens' story.

iv. The trial is based on liturgies and rituals where everybody performs a specific role, like in a theatrical play. Dickens' narration of the court day in *Bardell* is extremely theatrical[386]. The place is described as if it were a stage. People, their movements, and their words are reported as if it was all a staged performance, following a detailed script. The trial tends to expel spontaneity, and wishes to grant sincerity (e.g., of the witnesses) and truth (e.g., of the decision)

---

385 *Norton v. Melbourne* was a case of alleged "criminal conversation" brought in 1836 against William Lamb, Viscount Melbourne, then the Whig prime minister, by George Chapple Norton, the then-husband of Caroline Norton. The case had considerable echo in the public opinion. Dickens dealt with the case as a court reporter. The verdict went for the defendant. A report of the case is available at http://s3.amazonaws.com/cul-hydra/trial/sat2009/pdfs/sat2009.pdf (last access in November 2022).

386 TPP, chapter XXXIV.

thanks to solemnity and formalism. This is exactly the contrary of what happens in personal relationships, including love affairs and friendships, where spontaneity is the key. Not by chance, in *Bardell* it is exactly the spontaneity of Mr. Pickwick's friends (starting from Mr. Winkle), when heard as witnesses, that will prove fatal for the defendant. Mr. Winkle's testimony is one of the funniest moments in Dickens' story.

All this suggests that law and morals should simply be kept separate. Such a separation lies at the core of the Roman distinction between *ius* and *fas*, of the modern theory of sources of law, of eighteenth- and nineteenth-century legal positivism. Sadly (or luckily), law and morals cannot simply be separated, except on a merely formal and nominal plane. In the real world, they cannot but constantly interact with each other, sometimes with the mediation of comedy. Should the law try to keep morals at a distance by means of an efficiently engineered system of sources (but why should the law do that?), morals shall strike back anyway, influencing statutory interpretation and law enforcement, via the trial and the judicial decision.

The comic effects in the narration of *Bardell* are all based on the contrasts between the structural features of the law and the manifold, multi-faceted aspects of human nature, especially when it comes to that big mess called the heart. Dickens is not criticizing the law, the lawyers, or the judge. He is just caricaturizing them, in order to enable readers to understand how things go when you are involved in a litigation before a court – in general, and most of all when such litigation deals with something so personal and delicate as a love affair. Readers may think that the decision in *Bardell* is wrong, since they know from the previous chapters how much of a good-hearted man Mr. Pickwick is. Moreover, readers – who, unlike jurors, know anything about the persons and the facts – may have a reasonably bad opinion about the reputed solicitors Dodson & Fogg, who convinced Mrs. Bardell to sue, and about Mrs. Bardell herself, who probably let her meddling and plotting friend, Mrs. Sanders, persuade her to seek the services of Dodson & Fogg. On the other hand, at least in the first chapters of the book, Mr. Pickwick is undoubtedly naive, he utters his opinions without too much reflection, he often chooses words unhappily (just as he did when he addressed Mrs. Bardell), he is a bit too relaxed and light of heart with ladies. The problem with *Bardell* is precisely that Mr. Pickwick's choice of counsels was naïve, unthinking, and untimely, just like his initial approach to both Dodson & Fogg and to his barrister, the renowned Serjeant Snubbin, and the way he reported facts to his counsels.

Perhaps solicitor Perker and Serjeant Snubbin were good people, just like Pickwick. For sure, they will not prove to be good lawyers, at least in this case.

In search of the good lawyer

Suppose you were Mr. Pickwick, and you received the letter from Dodson & Fogg on behalf of Mrs. Bardell, claiming damages for the breach of a promise to marry, under threat of suing in court. Of course, you would be disappointed, since you had never had any real intention to marry her, and your relationship with her had always been within the boundaries of landlady-and-tenant. That day, you were just talking about the idea of hiring a manservant, as you did thereafter, in the person of Sam Weller. You would review the conversation, and realize that your choice of words was unfortunate, to say the least. Then, you would promptly seek the services of a lawyer, trying to choose the best one for the case.

Mr. Pickwick does not do this. He judges on the sole basis of his good faith and alleged knowledge of the human (Mrs. Bardell's) heart, ignoring completely the technicalities of the law. Just look at the following dialogue between Mr. Pickwick and his friend Wardle, which takes place immediately after Pickwick opened D&F's letter:

> 'It's a conspiracy,' said Mr. Pickwick, at length recovering the power of speech; 'a base conspiracy between these two grasping attorneys, Dodson and Fogg. Mrs. Bardell would never do it;—she hasn't the heart to do it;—she hasn't the case to do it. Ridiculous—ridiculous.'
> 'Of her heart,' said Wardle, with a smile, 'you should certainly be the best judge. I don't wish to discourage you, but I should certainly say that, of her case, Dodson and Fogg are far better judges than any of us can be.'
> 'It's a vile attempt to extort money,' said Mr. Pickwick.
> 'I hope it is,' said Wardle, with a short, dry cough. (TPP, 221)

The whole sense of the story is in Wardle's juxtaposition of "her heart" and "her case," which points at the hiatus between feelings and law, and between life and trials at court. Incidentally, Pickwick does not even know Mrs. Bardell's "heart," since he is so focused on himself to the point of not even wondering how Bardell may have interpreted his utterances. He absolves himself the very moment he condemns Dodson & Fogg. Armed with such self-confidence, he does not immediately seek a lawyer. He prefers to first visit his adversary's counsels, and then to send his manservant, Sam Weller, on a kind of undercover mission to Mrs. Bardell's household. Pickwick's visit to D&F symbolizes the indignation of the righteous before dishonest pettifoggers, the anger of justice before the distortions of the law. Tactically, it is a complete disaster.[387] Pickwick insults D&F, thus exposing himself to tortious

---

387 "Naturally Mr. Pickwick felt uncomfortable, and his first idea was to arrange the matter. This was a sensible course, and he ought at once to have put the matter into the hands of his friend Perker, with full powers to treat. But no. Mr. Pickwick's vanity and indiscretion made him meddle

liability.[388] Most of all, he reveals to two skilled practitioners like D&F his complete naivete, mixed with a touch of arrogance. Before D&F's eyes, Mr. Pickwick is a conceited idiot, gullible to the point of meeting his adversary's counsels without any assistance of a lawyer. The very moment Pickwick left their offices, Dodson & Fogg understood they had a very good chance of winning the case. The only information that Sam gleaned during his visit to Mrs. Bardell, and which was not apparent in the letter sent to his master, is that D&F were working on conditional fee. This, once again, sparks Mr. Pickwick's indignation, but it has no real legal relevance.

When it is already too late, Pickwick visits a solicitor. It is Mr. Perker, Mr. Wardle's attorney who became acquainted with Pickwick during the affair between Wardle's spinster sister and Mr. Jingle. In that case, Perker did not do anything significant, he just helped Wardle in reaching a settlement with Jingle (who got payment in order to stop seeing his fiancée).[389] Then, Mr. Perker had a role in the Eatanswill elections, where he acted as an agent for one of the candidates. In this capacity, he organized a disloyal staging, hiring people who had to impersonate his candidate's supporters during rallies.[390] There is no apparent reason for the choice of Perker, except for the previous and rather casual acquaintance with Mr. Pickwick. Let us assume that, at least according to Mr. Pickwick, Perker was a "good lawyer" meaning that he was a good-hearted person, since Pickwick knew nothing about Perker's professional skills. Personally, I am very doubtful about Mr. Perker's goodness of heart. Let us leave aside his dishonest behaviour at the Eatanswill rallies. Perker instructed his clerk, Mr. Lowten, to lie to a bankrupt client who was visiting his premises in search of news about his position. Clearly, Perker discriminates among his clients, granting preferential treatment

---

in the business behind his solicitor's back, as it where, and with damaging results to himself—a warning to all such amateurs. It must be said that Dodson and Fogg's behaviour at the extraordinary visit which he paid them was marked by a certain propriety. This very malapropos visit of Mr. Pickwick to the firm was, as I said, a mistake and damaged his case" (Percy Fitzgerald, *Bardell v. Pickwick*, 11).

388 "What is the charge, after all, against Messrs. Dodson and Fogg [...] They brought an action for breach of promise of marriage—some people think such actions should never be brought at all—[...] they made a little arrangement with regard to costs, unprofessional if you like, but still nothing to bring down upon them the denouncement to which they have been made subject. So far as Mr. Pickwick was concerned, he had absolutely nothing to complain of in their conduct" (Frank Lockwood, *The Law and Lawyers of Pickwick: A Lecture* [1894] (London: The Law Book Exchange, 2002, 68–69)).

389 TPP, chapter X.

390 TPP, chapter XIII.

to wealthy people like Pickwick.[391] Pickwick hears Lowten's lies, but gives no importance to the issue, although he is sure that Dodson & Fogg are rascals, because they work on conditional fee. Anyway, let us suppose that Mr. Pickwick, just like anybody else, has his own ideas of what is good and bad.

Had Pickwick reverted to a "bad lawyer" – someone unscrupulous but technically skilled, like *The Betrothed's* Azzeccagarbugli – Dr. Quibbler – he would have immediately realized how troublesome his situation was, and would have behaved accordingly. For example, he would have settled the matter from the very beginning, thus avoiding both the day in court and an unpleasant stay in the debtors' prison (consider that, at the outcome, Pickwick shall pay money in any case).

The initial dialogue between Mr. Pickwick and his solicitor Perker shows, once again, that Pickwick misunderstands the nature of the law and of the trial, confusing them with his own idea of good and bad:

> 'Ah, my dear Sir,' said little Mr. Perker, bustling up from his chair. 'Well, my dear sir, and what's the news about your matter, eh? Anything more about our friends in Freeman's Court? They've not been sleeping, I know that. Ah, they're very smart fellows; very smart, indeed.'
> As the little man concluded, he took an emphatic pinch of snuff, as a tribute to the smartness of Messrs. Dodson and Fogg.
> 'They are great scoundrels,' said Mr. Pickwick.
> 'Aye, aye,' said the little man; 'that's a matter of opinion, you know, and we won't dispute about terms; because of course you can't be expected to view these subjects with a professional eye. Well, we've done everything that's necessary. I have retained Serjeant Snubbin.'
> 'Is he a good man?' inquired Mr. Pickwick.
> 'Good man!' replied Perker; 'bless your heart and soul, my dear Sir, Serjeant Snubbin is at the very top of his profession. Gets treble the business of any man in court—engaged in every case. You needn't mention it abroad; but we say—we of the profession—that Serjeant Snubbin leads the court by the nose.' (TPP, 382)

Pickwick's misunderstandings are crystal-clear. He keeps looking for a good man, (i.e., someone who shares his idea of goodness), instead of a well-skilled lawyer. Perker is very soft in letting him know that Dodson & Fogg are outstanding practitioners, and he fails completely to warn Pickwick about the risks of the trial. Perker blames Pickwick for the delay in seeking him out, and for having undertaken

---

391 "There never was such a pestering bankrupt as that since the world began, I do believe!' said Lowten, throwing down his pen with the air of an injured man. 'His affairs haven't been in Chancery quite four years yet, and I'm d——d if he don't come worrying here twice a week. Step this way, Mr. Pickwick. Perker is in, and he'll see you, I know. Devilish cold,' he added pettishly, 'standing at that door, wasting one's time with such seedy vagabonds!' Having very vehemently stirred a particularly large fire with a particularly small poker, the clerk led the way to his principal's private room, and announced Mr. Pickwick." (TPP, 381–382).

unfortunate personal initiatives, but he never says clearly that there is a high risk that the case may be lost.[392] Rather, he seems to suggest that Pickwick is to blame for the eventual negative outcome of the trial.[393] Perker does not even examine with his client the possibility of settling the matter. Finally, when Mr. Pickwick states that he has no intention of paying any damages, even in the case of an unfavourable verdict, Mr. Perker omits this very fundamental information: "This way, you shall go to prison!" Instead, these are the final words in the conversation between these two on this critical issue:

> 'Very well, my dear Sir, very well,' said Perker. 'You know best, of course.' 'Of course,' replied Mr. Pickwick hastily. 'Where does Serjeant Snubbin live?' (TPP, 383)

Maybe Pickwick knew that he was risking imprisonment, or maybe he did not, but surely it was his solicitors' duty to expressly warn him. At this point, Pickwick insists on meeting Serjeant Snubbin personally, in order to convince the barrister of his innocence. When Perker manages to organize the meeting (something that is very unusual, for the obvious reason that the solicitor is there precisely to intermediate between the client and the barrister), Mr. Pickwick addresses the Serjeant with this astonishing allocution:

> 'Gentlemen of your profession, Sir, [...] see the worst side of human nature. All its disputes, all its ill-will and bad blood, rise up before you. You know from your experience of juries (I mean no disparagement to you, or them) how much depends upon effect; and you are apt to attribute to others, a desire to use, for purposes of deception and self-interest, the very instruments which you, in pure honesty and honour of purpose, and with a laudable desire to do your utmost for your client, know the temper and worth of so well, from constantly employing them yourselves. I really believe that to this circumstance may be attributed the vulgar but very general notion of your being, as a body, suspicious, distrustful, and over-cautious. Conscious as I am, sir, of the disadvantage of making such a declaration to you, under such circumstances, I have come here, because I wish you distinctly to understand, as my friend Mr. Perker has said, that I am innocent of the falsehood laid to my charge; and although I am very well aware of the inestimable value of your assistance, Sir, I must beg to add, that unless you

392 "'You know, my dear Sir, if you will take the management of your affairs into your own hands after entrusting them to your solicitor, you must also take the consequences.' Here Mr. Perker drew himself up with conscious dignity, and brushed some stray grains of snuff from his shirt frill." (TPP, 382–383)

393 "'And suppose the verdict is against me?' said Mr. Pickwick. Mr. Perker smiled, took a very long pinch of snuff, stirred the fire, shrugged his shoulders, and remained expressively silent. 'You mean that in that case I must pay the damages?' said Mr. Pickwick, who had watched this telegraphic answer with considerable sternness. Perker gave the fire another very unnecessary poke, and said, 'I am afraid so.'" (TPP, 383)

> sincerely believe this, I would rather be deprived of the aid of your talents than have the advantage of them. (TPP, 386–387)

No wonder Snubbin "had relapsed into a state of abstraction," long before the end of this "prosy" address. Basically, Pickwick is asking Snubbin not to do his job. He should not "lead the court by the nose" (something that, according to Perker, he was very good at). He should just rely on his own personal belief in Pickwick's innocence. Of course, Snubbin's beliefs about Pickwick's innocence are completely irrelevant, just like Pickwick's innocence itself is completely irrelevant, unless a jury can be convinced of it, following the rules of procedure, with the rules of evidence in the foreground.

Good Lawyers v. Bad Lawyers

From Mr. Pickwick's point of view, the court day in *Bardell*[394] should have been a good lawyers v. bad lawyers fight, whose outcome should have proved his own moral purity. As clarified by his conversations with both his solicitor Perker and his barrister Snubbin, Pickwick seeks a moral acquittal before a legal one, with the symmetrical (moral) condemnation of both Mrs. Bardell and her lawyers. Actually, the caricatural report of the case offered by Dickens is the narration of an ordinary trial, whose outcome is not determined by the lawyer's moral level, but by his professional skills.

Worthy of note, Dickens' report leaves both the judge and the jury in the background, while focusing on the dialectics between barristers and the strategies set forth in examining the witnesses. The judge has a purely formal role. It took the jury just an "anxious quarter of an hour" to decide the verdict, just as if the decision by the jurors was the mere automatic consequence of the victorious lawyers' strategies. In Dickens' view, lawyers do the real job in a trial.

In *Bardell*, the counsels for the plaintiff, with Serjeant Buzfuz as their frontman,[395] overweigh their adversaries. The trio of Perker, Snubbin, and the terrible junior barrister Phunky commits a series of awkward mistakes:[396]

394 Dickens gives a very detailed report of the hearing, in a court reporter's style, in chapter XXXIV of TPP.

395 "Buzfuz's great speech is one of the happiest parodies in the language. Never was the forensic jargon and treatment so humorously set forth—and this because of the perfect sincerity and earnestness with which it was done. There is none of the far-fetched, impossible exaggeration—the form of burlesque [...]. It is, in fact, a real speech, which might have been delivered to a dull-head-

i. the very choice of Phunky, a junior, very unexperienced and emotional member of the Bar, is completely wrong. Phunky is totally unknown to the judge (who misspells his surname as "Monkey") and his colleagues, and he lacks the skills to counteract Buzfuz's dialectical traps;
ii. the defendant calls no witnesses, leaving his opponent free to determine the evidentiary framework;
iii. Snubbin decides not to cross-examine the plaintiff's first witness (Mrs. Cluppins), "for Mr. Pickwick wished it to be distinctly stated that it was due to her to say, that her account was in substance correct." This is a fatal mistake. Cluppins is the plaintiff's key-witness, who reports the conversation between Pickwick and Bardell in which the alleged proposal of marriage was uttered. When the conversation took place, Mrs. Cluppins was eavesdropping, and by her own admission she did not have any clear view of the scene, but she just heard loud voices. Buzfuz himself offers a chance to his adversary, when he says to the witness "Well, Mrs. Cluppins, you were not listening, but you heard the voices." How can somebody who was "not listening" be a trusted witness of the real meaning of a conversation she was not listening to? In *Norton*, discrediting the witnesses for the plaintiff was the strategy that led the defendant to victory. It is worth adding that Snubbin commits this fatal mistake because he endorses his client's will to appear irreprehensible, disregarding completely the consequences that such an approach would produce on the trial;
iv. witness Mr. Winkle, one of Pickwick's closest friends, is confused to the utmost by the biased questions of Buzfuz's junior, the cunning Skimpin. Phunky does not realize how dangerous the cross-examination of such a witness could be. He ignores Snubbin's invitation to stop the cross-examination, and involuntarily induces the witness to reveal an embarrassing episode involving Mr. Pickwick and a young lady;[397]

---

ed audience without much impairing credibility. Apart from this it is a most effective harangue and most plausible statement of the Plaintiff's case" (Percy Fitzgerald, *Bardell v. Pickwick*, 44).

396 See the analysis of the defendant's strategies by William Renwick Riddell, "Plaintiff's Attorneys, Bardell v. Pickwick," *American Bar Association Journal* 8 (1922): 203–205.

397 "Amid the profound silence of the whole court, Mr. Winkle faltered out, that the trifling circumstance of suspicion was Mr. Pickwick's being found in a lady's sleeping-apartment at midnight; which had terminated, he believed, in the breaking off of the projected marriage of the lady in question, and had led, he knew, to the whole party being forcibly carried before George Nupkins, Esq., magistrate and justice of the peace, for the borough of Ipswich!" The reference is to the episode narrated in chapters XXII–XXIV of TPP.

v. witness Mrs. Sanders, a friend of Bardell's, is completely untrustworthy. She utters her firm beliefs that Pickwick was about to marry Bardell, but gives no reasons for it. Her entire testimony is but a series of assumptions, confused guesswork, and reports of gossip heard from unknown sources. If the counsels for the defendant had done their job properly, such a witness would have been considered counterproductive for the plaintiff;
vi. Dickens does not give a detailed report of Serjeant Snubbin's defence. We are told that he focused on the interpretation of the letters from Pickwick to Bardell, which were perhaps the weakest evidentiary element for the plaintiff. Dickens adds that Snubbin uttered "a very long and a very emphatic address [...] in which he bestowed the highest possible eulogiums on the conduct and character of Mr. Pickwick," and that "he did the best he could for Mr. Pickwick; and the best, as everybody knows, on the infallible authority of the old adage, could do no more." (TPP, 437) The problem is that Serjeant Snubbin's final defence could in no way overcome the very bad evidentiary framework.

Mr. Pickwick entered the court-house looking for a moral triumph, and he faced a complete judicial defeat. After the verdict, Mr. Pickwick claims once again his moral superiority towards Dodson & Fogg:

> They stopped in a side room while Perker paid the court fees; and here, Mr. Pickwick was joined by his friends. Here, too, he encountered Messrs. Dodson & Fogg, rubbing their hands with every token of outward satisfaction.
> 'Well, gentlemen,' said Mr. Pickwick.
> 'Well, Sir,' said Dodson, for self and partner.
> 'You imagine you'll get your costs, don't you, gentlemen?' said Mr. Pickwick.
> Fogg said they thought it rather probable. Dodson smiled, and said they'd try.
> 'You may try, and try, and try again, Messrs. Dodson and Fogg,' said Mr. Pickwick vehemently, 'but not one farthing of costs or damages do you ever get from me, if I spend the rest of my existence in a debtor's prison.'
> 'Ha! ha!' laughed Dodson. 'You'll think better of that, before next term, Mr. Pickwick.'
> 'He, he, he! We'll soon see about that, Mr. Pickwick,' grinned Fogg.
> Speechless with indignation, Mr. Pickwick allowed himself to be led by his solicitor and friends to the door. (TPP, 438–439)

Once again, Pickwick's position is unrealistic. It is the outcome of his own moral idea that the decision by the jury was unjust, and of his complete disregard for the whole legal-technical dimension of the issue. Pickwick definitely had a fair trial, the evidence was correctly presented to the jury, and both parties had equal chances to set forth their positions. Why, then, should the decision not be complied with?

Dickens' comic construction of the *Bardell v. Pickwick* litigation is two-sided. You can take Pickwick's point of view, and then you will laugh at the lawyers, the judge, the court-system, and the entire "lawyer-land"[398] theatre that is so wittily described by Dickens. You will probably reach the conclusion that justice does not belong to this world, but jurisdiction does (a very comical trite statement). You may add that, thank God, morals exist along with people of a high moral stance like Pickwick, who counteract the defaults of the law. Alternatively, you can take any of the involved lawyers' point of view, and laugh at Pickwick's ridiculous stubbornness in insisting that the law and the trial should just recognize him as a man of a high moral stance, a victim of a conspiracy between a swindler widow, her plotting friends, and some dishonest practitioners – just because this was his own idea of himself and of the entire matter. The choice is up to you. It is not difficult to imagine that the phantom of justice may be laughing at both Pickwick and the lawyers.

The wise man Pickwick and the final settlement

Surely, the outcome of *Bardell* is not illegal. Is it immoral? That outcome is not a consequence of the fact, nor of the law. It is determined by the trial, by the way each of the actors in the trial performed their role. Probably, had Dodson & Fogg and Buzfuz been on Pickwick's side, he would have won his case. Should we thus conclude that using a trial in order to reach a decision on human actions is an immoral choice? The law governs an immoral world, or better, a world where the very idea of morals constantly changes in time and in space, not to say person by person. Should we then substitute the trial with something more apt to Pickwick's morals, as Pickwick himself heartily invited his counsel Snubbin to do? Assuming that the law and the trial should be mere consequences of morals would be as flanked as assuming that law and morals are completely separate. The law and morals relationship should be seen within the framework of the ever-changing nature of the world, highlighted by the constant dwelling of comedy.

As it has been pointed out, the *Bardell* litigation is the real backbone of the plot in the novel. *The Pickwick Papers* would just be a series of unrelated episodes, sketching aspects of life in the English country and in the town of London, if it were not for the litigation, which offers Pickwick the chance for a transformation, and Dickens the chance to tell a real story. While in the first episodes Pickwick is basically a funny character, in the final part following his imprisonment, he turns

---

398 With the expression of John Glavin, "Pickwick on the Wrong Side of the Door," *Dickens Studies Annual* 22 (1993): 14.

into a kind of a wise old man, able to settle his own matters and help others in settling theirs. Dozens of chapters in the novel are dedicated to motion and funny adventures, at times bordering on the *pochade.* The final part, starting from Pickwick's residence at The Fleet, is in the key of settlement and stability. It is not just that Pickwick has grown older chapter by chapter, and that Dickens became tired and wanted to move to new and more ambitious projects. It is that, through *Bardell,* Pickwick understood the importance not only of living, but of experiencing the world. In Pickwick's story, just like in Pinocchio's, the law and the trial are part of the experience of the world. Dickens focuses on the law and the trial as factuality. They exist, they are part of the world, they can be part of our lives, as it happened to Dickens himself, who was a clerk, a court reporter, and a law student. Pickwick faced his litigation deciding to put his morals in the foreground. After his judicial defeat, he did not change his morals or his own idea of the law, but he learned that his morals are just a small part of the overall heterogeneity and complexity of the world, which includes the law, lawyers, and trials, of course.

In the end, Pickwick decides to settle, and the settlement includes paying Dodson & Fogg's fees,[399] something which Pickwick had solemnly declared he would never accept, immediately after the verdict for the plaintiff Bardell.[400] Pickwick

399 "[...] in the end Pickwick can go free, but only because the lawyers get their fees – as does Dickens. Or is it rather the publishers, Chapman and Hall, who, like an echo of Dodson and Fogg, get their fees from Pickwick? After all, Dickens was laboring for publishers who, like the lawyers within the novel, also had mercenary designs upon Pickwick" (Jonathan H. Grossman, "Representing Pickwick: The Novel and the Law Courts," *Nineteenth-Century Literature* 52 (1997): 171–197, 183).

400 Perker informs his client of the opportunity to settle with the following words: "You have now an opportunity, on easy terms, of placing yourself in a much higher position than you ever could, by remaining here; which would only be imputed, by people who didn't know you, to sheer dogged, wrongheaded, brutal obstinacy; nothing else, my dear Sir, believe me. Can you hesitate to avail yourself of it, when it restores you to your friends, your old pursuits, your health and amusements; when it liberates your faithful and attached servant, whom you otherwise doom to imprisonment for the whole of your life; and above all, when it enables you to take the very magnanimous revenge—which I know, my dear sir, is one after your own heart—of releasing this woman from a scene of misery and debauchery, to which no man should ever be consigned, if I had my will, but the infliction of which on any woman, is even more frightful and barbarous. Now I ask you, my dear sir, not only as your legal adviser, but as your very true friend, will you let slip the occasion of attaining all these objects, and doing all this good, for the paltry consideration of a few pounds finding their way into the pockets of a couple of rascals, to whom it makes no manner of difference, except that the more they gain, the more they'll seek, and so the sooner be led into some piece of knavery that must end in a crash? I have put these considerations to you, my dear Sir, very feebly and imperfectly, but I ask you to think of them. Turn them over in your mind as

is so much in the mood for settlement, that he even takes care of his adversary par excellence, the infamous Mr. Jingle, and his accomplice, Job Trotter.[401]

Then, finally, everything is settled. For Mr. Pickwick, maybe. But the world goes on, and the law with it...

---

long as you please. I wait here most patiently for your answer" (TPP, 593). Clearly, Perker once again adapts the facts to his client's sensibility.

401 TPP, chapter LIII.

Appendix 2
The Law and the Masochist's Contract: Notes on Gilles Deleuze's *Coldness and Cruelty*

Socrates and Plato

Chapter VII of Gilles Deleuze's 1967 introduction to Von Sacher Masoch's *Venus in Furs*, titled *Coldness and Cruelty*[402], deals with "Humor, Irony and the Law." The French philosopher starts from a "classical" view of the law, which he attributes to Plato, thus synthesized: "the law is only a representative of the Good in a world that the Good has more or less forsaken." With law being a "second best" for the Good, "The righteous man obeys the laws of the country of his birth or residence, and in so doing acts for the best, even though he retains his freedom of thought, freedom to think of the Good and for the sake of the Good." Although "quite conventional," this approach "nevertheless conceals elements of irony and humor which made political philosophy possible, for it allows the free play of thought at the upper and lower limits of the scale of the law." Socrates' death is an "exemplary illustration" of this, since "the laws place their fate in the hands of the condemned man, and ask that he should sanction their authority by submitting to them as a rational man."

According to Deleuze, "irony is the process of thought whereby the law is made to depend on an infinitely superior Good, just as humor is the attempt to sanction the law by recourse to an infinitely more righteous Best." Anyway, the philosopher adds that "the notion of law is not self-sufficient unless backed by force; ideally it needs to rest on a higher principle as well as on a consideration of its remote consequences." Therefore, the laws are nothing but ironic statements, dissimulating the Good. Humans know that the Good exists, but they do not know what the Good is. Humans need laws, but their knowledge (or rather we should say intuition) of the Good allows them to perceive the ironic nature of the laws themselves. If one looks at the practical outcomes of the law, the distance between the latter and the Good often appears, offering chances for humor.

The reflections in this book about the relationship between the law, the phantom of justice, and humor are quite syntonic with Deleuze's view. Deleuze does not clarify the role of "force": considerations above on the relationship between com-

402 Gilles Deleuze, *Coldness and Cruelty* [1967] (New York: Zone Books, 1991).

https://doi.org/10.1515/9783111286778-011

edy and dictatorships show that force cannot overcome the human capacity to see the comic aspect even of the strictest laws and enforcement apparatuses.

On the other hand, there seem to be some missing elements in Deleuze's reconstruction of Plato's idea of the relationship between laws, the Good, and laughter, on the one hand, and of Socrates' final choice to obey the laws, on the other. Both the *Republic* and the *Laws*, as seen in the essay above, show Plato's hostility towards laughter and humor, precisely because of their capacity to disrupt a society built upon a legal order that reflects a carefully sought-after idea of Good, which is the outcome of the philosophers' way of living and thinking. If there is a link between the laws and moral philosophy, seen as a search for the Good, then moral philosophy should share the same ironic/humorous nature of the law. The only possible knowledge would be a "gay science," alongside a "gay law." Nietzsche shows that things are not that easy. The path towards the "gay science" requires overcoming the traditional view of morals, through the transmutation of values (something very far from the classical idea of Good) and, at least according to Nietzsche, setting aside any idea of law as a source of non-arbitrary rules. Not by chance, Nietzsche did not theorise any "gay law," and he did not even dive into the problem of defining the rules of eutrapelia, though he did hint at them, as shown by his thoughts on the "unjust" scorn of Don Quixote. Since the *Laws* are a comprehensive treatise of how "good laws" should be drafted, within the perfectly engineered state described in the *Republic*, one may doubt that Plato would agree that "the Good has forsaken the world." The Good may be hidden and elusive, but the philosophers' task is precisely to find it, explain it to the others, and possibly practice it, as shown by Socrates' example. Maybe, in his early works Plato was more doubtful about the degree of precision that can be obtained in the knowledge of good, but, unlike Nietzsche, he would not appreciate being called "a buffoon."

Socrates' death is not the consequence of the "quite conventional" idea that, not (fully) knowing the Good, one must accept the law as a second best, even when the law is clearly unjust. Socrates accepts his fate, as he explains in the *Crito*, because he is bound by loyalty, and therefore by a common idea of Good, to the Athenian community which sentenced him to death. If Socrates had accepted Crito's proposal to escape, his behavior would have been immoral, unjust, and not merely illegal. The general principle stating that you must obey the rules of your community (and not merely the laws of "the country of birth or residence"), and accept its decisions even to your detriment, is a truthful, and not ironic expression of Good. Socrates, or Plato, apparently raise no objections. Maybe this is why at the end of the *Phaedo*, Socrates, moments before dying, reminds Crito to sacrifice a rooster to Asclepius. The god protected both from acting immorally (crazily), and prevented Socrates from betraying the fundamental reason for his philosophical search of the Good.

Deleuze sees the humorous side of law enforcement against Socrates in the fact that the final decision is in the hands of Socrates as a "rational man." I would rather say "as a loyal man." Socrates' acceptance of his sentence safeguards the link between law and the Good, by turning an unjust decision into an agreed outcome, which reinforces the communitarian bond among the Athenians. In some way, the Socrates-laws relationship is a win-win game. If Socrates had escaped, as suggested by Crito, the outcome would have turned into a lose-lose. Socrates would have lost his credibility as a philosopher and an educator, betraying his ideal of loyalty, and the laws would have lost their very foundation, represented by the common idea of Good which kept the Athenians together. The law would have turned into mere force, against communitarian agreement and not backed by any idea but the mere acceptance that the strongest prevails (something not Athenian at all).

Anyway, even admitting that Plato would accept the idea of the ironic/humorous nature of the law, it would still be hard to shift such an acknowledgement on a general plane and state, with Deleuze, that "irony and humor are the essential forms through which we apprehend the law." Such an acknowledgment would be the (disappointing) outcome of a thoroughly philosophical path, which, in any case, should be hidden from the general curiosity. The comic nature of the law should remain shaded, invisible to citizens / believers, or the law would fully lose its credibility, alongside any practical utility. Deleuze states that "the classical conception of the law found its perfect expression in Plato and in that form gained universal acceptance throughout the Christian world," but it is quite difficult to share the view that the Christian idea of the law is grounded in the awareness of its comic nature, or even that the very idea of a "comic law" could be accepted by classical Christian thinkers. Rather, those thinkers inherited from Plato and Aristotle their distrust towards laughter, which endangers any possible ideal, let alone any possible faith.

Deleuze's further statement, according to which "it is in this essential relation to the law" that irony and humor "acquire their function and their significance" seems a little too farfetched, unless we give to the word "law" a very broad meaning, which should include any statements (not necessarily juridical, or moral) which aim at having a general validity. Children laugh long before they learn what the law is, not only out of joy, but merely out of surprise, just when they see something pleasant and unexpected. Probably the sense of laughter arises, along with that of fear or horror, alongside the progressive perception of the ever-changing diversity of living.

It follows that the nexus between law and humor is not the mere effect of the comic nature of law, but of a dialectic relationship, if not a fight, between the law's pretense to issue general statements – with a capacity to transform humans and the world they live in – and the feeling of constant change, of life as a form of wandering, that grounds laughter.

Kant

Deleuze writes that "The final overthrow of the classical conception of the law was certainly not the result of the discovery of the relativity and variability of laws, since these were fully recognized and understood in this conception and were indeed an integral part of it." For sure, the Athenians knew that their laws were different from those of the Spartans, and that different communities agreed on different views of the Good, although this did not prevent them from finding some agreement, when needed.[403]

The French philosopher[404] sees the turning point between the classical and the modern idea of law in Kant's work:

> Whereas the classical conception only dealt with the laws according to the various spheres of the Good or the various circumstances attending the Best, Kant can speak of the moral law, and of its application to what otherwise remains totally undetermined. The moral law is the representation of a pure form and is independent of content or object, spheres of activity or circumstances. The moral law is THE LAW, the form of the law and as such it cannot be grounded in a higher principle. In this sense Kant is one of the first to break away from the classical conception of the law and to give us a truly modern conception.

Deleuze is not interested in the way Kant "salvages the Good in the system," but in his reconstruction of Kant's thought he adds that

> The law can no longer be grounded on the superior principle of the Good, but neither can it be sanctioned any more by recourse to the idea of the Best as representing the good will of the righteous. Clearly THE LAW, as defined by its pure form, without substance or object or any determination whatsoever, is such that no one knows nor can know what it is. It operates without making itself known.

There follows that anybody is constitutionally guilty of some breach of this unknown formal law: "This is the process by which the law manifests itself in its ab-

403 Plato, *Laws*, Vol. I, trans. Robert Greg Bury (Cambridge: Harvard Univ. Press, 1961), 191.
404 Deleuze, *Coldness and Cruelty*, 82–83.

solute purity, and proves us guilty." Kafka is quoted as an example. Deleuze does not distinguish between moral law and state law, nor does he dive into Kant's political philosophy. Thus, he attributes to Kant the idea of state law that characterizes legal positivism in its toughest expressions, breaking the nexus between state law and values and grounding the former exclusively on power. Actually, Kant emphasized the link between moral law and rationality, on the moral side, and that between acts of the state and rationality, as expressed by the general will in the ideal republican state, on the political side. Rationality, with its universal afflatus, is the element that keeps the system together, rather than being mere form. Of course, as a foundation for any possible law, Kant's rationality is something completely different from Socrates' loyalty (loyalty, unlike rationality, is a personal feeling, and in no case a universal parameter of judgment). It is not Kant who introduced the idea of guilt, or even some original and irredeemable guilt of humans, into Western thought. Rather, Kant may suggest the idea that an immoral behavior, such as a sexual perversion (let us not forget that Deleuze is dealing with sadism and masochism) is an irrational act, and therefore a possible form of mental sickness (and Deleuze's approach is clinical, just as it is philosophical). Moreover, Kant may suggest the idea that an illegal act is against reason/general will and thus it implies not only the fault of a breach of loyalty towards a given community, but a more serious fault, impinging once again in the realm of abnormality.

Anyway, I am not sure whether it is Kant's fault if monarchs and rule-makers in general progressively claimed to be reason incarnated, if reason tended to fade into power, if law became mere words of potentially oppressive power, and if the institutions turned from the assembly of the Athenians into the oppressive and unknowable mechanisms described by Kafka.

At this point, Deleuze introduces the psychoanalytic theme, which lies at the core of his work. Borrowing from Freud, and mostly from Lacan's complex reading of Sade with reference to Kant,[405] Deleuze emphasizes the link between the (moral?) law and repressed desires, claiming that the law, in order to perform its function, needs to remove its very object:

> The law cannot specify its object without self-contradiction, nor can it define itself with reference to a content without removing the repression on which it rests. The object of the law and the object of desire are one and the same, and remain equally concealed ... The comic is the only possible mode of conceiving the law, in a peculiar combination of irony and humor. In modem thought irony and humor take on a new form: they are now directed at a subversion of the law.

405 Jacques Lacan, "Kant with Sade" [1963], trans. James B. Swenson, Jr, *October* 51 (1989), 55–75.

The subversive power of laughter was well-known by Plato, and Aristotle too. Rather, after Nietzsche this power acquires a positive connotation, though without fully losing its threatening side. The real problem is with the concept of rationality. After Freud, the human mind can no longer be described using such a clear-cut notion. It becomes an arena where different forces fight each other, using complex strategies of attack and defense. This undermines Kant's system, insofar as it is no longer possible to use rationality as a test for universality. As shown by Lacan, using such a test may lead to paradoxical outcomes, such as universalizing Sade's law of pleasure by virtue of its rationality.

When assessing the possibility to extend this approach to state law, we should consider that state law has limited possibilities in resorting to removal strategies. In order to be obeyed, state law must be explicit (at least following the Western notion of law). It must mention the behavior it prohibits. On the other hand, legal positivism tends to cast a shadow on the link between law and morals – and therefore, in a Kantian perspective, rationality- to the point of holding that there is no such link, and that the legal system is self-determined. Thus, elusive moral law and explicit state law can coexist, with the former in a secondary position. Law basically becomes a matter of power, and rationality, sometimes along with morals, becomes a disguise for the exercise of power. Nietzsche clarified how any rules and any knowledge which constitute outcomes of the will to power, can only be grounded on lies. The strategy of the law is not removal, but lying. The task of the "gay science" is precisely to unveil these lies, thanks to the new knowledge which springs out of the "golden laughter," through the transmutation of values. Legal positivism and modern and contemporary constitutionalism can follow Nietzsche when he speaks about the link between law and power, but they cannot follow him on the path of the transmutation of values and on the critique against rationalism. They need to construe some "good power," that of the state, which stands on solid and equally "good" grounds set forth once and forever in the fundamental charters. Legal positivism needs a *Grundnorm* which is there to stay, and from which the rest of the legal order can be rationally and legally built. Thus, legal positivism somehow tries to keep Kant and Nietzsche together. It holds that the law is an outcome of the power of the state, and therefore it is not universal, nor can it necessarily be universalized. At the same time, legal positivism claims that the power of the constitutional state is a "good" power, which acts rationally starting from agreed values stated once and forever. As shown in the essay above, comedy does not, nor cannot accept such a construction. The Good, however it may be conceived, morality, and power can all be laughed at, but power is the most ridiculous. We humans do not know exactly what "good" is, though we search for it, but we experience personally what "power" is in the form of ambition for power and/or submission to power. We suspect that the "good power" may be an oxymoron, but we know that we cannot do without some form of power. The more ridiculous such power shall prove to be, the less powerful it shall be.

Sade

Deleuze hits the bull's eye when, referring to Kafka's *The Trial*, he writes that "A spurious sense of tragedy dulls our intelligence; how many authors are distorted by placing a childishly tragic construction on what is more often the expression of an aggressively comic force!" When listening patiently to someone else's griefs, a sense of tragedy inspires a feeling of empathy and depth of thought, along with the pleasure of being part of an elite, which can follow the path of moral growth and a final catharsis. Comedy, on the contrary, is seen as trivial, popular, involving a sense of distance and indifference towards the ridiculed victim. Comedy often shows that we, the spectators, are exactly in the position of the one who is ridiculed, but we are not "intelligent" enough to understand it. We are supposed to be laughing at somebody else, but we are laughing at ourselves, and the ridiculed one is laughing back at us.

Sade does not escape this rule. Deleuze takes him seriously and focuses on his political philosophy, criticizing tyranny, and the law as an outcome of tyranny:

> It is irrelevant whether we see the law as the expression of the rule of the strongest or as the product of the self-protective union of the weak. Masters and slaves, the strong and the weak, all are creatures of secondary nature; the union of the weak merely favors the emergence of the tyrant; his existence depends on it. In every case the law is a mystification; it is not a delegated but a usurped power that depends on the infamous complicity of slaves and masters.[406]

On the other hand, we should not forget that these teachings against tyranny and the law come from characters who philosophize in the boudoir, during brief intermissions between complex performances of group sex, whose outcome is to show that the ultimate foundation of being is a search for unlimited personal pleasure. The point that Deleuze apparently misses is that in this scenario power and pleasure are synonyms. Sade's characters praise anarchy and despise the law when they are talking about politics, but they deny their own teachings when sex and pleasure are at stake, and sex and pleasure are what matters to them. They do not abolish the Good, or rationality, but they simply substitute it with Evil, which becomes the *Grundnorm.* While Socrates admitted that he did not know exactly what the Good was, though he was living in search of it, Sade's "philosophers" do know

406 Deleuze, *Coldness and Cruelty*, 86.

very well what Evil is; they know it, teach it, and practice it, leaving no room for doubts of any sort. They are "one-dimensional men," carrying on their peculiar idea of "education" as something that must be passed on to their pupils. Sade's masters do not despise rules and laws at all, nor tyranny even, when it comes to sex as a demonstration of the primacy of Evil. Just think of the *120 journées de Sodome*, where everything is deeply regulated by specific roles and procedures, which include even specific timetables for each single sexual misdemeanour. It is not surprising that Horkheimer and Adorno saw in Sade's "sexual teams" an announcement of the forthcoming model of capitalistic business organization, where anything is governed by the monolithic principle of efficiency, and of the consumerist society based on mass production-distribution-consumption. It is not surprising, as well, that Pier Paolo Pasolini, in his 1975 cinematographic rendition of the *120 journées* set during the last days of the Fascist dictatorship, saw in Sade's "libertines" an emblem of the limitless cruelty and self-referentiality of totalitarianisms.

I cannot agree with Deleuze when he writes that, in Sade,

> [...] the idea of absolute evil embodied in primary nature cannot be equated either with tyranny – for tyranny still presupposes laws – or with a combination of whims and arbitrariness; its higher, impersonal model is rather to be found in the anarchic institutions of perpetual motion and permanent revolution.[407]

In Sade, absolute evil is the law, and the law of absolute evil is completely fixed, undisputable, and motionless. It is far more static than any Kantian idea of a universal law. When Sade's libertine philosophers preach anarchy, they are not talking seriously, or maybe they are just talking about a trivial matter, i.e., politics, which is powerless against the only real power, the search for pleasure, pushed by the Law of Supreme Evil. Sade tries to shift the Supreme Evil from any sensible or emotional dimension of life, uplifting it to an unattainable "primary nature," but this does nothing but reinforce the normative nature of the Supreme Evil, at least insofar as the alleged primary nature is completely non-disposable by humans.

Still talking about Sade, Deleuze adds that

> The fact that anarchy can only exist in the interval between two regimes based on laws, abolishing the old to give birth to the new, does not prevent this divine interval, this vanishing instant, from testifying to its fundamental difference from all forms of the law.[408]

407 Deleuze, *Coldness and Cruelty*, 87.
408 Deleuze, *Coldness and Cruelty*, 87.

Yet, Sade's sexual/criminal enterprises are wholly based on detailed rules, which, although turned upside-down, are still laws. From the point of view of someone who is not a sadist, they are simply bad laws, just like racial laws are bad laws from the point of view of anyone who is not a racist. Sade does not tell of one single moment of "divine anarchy." In his petrified world, no transmutation of values is possible. Deleuze, quoting *Juliette*, writes that in Sade:

> Sensuality is movement. In order to convey the immediacy of this action of one soul against another, Sade chooses to rely on the quantitative techniques of accumulation and acceleration, mechanically grounded in a materialistic theory: reiteration and internal multiplication of the scenes, precipitation, over-determination. (The subject is at once parricide, incestuous, murderer, prostitute and sodomite.)[409]

This frantic reiteration of always identical acts, this accumulation of sins, misdemeanours, and crimes is only apparent movement. It is like the movement of a hamster spinning a wheel: completely useless and self-referential, not even natural but the mere outcome of imprisonment. Unlike hamsters, Sade is self-imprisoned by his own idea-obsession of the Supreme Evil as the only possible primary nature, and the only possible law.[410]

On the other hand, Sade may be joking when he talks about sex and crime, just as he is joking when he talks about politics or philosophy. But his science is never gay, because, bound as he is by repetition, he misses the link between comedy, laughter, and change. Thus, only the law remains.[411] Sade's laughter is like a useless echo in empty hallways, after the cries of the victims have faded away. Anyway, at

---

409 Deleuze, *Coldness and Cruelty*, 70.

410 Deleuze does not miss the importance of repetition in Sade, and in Masoch: "Beneath the sound and fury of sadism and masochism the terrible force of repetition is at work. What is altered here is the normal function of repetition in its relation to the pleasure principle: instead of repetition being experienced as a form of behavior related to a pleasure already obtained or anticipated, instead of repetition being governed by the idea of experiencing or reexperiencing pleasure, repetition runs wild and becomes independent of all previous pleasure. It has itself become an idea or ideal" (Deleuze, *Coldness and Cruelty*, 120). Thus, repetition seems to become the real core of Sade's "primary nature." This petrified idea goes against any idea of the link between humor and transformation, or of anarchy, or of creative movement. It is an expression of the law at its heights.

411 And, once again, Deleuze does not miss the point, when he underlines the super-egoic nature of sadism: "Sadism likewise tells a story. It relates how the ego, in an entirely different context and in a different struggle, is beaten and expelled; how the unrestrained superego assumes an exclusive role, modeled on an inflated conception of the father's role – the mother and the ego becoming its choice victims" (Deleuze, *Coldness and Cruelty*, 131).

least to this reader, both Sade's lengthy lessons in immorality and his hundreds-of-pages-long tales in pornology[412] tend to sound boring.

The Law and the Masochist's Contract

About Masoch, Deleuze points out that:

> The way in which Masoch defines his idealism or "supersensualism" seems at first sight rather trivial. Why believe in the idea of a perfect world? asks Masoch in *The Divorced Woman*. What we need to do is to "put on wings" and escape into the world of dreams. He does not believe in negating or destroying the world nor in idealizing it: what he does is to disavow and thus to suspend it, in order to secure an ideal which is itself suspended in fantasy. He questions the validity of existing reality in order to create a pure ideal reality, an operation which is perfectly in line with the judicial spirit of masochism.[413]

So, does the law have a masochist spirit, symmetrical to the "judicial spirit" of masochism, insofar as it tries to "create a pure ideal reality," or, to be more precise, to transform the existing reality into a better one, according to its own will, which shall impose itself on its subjects? The English translation of Deleuze's work uses the word "fantasy," but the French original reads: "Il ne s'agit donc pas de nier le monde, ou de le détruire, mais pas d'avantage de l'idéaliser; il s'agit de le dénier, de le suspendre en le déniant pour s'ouvrir à un idéal lui-même suspendu dans le phantasme."[414] "Phantasme," ghost, and not "fantasy." As we have seen in the essay above, the law has a lot to do with ghosts, and mostly with the phantom of justice. It chases this ghost and is constantly confronted with it by comedy. Thus, Masoch calls the law to act as a key, as a medium linking the "real" world with the universe of ghosts. The law should let the ghosts inspire humans, lifting their spirits towards "supersensualism." This is exactly the task that Masoch assigns to the law, by means of his use of the contract in his relationships with women. Should the law accept this mission, there would be no room left for comedy, and humor. On the other hand, following Masoch's scheme, in order to perform such a function the law should "disavow" and "suspend" the world, moving towards the sphere of idealism where ghosts dwell, at least according to Masoch.

---

412 "[...] the work of Sade and Masoch cannot be regarded as pornography; it merits the more exalted title of "pornology" because its erotic language cannot be reduced to the elementary functions of ordering and describing" (Deleuze, *Coldness and Cruelty*, 18).

413 Deleuze, *Coldness and Cruelty*, 32–33.

414 Gilles Deleuze, *Présentation de Sacher-Masoch. Le froid et le cruel* (Paris: Les éditions de minuit, 1967), 30.

This is the really hard part. The law cannot but refuse this method and, consequently, it cannot but grant the perennial survival of comedy, and humor.

Let us supersede this issue for the time being, and turn for a while to Deleuze's remarks about Masoch's attitude towards the law and comedy. According to the French philosopher:

> The masochist regards the law as a punitive process and therefore begins by having the punishment inflicted upon himself; once he has undergone the punishment, he feels that he is allowed or indeed commanded to experience the pleasure that the law was supposed to forbid. The essence of masochistic humor lies in this, that the very law which forbids the satisfaction of a desire under threat of subsequent punishment is converted into one which demands the punishment first and then orders that the satisfaction of the desire should necessarily follow upon the punishment.[415]

The statement that the masochist "regards the law as a punitive process" contradicts the previous argument about the "judicial spirit" of masochism, and the role of the law in assuring the "elevation" of humans (or rather I should say of the masochist) from the actual world to the world of "supersensuality." The punishment is completely part of the staging of the masochist's ritual, performed by a woman who should transform herself into a goddess-like figure, an unattainable "work of art," whose superior nature is proven precisely by her capacity to rightly punish. The contract, and therefore the law, should enforce the masochist's wish to have the woman undergoing such a transformation. The woman is bound by the contract (by the law) to transform herself into the Venus in furs, to the full benefit of the masochist, and surely not to her own benefit (masochism thus reverses the classical master-and-slave relationship). Sade sees in the law a barrier to pleasure, which involves breaking the law, and substituting it with a stricter and thick headed one. According to Masoch, on the contrary, the law is not at all supposed to "forbid pleasure," or to "forbid the satisfaction of a desire under threat of a subsequent punishment." The law is the hallway to a higher kind of pleasure, aesthetic and ideal, within which punishment marks the distance between the masochist and his woman-idol. The masochist feels and accepts such a distance (Deleuze's "coldness"), which was created by his own will, even against the loving feelings of the woman. Thus, the masochist elevates himself, thanks to the transformative power that the law exercised on the woman via the contract, to a higher level of existence (somehow remembering the annihilating experience of the sublime). Within such an ideal of the law, there is no room for comedy, let alone for

415 Deleuze, *Coldness and Cruelty*, 88–89.

humor. Masoch takes the law damn seriously. The problem is that the law does not take *him* seriously.

Let us turn back to the law and ghosts, and have a closer look at the masochist's contract.

Deleuze points out that:

> In Masoch's personal adventures as well as in his fiction, and in his particular case as well as in the structure of masochism in general, the contract represents the ideal form of the love-relationship and its necessary precondition. A contract is drawn up between the subject and the torturess, giving a new application to the idea of the jurists of antiquity that slavery itself is based on a contract. The masochist appears to be held by real chains, but in fact he is bound by his word alone. The masochistic contract implies not only the necessity of the victim's consent, but his ability to persuade, and his pedagogical and judicial efforts to train his torturer.[416]

The Parisian philosopher adds that Masoch's contracts become "increasingly cruel and restrictive toward one of the parties (in this case the initiator of the contract)," and that "the tightening of the contractual bond indicates that the function of the contract is to lay down the law, which, once established, becomes increasingly cruel and restrictive toward one of the parties (in this case the initiator of the contract)." Although he notes that there is some effort (contractual obligation) of the victim to "train his torturer," Deleuze seems to overlook the peculiar aspect of the masochist's contract. This peculiarity distinguishes the masochist's contract from any idea of slavery and from any ancient example of volunteered slavery, just as from more recent examples, such as the contracts of servitude provided for by the indentured system in the British colonies. The masochist's contract is entirely to the benefit of the slave, and not at all to the benefit of the mistress. In *Venus in Furs*, although the contract of slavery is drafted by Wanda, it is the outcome of Severin's prolonged efforts to persuade her to discover her "real nature," to the point of incarnating Severin's aesthetic ideal. Surely, it is not Wanda's contract, but the masochist's contract. The excerpt of Wanda von Sacher Masoch's memoires added as an appendix to Deleuze's work constantly underlines that her husband was the actual director of their adventures, acting as a real manipulator: "My husband possessed a dangerous eloquence that was gripping, if not convincing, and whoever found themselves exposed to it without warning never failed to succumb to its influence."[417] The "increasing cruelty" of the law is not an outcome of the law, but of changes to the contract which are inspired, if not actually written, by Masoch. He

416 Deleuze, *Coldness and Cruelty*, 75.

417 Wanda von Sacher-Masoch, "The Adventure with Ludwig II," in *Coldness and Cruelty*, 281–293, 287.

is not disappointed at all with such increases in cruelty, since they do nothing but to push the woman-mistress one step closer to his ideal.

At this point, Deleuze focuses on the distinction between the law, trusted by Masoch, and despised by Sade, and the Saint-Just style institutions, praised by Sade:

> Granted that both the contract and the law are in the nature of mystifications, the law being used by despotism for its own purposes, and granted that the institution is the only form of political organization that differs essentially from both law and contract, where should we look to for the perfect institution – the one that banishes contracts and allows only the barest minimum of laws? In reply, Sade points to the ironic possibility, under these conditions, of making atheism, calumny, theft, prostitution, incest and sodomy – even murder – into institutions, and shows furthermore that they are necessarily the types of the ideal institution, the institution in perpetual motion.[418]

The law v. institutions juxtaposition is simply misleading. The institutions exist properly because of some laws, which baptize them as "institutions." It does not matter whether such law comes from the institution itself, or from some other source, if it is obeyed. An institution can be based on the idea of the rule of law, as developed by modern constitutionalism, or on atheism, etc., but in any case, it is always grounded on rules. What changes is the different quality of the founding rule. Moreover, no institution, not even an absolute monarch, acts as a pure rule-maker, which must obey no rule. Even the most powerful institution shall follow a supreme rule, that may be stated as follows: "act in the way which safeguards your power," or, in other words, "never lose your power," and eventually your head alongside it, as what happened to Saint-Just. The very idea of an "institution in perpetual motion" is contradictory: institutions disapprove motion, because motion will overwhelm them, and finally substitute them with new institutions. Once again, motion, in Sade, is only apparent, it is stillness under disguise.

On the contrary, the masochist's contract is aimed at motion, at transformation, at chasing an ideal (attaining to the world of ghosts). Here, Deleuze seems to fall into the traps of Masoch's "dangerous eloquence":

> [...] the contract-law relationship involves in a sense a mystification. To imagine that a contract or quasi contract is at the origin of society is to invoke conditions which are necessarily invalidated as soon as the law comes into being. For the law, once established, violates the contract in that it can apply to a third party, is valid for an indeterminate period and recognizes no inalienable rights. This process of invalidation of the contract by the law is reflected, as we have seen, in the peculiar progression of Masoch's successive love-contracts [...] Since the law results in our enslavement, we should place enslavement first, as the dreadful object

418 Gilles Deleuze, *Coldness and Cruelty*, 78–79.

> of the contract. One could even say, as a general rule, that in masochism the contract is caricatured in order to emphasize its ambiguous destination.[419]

Enslavement is not the outcome of the law, but of the masochist's will, which he asks the law to cooperate with, via the enforcement of the contract. Masoch places enslavement first not because he aims at pre-empting the law, but because the mistress becomes more and more close to his ideal, his ghost, as she gets harsher, performing her contractual obligations to the masochist's benefit. Masoch's trick is to convince Wanda that the Venus in furs is "her real nature," while it is really his own ghost. Using the same trick, Masoch convinces Deleuze that enslavement is in the nature of the law, which uses the contract as an alibi, while enslavement is the core of Masoch's ideal, and Masoch asks the law to cooperate in reaching this ideal, granting enforcement of stricter and stricter contracts. Deleuze is aware of the masochist's egoistic nature, but he seems to forget it when he deals with the masochist's relation with the law. Masoch's contracts can be "caricatures" for the non-masochist reader, but surely not for Masoch.

Of course, the masochist's contracts are legally unenforceable. Thinking of today's law, the reason for this unenforceability can be traced to the inalienable nature of some rights involved by Masoch's contracts, like the right to life, and/or in the fact that those contracts do not pursue interests which may be legally protected. This was not a problem under laws of the past which allowed slavery, including volunteered slavery, but, as we have seen, the masochist's contract provides for a "reversed slavery," to the benefit of the slave. Paradoxically, under those contracts the slave could sue the mistress for non-performance of her duty to properly act as a mistress. We can reasonably suppose that no slavery law would ever enforce such a claim. So, the unenforceability of the masochist's contracts stands on a deeper level than that of modern theories of inalienable rights, or techniques of legal control and limitations on private autonomy.

Let us turn back to the method that the law should follow, according to Masoch. The law should "suspend the world," and work as a medium towards the beyond, where ghosts dwell. It should lift the humans' spirits towards the ghosts, thus allowing the shift from sensuality (the way humans act in the world) to "supersensuality" (Masoch's Apollonian ideal). This way, comedy and humor would be pushed out of the scene. Sadly, this is something that the law, or at least human law, could never do, or even accept to try. The law cannot suspend the world: it is in the world and of the world. It aims at transforming the world by acting in the world. Should the law ever try to "suspend" the world, it would reveal its complete

419 Deleuze, *Coldness and Cruelty*, 91–92.

uselessness, to the point of reaching the paradox of suspending itself. The law chases the phantom of justice, but it does that in the world, like a metaphorical ghostbuster. This is why it offers unlimited opportunities to comedy, and humor. On the contrary, it is exactly the idea of suspending the world, and itself as a part of the world, that sounds hilarious to the law. This way, the law would fall, with Wanda and Deleuze, into the trap of Masoch's eloquence, i. e., it would assume that its true "spirit" is a masochist one. The law would become a Venus in furs, an apparent mistress, and a real slave of her own servant. But the law is too skilful, it has inhabited this planet too long to be cheated by this kind of tricks.

Think of the law of contracts, and read this clause of the Masoch – Fanny von Pistor contract:

> In short, the subject shall obey his sovereign with complete servility and shall greet any benevolence on her part as a precious gift; he shall not lay claim to her love nor to any right to be her lover. On her behalf, Fanny von Pistor undertakes to wear furs as often as possible, especially when she is behaving cruelly.[420]

Concentrate. Close your eyes. You will hear the law giggling.

---

420 Published as Appendix II to Deleuze, *Coldness and Cruelty*, 277.

Bibliography

Adler, Hermann, "Jewish Wit and Humor," *The Eclectic Magazine* 57 (1893): 530–538.

Ajani, Gianmaria, Barbara Pasa, and Domenico Francavilla, *Diritto comparato. Lezioni e materiali* (Turin: Giappichelli, 2018).

Andersen, Hans Christian, "The Emperor's New Clothes," in *Andersen's Fairy Tales*, trans. Jean Hersholt (New York: Heritage Press, 1942), 79–87.

Arendt, Hanna, *The Origins of Totalitarianism* [1946–1948] (New York: Schocken Books, 2004).

Aristophanes, *The Wasps*, ed. Anya Elizabeth Leonard (Classical Wisdom Weekly). Available online: https://classicalwisdom.com/wasps/.

Aristotle, *Parts of Animals*, trans. A. L. Peck (Cambridge, MA: Harvard Univ. Press, 1961).

Aristotle, *The Nicomachean Ethics*, trans. David Ross (Oxford: Oxford Univ. Press, 1998).

Ascarelli, Tullio, "Antigone e Porzia," in *Problemi giuridici* (Milan: Giuffrè, 1959), 107–117.

Aspesi, Natalia, "Villaggio in cerca d'amore," *La Repubblica* (September 8, 1992).

Aub, Max, *Crimenes ejemplares* [1957] *Crimenes ejemplares/ Exemplary Crimes* (Thule Ediciones, 2007); Italian trans. Lucrezia Panunzio Cipriani, *Delitti esemplari. Gli insopportabili incontri della quotidianità trasformati in delitti senza castigo* (Palermo: Sellerio, 1981).

Aubry, Charles and Charles Rau, *Cours de droit civil français d'après la méthode de Zachariae* (Paris, 1869). Available online: https://gallica.bnf.fr/ark:/12148/bpt6k5858422r/f10.image.texteImage (last access in March 2021).

Auden, Wystan Hugh, "Law like Love" [1939], in *Collected Shorter Poems 1927–1957* (London: Faber & Faber, 1969): 154–155.

Banfi, Emilio, "Il linguaggio comico: tra pragmatica e strategie linguistiche," in *Sei lezioni sul linguaggio comico,* ed. Emilio Banfi (Trento: Università degli Studi di Trento, 1995), 17–70.

Barbieri, Daniele, "Ridere con ritmo. Meccanismi tensivi e iterazione nel testo comico," in *Il Comico: approcci semiotici. Documenti di lavoro e prepubblicazioni,* eds. Daniele Barbieri, Giovanni Bottiroli, and Alessandro Perissinotto (Urbino: Centro internazionale di Semiotica e Linguistica, 2001), 1–26.

Bartezzaghi, Stefano, "Così Fantozzi," in Paolo Villaggio, *Fantozzi rag. Ugo* (Milan: Rizzoli, 2013), 1–8.

Barthes, Roland, *Le degré zéro de l'écriture* suivi de *Nouveaux essais critiques* (Paris: Seuil, 1972).

Bataille, George, *Oeuvres complètes* (Paris: Gallimard, 1973).

Baudelaire, Charles, "On the Essence of Laughter" [1885], trans. and ed. Jonathan Mayne, in *The Mirror of Art. Critical Studies by Charles Baudelaire* (New York: Doubleday, 1956): 131–153.

Bauman, Zygmunt, *Identity: Conversations with Benedetto Vecchi* (London: Polity Press, 2004).

Becker, Gary S., "Crime and Punishment: An Economic Approach," *Journal of Political Economy* 76 (1968): 169–217.

Bergson, Henri, *Le rire: Essai sur la signification du comique* (1900); Italian trans. Arnaldo Cervesato and Carmine Gallo, *Il riso. Saggi sul significato del comico* (Bari: Laterza, 1999), preface by Beniamino Placido.

Bergson, Henri, *Laughter. An Essay on the Meaning of the Comic* [1900], trans. Cloudesley Brereton and Fred Rothwell (London: McMillan, 1911).

Bertozzi, Marco, "Hobbes e Canetti. Il riso come maschera dell'arcaico," *Animal Ridens – I castelli di Yale online*, 5.2 (2017): 279–287.

Bierce, Ambrose, *The Unabridged Devil's Dictionary: The Cynic's Word Book – Satirical, Ironic and Humorous Definitions* [1911] (Athens: Univ. of Georgia Press, 2001). Also online: http://www.thedevilsdictionary.com (last access in February 2023).

https://doi.org/10.1515/9783111286778-012

Biscaretti di Ruffia, Paolo and Gabriele Crespi Reghizzi, *La Costituzione sovietica del 1977* (Milan: Giuffrè, 1990).
Blumemberg, Hans, *The Laughter of the Thracian Woman. A Protohistory of Theory* [1987], trans. Spencer Hawkins (London: Bloosmbury, 2015).
Bombelli, Giovanni, "'Comunità': tra identità e diritto," in *Luoghi della filosofia del diritto. Idee Strutture Mutamenti*, ed. Bruno Montanari (Turin: Giappichelli, 2012), 233–273.
Borges, George Luis, *The Analytical Language of John Wilkins of 1952*, Jorge Luis Borges, *Other Inquisitions*, trans. Ruth LC. Simms (Austin/London: Univ. of Texas Press, 1964), 101–105.
Bosco, Umberto, *Introduzione* al Canto XXI, in Dante Alighieri, *La Divina Commedia. Inferno* (Florence: Le Monnier, 1979).
Bottiroli, Giovanni, "Il comico delle articolazioni," in *Il Comico: approcci semiotici. Documenti di lavoro e prepubblicazioni*, eds. Daniele Barbieri, Giovanni Bottiroli, and Alessandro Perissinotto (Urbino: Centro internazionale di Semiotica e Linguistica, 2001), 303–305. Available online: https://giovannibottiroli.it/it/letteratura/altro/71-il-comico-delle-articolazioni.html (last access in February 2023).
Brant, Sebastian, *The Ship of Fools*, trans. Alexander Barclay (Edinburgh: W. Patterson, 1874).
Campanella, Tommaso, *La Città del Sole. Scritti scelti* (Nuoro-Soveria Mannelli: Ilisso- Rubbettino, 2006).
Canetti, Elias, "The First Book: Auto da Fè" [1973], trans. Joachim Neugroschel, in Elias Canetti, *The Conscience of Words. Essays* (New York: Seabury Press, 1979), 203 – 213.
Canetti, Elias, *Auto da fé* [1935], trans. C.V. Wedgwood (New York: Stein and Day, 1946).
Canetti, Elias, *Crowds and Power* [1960], trans. Carol Stewart (New York: Seabury Press, 1978).
Carbone, Paola and Giuseppe Rossi, "Celsus and Chatwin Go Walkabout," *Pólemos*, 9.1 (2015): 175–197.
Carbone, Paola and Giuseppe Rossi, "Ethics and Law at Play on the Football Pitch," in *Fables of the Law. Fairy Tales in a Legal Context*, eds. Daniela Carpi and Marett Leiboff (Berlin: De Gruyter, 2016), 209–243.
Carbone, Paola and Giuseppe Rossi, "Who is the Monster? Laughing at Friends and Foes," in *Monsters and Monstrosity. From the Canon to the Anti-Canon: Literary and Juridical Subversions*, ed. Daniela Carpi (Berlin/Boston: De Gruyter, 2019), 157–179.
Carpi, Daniela, "'Law and…': A Proposal for Further Interdisciplinary Approaches," in *Recht und Literature im Zwischenraum/Law and Literature in-Between: Aktuelle inter-und transdisziplinäre Zugänge/Contemporary Inter-and Transdisciplinary Approaches*, eds. Christian Hiebaum, Susanne Knaller, and Doris Pichler (New Brunswick/London: transcript Verlag, 2015), 105–117.
Cartari, Vincenzo, *Le imagini de i dei de gli antichi* (Venezia: Giordano Ziletti, 1571). Available online: https://gallica.bnf.fr/ark:/12148/bpt6k59561r/f495.item (last access in February 2023).
Cattaneo, Fabrizio, *L'idea di repubblica da Kant a Habermas* (Turin: Giappichelli, 2013).
Chrétien de Troyes, *Perceval. The Story of the Grail*, trans. Nigel Bryant (Cambridge: D.S. Brewer, 1986).
Cicero, Marcus Tullius, *De officiis*, ed. Michael Winterbottom (London: Clarendon Press, 1994).
Cipolla, Carlo M., *The Basic Laws of Human Stupidity* [1976] (New York: Doubleday, 2021).
Collodi, Carlo, *Pinocchio* [1881] (London: Bloomsbury Books, 1994).
Cross, Frank B., *The Theory and Practice of Statutory Interpretation* (Stanford, CA: Stanford Univ. Press, 2009).
Curtis, Dennis E. and Judith Resnik , "Images of justice," *Yale Law Journal*, 96 (1986): Yale Law Journal 96 (1987): 1727–1772.

Curtis, Dennis E. and Judith Resnik, *Representing Justice: Invention, Controversy and Rights in City-States and Democratic Courtrooms* (New Haven/London: Yale Univ. Press, 2011).

Davis, Ben, "Guy Smiling," review of "Yue Minjun and the Symbolic Smile," Oct. 14, 2007–Jan. 6, 2008, at the Queens Museum of Art, Flushing Meadows Corona Park, Queens, N.Y. 11368, *Artnet Magazine* (2017). Available online: http://www.artnet.com/magazineus/reviews/davis/davis11 – 12 – 07.asp (last access in February 2023).

De Amicis, Edmondo, *Heart. A School-Boy's Journal* [1886], trans. Isabel F. Hapgood (New York: Crowell & Co., 1901).

de Cervantes, Miguel, *Adventures of Don Quixote de La Mancha* [1605], trans. Charles Jarvis (New York: Crowell & Co., without year).

Dentith, Simon, *Bakhtinian Thought* (London/New York: Routledge, 1995).

De Quincey, Thomas, *Murder considered as one of the fine arts* [1827–1839] (United Kingdom: Penguin Random House, 2015).

Descartes, René, *The Passions of the Soule* [1649], translator unknown (London: Martin & Ridley, 1650).

Diderot, Denis, *Essai sur les règnes de Claude et de Néron, et sur la vie et les écrits de Sénéque, pour servir d'introduction à la lecture de ce philosophe* [1782]. Available online https://obvil.sorbonne-universite.fr/corpus/critique/diderot_claude-neron/#body-2 (last access in January 2023).

Donà, Massimo, *Filosofia dell'errore. Le forme dell'inciampo* (Milan: Bompiani, 2012).

Donati, Benvenuto, *Lodovico Antonio Muratori e la giurisprudenza del suo tempo* (Modena: Università degli Studi, 1931).

Dovlatov, Sergej, *The Zone. A Prison Guard Notes* [1985], trans. Anne Frydman (London: Alma Classics, 2013).

Doyle, Arthur Conan, *The Hound of the Baskerville* [1901–1902], in *The Complete Sherlock Holmes Long Stories* (London: John Murray and Jonathan Cape, 1973).

Dworkin, Ronald, *Justice for Hedgehogs* (Cambridge, MA: Harvard Univ. Press, 2011).

Dworkin, Ronald, "What is a Good Life?," *New York Rev. of Books* (February 10, 2011). Available online: http://www.nybooks.com/articles/2011/02/10/what-good-life/ (last access in February 2023).

Eco, Umberto, "Elogio di Franti," in *Diario minimo* (Milan: Mondadori, 1963), 85–96.

Eco, Umberto, *Il costume di casa. Evidenze e misteri dell'ideologia italiana negli anni sessanta* (Milan: Bompiani, 2012).

Eco, Umberto, "The Comic and the Rule" [1981], trans. William Weaver in *Travels in Hyperreality. Essays* (San Diego: Harcourt Brace Jovanovich, 1986), 269–278.

Ercoli, Lucrezia, *Filosofia dell'umorismo* (Rome: Inschibolleth, 2013).

Falcioni, Daniela, *Natura e libertà in Kant. Una interpretazione del progetto per la pace perpetua* [1795] (Rome: Bulzoni, 2000).

Famularo, Mara, "Marjane Satrapi e la rivoluzione di *Persepolis*," *Fumettologica* (November 22, 2019). Available online: https://www.fumettologica.it/2019/11/marjane-satrapi-persepolis/ (last access in February 2023).

Ferlinghetti, Lawrence, *Little Boy* (London: Faber & Faber, 2019).

Ferrajoli, Luigi, "Garantismo e poteri selvaggi," *Teoria politica* 8.3 (1998): 11–24.

Fischer, Mark A., E. Gabriel Perle, and John Taylor Williams, *Perle, Williams and Fischer on Publishing Law* (New York: Wolters Kluwer, 2015).

Foucault, Michel, "The Ethics of the Concern of the Self as a Practice of Freedom" [1984], in *Ethics Subjectivity and Truth*, ed. Paul Rabinow, trans. P. Aranov, and D. McGrawth (New York: New Press, 2003), 281 – 301.

Foucault, Michel, "Truth and Juridical Forms," in *Power*, ed. James D. Faubion, trans. R. Hurley (New York: New Press, 2000), 1 – 89.

Foucault, Michel, *The Order of Things. An Archaeology of the Human Sciences* [1966] (New York: Pantheon Books/Random House, 1970).

Franca, Marcilio, "The Blindness of Justice: An Iconographic Dialogue between Art and Law," in *Law and the Senses*, eds. Andrea Pavoni, Danilo Mandic, Caterina Nirta, Andrea Philippopoulos-Mihalopoulos (London: Westminster Univ. Press, 2018), 159–196.

Freud, Sigmund, "Humor" [1927], in *Collected Papers*, ed. James Strachey (London: Hogarth Press, 1950), V, 215–221.

Freud, Sigmund, *Der Witz und seine Beziehung zum Unbewußten* (1905), *The Joke and Its Relation to the Unconscious*, trans. John Carey (London: Penguin, 2003).

Fry, William F., *Sweet Madness: A Study of Humor* (Palo Alto, CA: Pacific Books, 1963).

Frye, Northrop, *Anatomy of Criticism: Four Essays* [1957] (Princeton: Princeton Univ. P, 1973).

Frye, Northrop, Troni Y. Grande, and Garry Sherbert, *Northrop Frye's Writings on Shakespeare and the Renaissance* (Toronto: Univ. of Toronto Press, 2010).

Gatti, Andrea, "Egoismi e incongruenze. Estetiche del riso in età moderna," *I castelli di Yale online*, 5.2 (2017): 289–303.

Gilmore, Grant, *The Ages of American Law* [1977] (New Haven/London: Yale Univ. Press, 2014)

Gordon, James D., "Introduction: Humor in Legal Education and Scholarship," *BYU Law Review* 2 (1992): 313–323. Available online: https://digitalcommons.law.byu.edu/lawreview/vol1992/iss2/1 (last access in February 2023).

Gruner, Charles R., *The Game of humor: A Comprehensive Theory of Why We Laugh* (New Brunswick/London: Routledge, 2000).

Guareschi, Giovannino, *Italia provvisoria: album del dopoguerra* (Milan: Rizzoli, 2012).

Hašek, Jaroslaw, *The Good Soldier Šveik and His Fortunes in the World War* [1921–1923], trans. Cecil Parrott (London: Penguin, 1973).

Hattenstone, Simon, "Interview Confessions of Miss Mischief," *The Guardian* (March 29, 2008). Available online: https://www.theguardian.com/film/2008/mar/29/biography (last accessed in February 2023).

Heller, Joseph, *Catch 22: A Novel* [1961] (New York: Simon & Schuster, 2011).

Heritier, Paolo, "Nessi multiformi tra diritto e narrazione," *Tigor: rivista di scienze della comunicazione* 1 (2010): 4–13.

Heritier, Paolo, *Estetica giuridica* (Turin: Giappichelli, 2012).

Hindman, Elizabeth B., *Rights vs. responsibilities: The Supreme Court and the media* (Westport: Greenwood Publishing Group, 1997).

Hobbes, Thomas, *Elements of Law, Natural and Politic* [1650] (London: Frank Cass & Co., 1969).

Hobbes, Thomas, *Leviathan, or The Matter, Forme and Power of a Common Wealth Ecclesiastical and Civil* [1651] (Oxford: Oxford Univ. Press, 1996).

Horkheimer, Max and Theodor W. Adorno, *Dialectic of Enlightenment* [1947], trans. John Cumming (New York: Seabury Press, 1972).

Hrabal, Bohumil, *Dancing Lessons for the Advanced in Age* [1964], trans. Michael Henry Heim (New York: Harcourt, Brace & Co., 1995).

Hugo, Victor, *The Last Day of a Condemned Man* (Hastings, UK: Delphi Classics, 2015).

Hugo, Victor, *The Man Who Laughs* [1869] (New York: Sears & Co.).

Hutcheson, Francis, *Reflections Upon Laughter and Remarks Upon the Fable of the Bees* [1725] (Glasgow: D. Baxter, 1750).

Italia, Vittorio, "Alessandro Manzoni, le 'grida' contro I 'bravi' e le 'linee guida' sugli appalti pubblici," *Società e diritti* 2.3 (2017): 21–28.

Jankélévitch, Vladimir and Béatrice Berlowitz, *Quelques parts dans l'inachevé* (Paris: Gallimard, 1978).

Jullien, François "No possible Subject," in *Yue Minjun, L'ombre du fou rire* (Paris: Fondation Cartier pour l'art contemporain, 2012), 31.

Kant, Immanuel, *Anthropology from a Pragmatic Point of View* [1798], trans. Mary J. Gregor (The Hague: Nijhoff, 1974).

Kant, Immanuel, *Critique of Judgment* [1790], trans. Werner S. Pluhar (Indianapolis/Cambridge: Hackett, 1987).

Kant, Immanuel, *Critique of Practical Reason* [1788], trans. T.K. Abbott (New York: Prometheus Books, 1996).

Kant, Immanuel, *The Philosophy of Law* [1797], trans. W. Hastie (Edinburgh: T. &. T. Clark, 1887).

Kawakami, Fumito, Masaki Tomonaga, and Juri Suzuki, "The First Smile: Spontaneous Smiles in Newborn Japanese Macaques (Macaca fuscata)," *Primates* 58 (2017): 93–101.

Keaton, Buster and Charles Samuels, *My Wonderful World of Slapstick* (New York: Doubleday & Co., 1960).

Kelsen, Hans, and Richard Potz, *Secular Religion. A Polemic against the Misinterpretation of Modern Social Philosophy, Science and Politics as "New Religion"* [1964] (Vienna/New York: Springer, 2012).

Konig, David Thomas, Paul Finkelman, and Christopher Alan Bracey, (eds.), *The Dred Scott Case: Historical and Contemporary Perspectives on Race and Law* (Athens: Ohio Univ. Press, 2010).

Lacan, Jacques, "Kant with Sade" [1963], trans. James B. Swenson, Jr, October 51 (1989), 55–75.

Le Goff, Jacques, "Rire au Moyen Àge," *Cahiers du Centre de Recherches Historiques* 3 (1989): 1–14.

Leopardi, Giacomo, *Discorso sopra lo stato presente dei costumi degl'Italiani*, in *Pensieri Moralisti Greci. Volgarizzamenti e scritti vari*, ed. Alessandro Donati (Rome/Bari: Laterza, 1932).

Leopardi, Giacomo, *Tutte le opere*, eds. Walter Binni and Enrico Ghidetti (Florence: Sansoni, 1969).

Leopardi, Giacomo, *The Poems (Canti)*, trans. J.M. Morrison (London: Gay and Bird, 1900), 128–140.

Leopardi, Giacomo, *Zibaldone*, ed. Michael Caesar and Franco D'Intino (New York: Farrar, Strauss and Giroux, 2015).

Leopardi, Giacomo, *The Moral Essays* [1827], trans. Patrick Creagh (New York: Columbia Univ. Press, 1983).

Lerner, Gad, "Il Don Chisciotte sconsolato che generò l'umorismo ebraico," introduction to S. Alechem, in *La storia di Tewje il lattivendolo* (Milan: Feltrinelli, 2000), 5–10.

Ljapon, M.V., "O 'grammatike' jumora i strategii ostroumija," in *Logičeskij analiz jazyk. Jazykovy mechanizmy jumora*, ed. N.D. Arutjunova (Moscow: Indrik, 2007), 308–328.

Lorenz, Konrad, *On Aggression* [1963] (London and New York, 200rutjunova (Indrik., 2). Available online: https://monoskop.org/images/d/d0/Lorenz_Konrad_On_Aggression_2002.pdf (last access in February 2023).

Lukàcs, György, "La tragedia di Heinrich von Kleist," in *Realisti tedeschi del XIX secolo* (Milan: Feltrinelli, 1962).

Mannuzzu, Salvatore, *Il fantasma della giustizia* (Bologna: Il Mulino, 1998).

Manzin, Maurizio, "La questione retorica alle origini dell'umanesimo giuridico," in *Retorica, processo, verità*, ed. Francesco Cavalla (Padua: Cedam, 2005), 127–150.

Manzin, Maurizio, "Del contraddittorio come *principio* e come *metodo*," in *Audiatur et altera pars. Il contraddittorio tra principio e regola*, eds. Maurizio Manzin and Federico Puppo (Milan: Giuffrè, 2008), 3–22.

Manzoni, Alessandro, *The Bethroted* [1825], trans. B. Penman (London: Penguin, 1972).
Margiotta, Costanza, “La schiavitù tra diritto, memoria e ricerca storica: il caso francese,” in *Il senso della Repubblica. Schiavitù*, ed. Thomas Casadei and Sauro Mattarelli (Milan: F. Angeli, 2009).
Marx, *I Fratelli Marx, legali da legare!* (Milan: Bompiani, 1996).
Masters, Edgar Lee, *Spoon River Anthology* [1914–1915] (New York: McMillan, 1916).
Mattei, Ugo, *Common law. Il diritto anglo-americano* (Turin: Utet, 1992).
McNeese, Tim, *Dred Scott v. Sandford. The Pursuit of Freedom* (New York: Chelsea House, 2007).
Melosi, Laura. “Ius Leopardi: legge, natura, civiltà,” *Ius Leopardi* (2016): 1–111.
Minois, Georges, *Histoire du rire et de la dérision* (Paris: Fayard, 2000).
Mori, Luca, “Il ‘ridere’ come rottura nelle cornici di senso: esplorazione filosofica a partire da un chiasma platonico,” *Itinera* 6 (2013): 156–174.
Morreal, John, *Taking Laughter Seriously* (Albany: State Univ. of New York Press, 1983).
Morreal, John, *Comic Relief. A Comprehensive Philosophy of Humor* (New York: Wiley Blackwell, 2009).
Morretta, Alison, *Slavery and Citizenship: the Dred Scott Case* (New York: Cavendish Square, 2018).
Muratori, Ludovico A., *Dei difetti della giurisprudenza* (Trento: Stamperia Paroniana, 1743).
Nerozzi, Patrizia and Mara Logaldo, “Intertextuality and Parody of Law in *The Third Policeman* by Flann O’Brien: a Literary and a Linguistic Reading,” *Pólemos*, 10.2 (2016): 431–452.
Nicolini Coen, Cosimo, “Heidegger e Kelsen lettori di Nietzsche: il nodo del rapporto tra metafisica e umanismo,” *Poli-Femo* 15 (2017): 151–168.
Nietzsche, Friedrich, *Thus Spoke Zarathustra. A Book for Everyone and No One*, trans. R.J Hollingdale (London: Penguin, 1969).
Nietzsche, Friedrich, *The Gay Science*, trans. W.A. Kaufmann (New York: Vintage Books/Random House, 1974).
Nietzsche, Friedrich, *Beyond Good and Evil. Prelude to a Philosophy of the Future* [1886], trans. W. Kaufmann (New York: Vintage Books/Random House, 1989).
Nietzsche, Friedrich, *Human, All Too Human. A Book for Free Spirits* [1878], trans. Marion Faber and Stephen Lehmann (Lincoln: Univ. of Nebraska Press, 1996).
Nietzsche, Friedrich, “Schopenhauer as Educator” [1874], trans. R.J Hollingdale, in *Untimely Meditations* (Cambridge: Cambridge Univ. Press, 1983), 125 – 194.
Nietzsche, Friedrich, “On the Genealogy of Morals” [1887], trans. W. Kaufmann and R.J. Hollingdale, in *On the Genealogy of Morals and Ecce Homo* (New York: Vintage Books/Random House, 1989), 24–166.
O’Brien, Flann, *The Third Policeman* [1939–1940] (London: Harper Collins, 2007).
Odifreddi, Piergiorgio, *C’era una volta il paradosso. Storie di illusioni e verità rovesciate* (Turin: Einaudi, 2001).
Palmer, Jerry, *Taking humor Seriously* (London: Routledge, 2003).
Palmiste, Clara, “La Francia e la schiavitù: storia, memoria e politica,” *Passato e presente*, 69 (2006): 1–6.
Pascal, Blaise, *Pensieri* [1669] (Turin: Einaudi, 1997).
Piana, Giovanni, *Interpretazione del ‘Mondo come volontà e rappresentazione’ di Schopenhauer* (London: Lulu, 2013).
Pirandello, Luigi, *L’umorismo* [1908] (Milan: Garzanti, 1995).
Placido, Beniamino, Preface to Henri Bergson, *Il riso. Saggi sul significato del comico*, trans. A. Cervesato and C. Gallo (Bari: Laterza, 1999).
Plato, *Laws*, I, trans. Robert Greg Bury (Cambridge: Harvard Univ. Press, 1961).
Plato, *Republic*, trans. Robin Watterfield (Oxford: Oxford Univ. Press, 1994).

Plato, *Theaetetus*, trans. Robin A.H. Waterfield (London: Penguin, 1987).

Post, Robert C., "The Constitutional Concept of Public Discourse: Outrageous Opinion, Democratic Deliberation, and Hustler Magazine v. Falwell," *Harvard Law Review* 103 (1990): 601–686. Available online: http://digitalcommons.law.yale.edu/fss_papers/210 (last access in February 2023).

Pothier, Robert Joseph, *Pandectae Justinianeae* [1748] (Paris, 1818).

Prezzo, Rosella, *Ridere la verità. Scena comica e filosofia* (Milan: Cortina, 1994).

Prosperi, Adriano, *Giustizia bendata. Percorsi storici di un'immagine* (Turin: Einaudi, 2009).

Rabelais, François, *Gargantua & Pantagruel* [1532], trans. Thomas Urquhart and Peter LeMotteux (New York: Dodd, Mead & Co., 1900).

Richman, Steven, "Edgar Lee Masters and the Poetics of Legal Realism," *Cal. WL Rev.* 31 (1994): 103.

Ripepe, Eugenio, "Ogni persona è più persone in una. *Il mercante di Venezia*, l'identità individuale come identità plurale e l'impossibilità di ro(con)durre la giustizia al diritto o il diritto alla giustizia," in *Dei confini, dell'identità e di altri demoni. La diversità tra letteratura e diritto*, eds. Daniele M. Cananzi and Antonio Salvati (Turin: Giappichelli, 2018), 37–60.

Rossi, Giuseppe, "Contraddittorio processuale e formazione della regola di diritto," in *Audiatur et altera pars. Il con-traddittorio tra principio e regola*, eds. Maurizio Manzin and Federico Puppo (Milan: Giuffrè, 2008), 321–341.

Rossi, Giuseppe, "The Search for the 'Workable Legal Precept' in a Context of Incoherence and Uncertainty: Reflections on Roscoe Pound's Theory of Judicial Empiricism from a European Perspective," *Comparative Law Rev.* 8 (2017). Available online: http://www.comparativelawreview.unipg.it/index.php/comparative/article/view/131 (last access in February 2023).

Rossi, Giuseppe, *La pubblicità dannosa. Concorrenza sleale, "diritto a non essere ingannati", diritti della personalità* (Milan: Giuffrè, 2000).

Sacco, Rodolfo, *Introduzione al diritto comparato* (Turin: Giappichelli, 1990).

Salmon, Laura, *I meccanismi dell'umorismo: dalla teoria pirandelliana all'opera di Sergej Dovlatov* (Milan: F. Angeli, 2018).

Sartre, Jean Paul, "Play," in *The Philosophy of Jean Paul Sarte*, ed. R. D. Cumming (New York: outledge, 1965).

Satrapi, Marjane, *Persepolis I and II: The Story of a Childhood and The Story of a Return* (London: Random House, 2008).

Sbriccoli, Mario, "La benda della giustizia. Iconografia e leggi penali dal Medioevo all'età moderna," in *Storia del diritto penale e della giustizia* (Milan: Giuffrè, 2008), 155 – 208.

Schepis, Maria Felicia, *Colui che ride. Per una ricreazione dello spazio politico* (Milan: F. Angeli, 2011).

Schopenhauer, Arthur, *Essays from the Parerga and Paralipomena* [1851], trans. T. Bailey Saunders (London: Allen & Unwin, 1951).

Schopenhauer, Arthur, *Supplements to "The World as Will and Representation"* [1844], trans. E.F.J. Payne (New York: Dover Inc., 1969).

Schopenhauer, Arthur, "The Art of Controversy" [1831], trans. T. Bailey Saunders, in *The Art of Controversy and Other Posthumous Papers* (London: Swan Sonnenschein & Co., 1896).

Schopenhauer, Arthur, *The World as Will and Representation* [1818], trans. E.F.J. Payne (New York: Dover Inc., 1969).

Seneca, Lucio Anneo, *Ad Lucilium, Epistulae morales* (London: William Heinemann and New York: G. P. Putnam's Sons, 1923), trans. Richard M. Gummere. Available online https://en.wikisource.org/wiki/Moral_letters_to_Lucilius/Letter_109 (last accessed in July 2022).

Seneca, Lucio Anneo, "Of Peace of Mind," trans. Aubrey Stewart, in *Minor Dialogues together with the Dialogue on Clemency* (London: Bell & Sons, 1889), 250–287.
Shaftesbury, Anthony, "Sensus Communis, An Essay on the Freedom of Wit and Humor" [1709], in *Characteristicks of Men, Manners, Opinions, Times* (Indianapolis: Liberty Fund), I, 37 – 94.
Simone, Anna, *Rappresentare il diritto e la giustizia nella modernità. Universi simbolici, iconografia, mutamento sociale* (Milan: Mimesis, 2015).
Simons, Kenneth W., "Dworkin's two principles of dignity: an unsatisfactory nonconsequentialist account of interpersonal moral duties," *BUL Rev.* 90 (2010): 715–735.
Smith, Wesley D., *Hippocrates: Pseudepigraphic Writings* (Leiden: Brill, 1990).
Smolla, Rodney A., "Emotional Distress and the First Amendment: An Analysis of Hustler v. Falwell," *Arizona State Law Journal* 20 (1988): 423–474.
Solženicyn, Aleksandr, *One Day in the Life of Ivan Denisovich* [1962], trans. Gillon Aitken (Frogmore St. Albans: Triad/Panther, 1978).
Stefani, Piero, "Riso ed ebraismo," *Servitium* 23 (1999): 247–258.
Stella, Gian Antonio, *Bolli, sempre bolli, fortissimamente bolli. La guerra infinita alla burocrazia* (Milan: Feltrinelli, 2014).
Stolleis, Michael, *L'occhio della legge. Storia di una metafora* (Rome: Carocci, 2007).
Tagliapietra, Andrea, "Rido dunque potrei essere. La singolarità e le conseguenze del comico," *Animal Ridens, I castelli di Yale online* 5.2 (2017): 247–265.
Telfer, Elizabeth, "Hutcheson's Reflections upon Laughter," *The Journal of Aesthetics and Art Criticism* 53.4 (1995): 359–369.
Terranova, Giuseppe, *Elogio dell'approssimazione. Il diritto come esperienza comunicativa* (Pisa: Pacini Giuridica, 2005).
Tolstoy, Leo, *War and Peace* [1865–1869] (London: Penguin, 1997).
Tosi, Renzo, "Sulla genesi di alcuni proverbi," in *Καλὸς καὶ ἀγαθὸς ἀνήρ· διδασκάλου παράδειγμα – Homenaje al Profesor Juan Antonio López Férez*, eds. Luis Miguel Pino Campos and Germán Santana Henriquez (Madrid: Ediciones Clásicas, 2013), 813–819.
Treu, Martina, "'Guidaci a passo di danza' ... Cori comici sulla scena," in *Συναγωνίζεσθαι. Studies in Honour of Guido Avezzù*, eds. Silvia Bigliazzi, Francesco Lupi, and Gherardo Ugolini (Verona: Skenè. Studies, 2018), 859–881.
Treu, Martina, "Il popolo e i suoi servi," *STRATAGEMMI – Prospettive Teatrali*, 038–039.2 (2018) 1 (2019): 97–112. Available online: https://www.stratagemmi.it/wp-content/uploads/2020/03/Stratagemmi-38–39-web.pdf (last access in May 2020).
Tully, Annie, "An interview with Marjane Satrapi," *Bookslut* (October 2004). Available online: http://www.bookslut.com/features/2004_10_003261.php (last access in June 2020).
Twining, Willian, and David Myers, *How to Do Things with Rules. A Primer of Interpretation* (Cambridge: Cambridge Univ. Press, 1976).
Ulianov (Lenin), Vladimir Ilič, *State and Revolution* [1917] (New York: International Publishers, 1932).
Verne, Jules, *A Fantasy of Dr. Ox* [1872], trans. Andrew Brown (London: Hesperus Press, 2003).
Vico, Gianbattista, *Vici vindiciae* [1729], in *Giambattista Vico: Keys to the "New Science": Translations, Commentaries, and Essays*, eds. Thora Ilin Bayer and Donald Phillip Verene (Cornell: Cornell Univ. Press, 2008).
Watson, Emma, "Emma Watson Interviews Persepolis' Author Marjane Satrapi," *Vogue* (August 1, 2016). Available online: https://www.vogue.com/article/emma-watson-interviews-marjane-satrapi (last access in February 2023).

Index

https://doi.org/10.1515/9783111286778-013

Printed in the USA
CPSIA information can be obtained
at www.ICGtesting.com
CBHW031237090924
14023CB00002B/44

9 783111 285399